A n n   B a r n

OVER 130 RECIPES!

Eat Super, Be Super!

**Your Superfood Guide
to Allergen and Gluten Free,
Plant-Based Living**

Published by NatPro Publishing Corp. 947 Alness Street, Toronto, Ontario. M3J 2J1

The Library and Archives Canada has cataloged this NatPro Publishing Corp. publication as follows:

Barnes, Ann

Eat Super, Be Super!: A book I by Ann Barnes — 1st ed.

ISBN: 978-0-9919292-0-7

Published and manufactured in China.

10   8   7   6   5   4   3   2   1   0

This book is dedicated to:

All of my friends and acquaintances who confided in me about their food intolerances
and allergy issues and expressed their frustration about how to eat healthy great tasting food;
my two youngish children who provide me with the greatest sense of awe
and who keep me constantly motivated to improve upon my many imperfections;
to my grown son JJ who is one of the most intelligent people I know
and one of the few who can consistently make me snort-laugh;
to my husband for his continued support, love, honesty and superior taste-testing skills;
and to our old Yellow Lab Titi who has attempted to eat more of my discarded bad-tasting
gluten free packaged food than she ever thought glutinously possible.

Table of Contents

Go-Mango-Go Porridge, see p. 113

Introduction

WELCOME TO MY WORLD!

That Cupboard

I have one corner cupboard in my kitchen that makes me upset — so I never open it. It is the cupboard where I house all of my ridiculously expensive food items and ingredients that are really good for me but taste horrible.

My bags and bottles of slippery elm bark, acai, camu camu, to name but a few, all sit waiting to be used in some smoothie that tastes and looks like it came from the bottom of a lake. When I am brave enough to open this cupboard, these expensive items stare at me while I recall my great healthy intentions upon purchase. I've spent so much on each one of them that I cannot bring myself to find them a new home, but I also cannot bring myself to use them on a daily basis due to their unfortunate flavors. So now I just don't open "that cupboard".

Superfoods

I don't think I am alone in this "that cupboard" issue. The reality for most people is that no matter how healthy something is for you, if it doesn't taste good, you won't be likely to eat it... not to mention picky hubs' or children. Now before putting down this book and rushing out to buy a bag of chips and an über-caloric milkshake chaser, know that there are incredible options for great tasting Superfoods that have incredible medicinal health benefits.

If you are busy and on-the-go then these natural whole Superfoods are quick and easy sources of vitamins, minerals, fiber, healthy fats and protein with other medicinal compounds. Not only are these foods great and easy to use on their own, but due to their consistency and flavors are also easily used in great tasting recipes. By using these Superfoods daily you can fuel your body and enable it to work at a more efficient level. By choosing food wisely, it should work harder for you so your body does not have to work as hard.

Get On With It

When I decided to write this cookbook I knew that I wanted to help people learn about the incredible nutritional benefits of Superfoods. I also wanted to provide great tasting recipes that the whole family can enjoy.

Unfortunately, many people now wrestle with finding time to eat as a family and to follow a meal plan (did you just shake your head "yes" in agreement?). Now, I am not going to lecture you about this but I am going to make a suggestion: if you feel like you have no time to cook or prepare your own meals, then for one week, on each day, add up all the time spent: writing inane tweets (I do it!) or text messages, squatting on Facebook, watching TV, or cruising YouTube for yet another video on "weird squirrel tricks".

When you add up all this time you will likely find that if you can cut down time spent doing these things you will have more time to invest in your and your loved ones' health.

So, the bottom line is: Get Cookin'!

"Food Issues"

The other issues that many people wrestle with are what I like to call "food issues". I have seen people panic over dinner parties or family holiday meals due to the fact that they have a loved one who is vegan, gluten-free, or has other food intolerances to high allergen items such as egg, nuts, soy and corn.

These intolerances and allergies are real and when you have an allergy or sensitivity (or many), the result of eating 'contaminated food' can have very scary and real effects. Many of these high allergen foods are not great choices overall: wheat, soy and corn all cause inflammation. And even those with no intolerance can hugely benefit from reducing intake and enjoying a Superfood version.

Since deciding to be vegan/vegetarian and, more recently, gluten-free, I have found that many of the prepared foods that cater to these "food issues" either taste like packing materials and/or have no nutritional value.

I am tired of eating food that even my super-sized 10 year old Labrador dog named Titi turns her nose up at. I couldn't get her to eat my (yet again) tossed out prepared, nutrient dead, processed gluten-free pizza crust to save her overweight life... this coming from a dog whose nickname is "goat". The result is that for food intolerances or allergies, when shopping for prepared foods you often trade in one problem (intolerance) for another (nutrient deficiencies).

So once again: why eat it?

I am very grateful for this incredible opportunity to be welcomed into your world and your home, and to be able to share in what I have learned in my own personal journey for health and betterment. I wrote this cookbook for all of you out there who want to eat allergen free and plant-based dishes that are delicious AND Superfood nutritious. I hope to encourage you to take the time to do it.

My whole food motto is very simple:

1. If it doesn't taste good don't bother eating it;

2. Make sure that your food is nutrient dense while reducing food intolerances — that way food works harder for you; and

3. Take the time to truly feed yourself and your loved ones from the inside out.

Additionally, I have revisited some of my fond childhood food memories of dishes that my dearly departed Mom infused daily with liberal amounts of oil, eggs, butter and cream. The result of my efforts are many recipes that were once a traditionally unhealthy dish (which was great tasting) but when made with simple Superfood ingredients, become a wonderfully rich tasting nutrient dense dish that everyone can enjoy. The possibilities are endless.

So, welcome to my information packed cook book dear friend. I hope that you learn a little and can then enjoy these delicious, healthy recipes powered by Superfoods that are all: plant-based, wheat-free, nut-free, and soy-free. My greatest wish is that these recipes may serve as a source of nutritional and healing comfort for you and your loved ones: now and for the many years to come.

With all of my best wishes,
Ann

Cutie Frutie Morning Salad, see p. 123 and Strawberry Slammer Jammer, see p. 120

Full Disclosure

My legal background has served me well. Although my years spent acting as an in-house corporate/ entertainment lawyer for various companies seems like another lifetime, the fundamentals are still with me. Which is why I feel the need to disclose my own interests in Superfoods.

Years ago, while I was still living in the core of a big city and busy climbing the corporate horizontal ladder while acting as General Counsel for a media company, my husband (a food developer) had the opportunity to get involved in a branded variety of chia. As a result of that, my life shifted and eventually led me down the path of quitting my corporate job (yah!) and joining my hub' to begin working in the world of natural health food. Which, quite honestly, is often not so "natural" after all… but that's *another* book! As a result of this shift, and our personal passion for farmers and great food, we ended up buying a hemp company which has expanded into an entire line of Superfoods called "Mum's Original".

I am personally really proud of what we have done and how we have done it. As a family, we highly value the true gift of food and now know how painstakingly hard it is to grow consistently, and to ensure that the integrity of the food survives all aspects of the food chain: from the seed itself, to the growing practices, to who grows it, to how it is processed once the crop has been taken down, to the final step of packaging.

Our desire to learn resulted in us deciding to sell everything, pack up our bags and leave the big city for a simpler life. We are now the proud but VERY humble owners of an hundred acre farm, which frankly is not as well functioning as we want. I now know firsthand, how important each level of the food chain is in maintaining (or destroying) the quality of all of the food that is grown.

I have learned so much in my role as Co-Founder of Mum's Original and in owning our own farm. It is not easy, nor is it usually financially prosperous, to grow good quality food. My passion grows daily for the nutritional benefits of Superfoods and for my daily awe of the incredible growers who are conscientious and create such gifts from the ground. It is the growers of these incredible foods who make a difference every time we sit down to eat a healthy non-processed organic meal.

So, with full disclosure: I love what I do and my knowledge of how truly incredible whole food can be. The Superfoods I have chosen for my line is what I love to personally use and cook with every day. That is not to say that there are not other great foods out there — I just find the ones I've chosen to be the best bang for the nutritional and taste-bud buck.

In this book, I have only referred to the specific Mum's Original products, Delores Hempseeds and the Slow Roasted Hempseeds, as they are truly distinctive in flavor and consistency as compared to other hemp varieties and products out there. Their distinctive flavors do impact the tastiness of the recipes so I have noted them in the recipe section.

So with that out there, let's now get started!

Bestest Biriyani, see p. 262

Part One:
Body Basics

FOOD CHOICES: WHAT'S NEW?

Superfoods are not new as they have been enjoyed by ancient civilizations for thousands of years. Although the Superfoods were so well understood and utilized by aboriginal and traditional societies, our 20th and 21st century focus on commercialized food crops has resulted in decades of minimal knowledge and disregard of these traditional Superfoods.

Our North American way of eating over the last 100 years has been based upon commercial farming and food production practices adopted to save money and increase yields. This commercial food shift has resulted in:

- Plant seeds that are genetically altered and mutated (GMO) which has been done on the premise that such genetic modification will improve crop (financial) yields;

- Soil steeped in chemical fertilizers and stripped of all minerals as monoculture agricultural systems plant the same crops over and over. With the result that the soil is overworked, undernourished and drained;

- Crops being sprayed with raw manure or chemical based pesticides and herbicides;

- Fruits and vegetables sprayed with chemical compounds to make them look unnaturally colorful and shiny;

- Meat that comes from caged animals who are fed hormones and GMO food, which is then often chemically treated with nitrates (known carcinogens) and deep fried in anti-foaming agents and chemical preservatives that are butane and silicone based (hello fast food chicken fingers! BLAH!);

- A high acidity rate in our processed foods contributing to constant inflammation and weight gain as the body tries to dilute the acid by flushing cells with water;

- Food that is comprised of empty calories; and

- Highly processed "dead foods" that are chemically charged with added preservatives, coloring that are high in sugar and bad fats (trans fatty acids and saturated fat) with little or no fiber.

Our North American cultural acceptance of this "frankenfood", especially in the last 20 years, has now been transplanted around the world and this new-flab diet has been given a new name: what was once the "Western Diet" has now been replaced with the holistic and all-inclusive "Industrial Global Diet".

So ironically, as second and third world countries build their economies and become wealthier, the worse is the food their people eat, and the sicker and more disease ridden they get.

The huge impact (no pun intended) on these wealthy populations has resulted in alarming predictions globally. The World Health Organization (WHO) has estimated that:

- At least 2.8 million adults die each year as a result of being overweight or obese;[1]

- 44% of the diabetes burden, 23% of the ischemic heart disease burden, and between 7% and 41% of certain cancer burdens are attributable to people being overweight and obese; and

- There are shocking statistics that there are currently more than 1.4 billion adults who are overweight, and one in ten of the world's adult population is obese.

In addition, the International Diabetes Federation has predicted that in 15 years, childhood type 2 diabetes will increase by 50%, and by the year 2021, 552 million adults will have type 2 diabetes and an additional 398 million adults will be at risk.[2]

Not only is this new diet making us fat and disease ridden, but dramatic increases in allergies and food intolerance may also be related to our mutated "frankenfood" (I will discuss this in detail later in the book).

Basically, we are consuming substantially more food that has less nutrition benefit while we are simultaneously getting dramatically fatter and sicker. So we now know that the Industrial Global Diet does not work for anyone: not for our children, adults, animals, and definitely not for the health of our planet.

In addition, the World Allergy Organization (WAO) in their most recent report on International allergy trends reports that:

> "The prevalence of *allergic diseases worldwide is rising dramatically* in both developed and developing countries. These diseases include asthma; rhinitis; anaphylaxis; drug, food, and insect allergy; eczema; and urticaria (hives) and angioedema. This increase is *especially problematic in children, who are bearing the greatest burden of the rising trend* which has occurred over the last two decades."[3]

> The WAO recognizes allergies as a global health crisis. There is a steady increase in the prevalence of allergic diseases globally, with about 30-40% of the world population now

being affected by one or more allergic conditions, with forecasts that allergic problems will increase further as air pollution and the ambient temperatures increase.[4]

The good news is that due to these alarming and dramatic results, there is a rising tide and a newfound focus on a "back to basics" approach to eating traditional nutrient-rich food that is allergen free; with Superfoods leading the pack. More and more people are taking health and wellness into their own hands... and forks. Some are taking action because they are forced to due to a diagnosis of an allergy or illness, and many just because they recognize that they feel happy and energized when they eat whole Superfoods.

Positively, these Superfoods are now being accepted and used by many, including: the Superfoodies, the nutrition focused, professional athletes, and slowly but surely the critical mass of consumers. Their combinations of medicinal effects, superlative nutritional benefits, and enjoyable tastes have been ancient secrets that are only now being truly understood from our North American based scientific perspective.

The benefits of eating these Superfoods go above and beyond the traditional choices of other plant-based food sources such as: nuts, seeds, fruits and vegetables (and obviously goes WAY beyond processed "dead" food). Although incredible choices for flavor, fiber, and some other nutrients, the Superfoods are so dense that they are truly the best and easiest way to get your body super-fueled. Even better; they are not common allergens so most people can enjoy them without issue.

The body is a wonderful machine and if you feed it with foods that do not cause allergic responses and which are incredible whole foods, especially Superfoods, you are giving your body the building blocks it needs to repair and regenerate. In order to make the right choices daily, it is important to understand how intertwined and incredible the body is. To help you make better choices, let's review:

- The very basics of nutrition as means of knowing how your body works will help you to make better and more informed choices when grocery shopping, standing in front of your fridge, or before you take that first bite;

- What foods are high triggers for allergens and food intolerance; and

- Why Superfoods are truly SO super for so many.

BACK TO BODY BASICS

I like to think of the body as a house that you are constantly building and repairing. For any home, you want a secure foundation that is free from cracks and fissures. You also want strong and sturdy walls and pillars that can hold up your roof, and that remains free from leaks. With everything working properly, you can ensure that you are safe and cozy, and well protected from the not-so-nice inclement elements.

Likewise, everything that you eat has an effect upon the "house of you". The foundation upon which all nutrition rests is called macronutrients. These three elements include: carbohydrates, fats and protein. And as you might guess, every type of food includes at least one of the three macronutrients.

These three nutrients serve as the main pillars of nutrition. If you think of these as the foundation, walls, and pillars of your "house of health", it becomes clear that it is important to keep these pillars strong and well supported. Without them the sides of your house will become compromised and will, over time, weaken and start to lean or fall apart.

If left unchecked, the failing support will also affect the ability of your roof to remain secure and the protective awning will also eventually become compromised and start to leak, leaving you to face the harsh elements on your own. Brrrrrr.

Where the macronutrients are concerned, it is important to understand that not all macronutrients carbohydrates, fats, or protein are created equal. There are great choices to make under each pillar, and some can be really bad ones. So, getting back to our motto of "make your food work", let's look at what the best choices are for each of our pillars in your "house of health".

Fats

Food fats are one of the three major nutritional pillars of your diet (with the other two being protein and carbohydrates). Fats found in food consist of a wide group of compounds that are sources of energy. They can come in liquid form (oil — like olive oil) or solid form (fats — like butter) when at room temperature. Good food fats are essential to our bodies and are important for brain development, absorption of vitamins, reducing blood clotting and controlling inflammation. It is also the vanity food as it helps to keep our skin, nails, and hair healthy.

The term "fat" tends to get a bad rap as it is often confused with fat molecules. Fat molecules are simply the units of stored energy (calories) from the over consumption of food. Basically, whatever calories that you eat (carb, fat, or protein), that your body cannot use up right away, are converted into these molecules, and are then tucked away in your fat cells for future energy. The only problem? Your body uses up these fat reserves only after using its first choice of fuel: carbohydrates (which is why fat cells are harder to get rid of as they like to "stick" around).

Food fats can vary in nutritional benefits, and most food is comprised of a combination of fats with a higher concentration of one specific type. So, what exactly are these different types of food fats?

Polyunsaturated Fats

These include corn oil, safflower oil, walnut oil, fish oils, and oily fish (herring, salmon, mackerel, and halibut), grains, eggs and soybeans. These fats, in oil form, are the most unstable of all food fats as they can go rancid when exposed to sunlight, air, or heat. In limited amounts they can help reduce the bad cholesterol (low-density lipoprotein — LDL) levels in your blood and lower your risk of heart disease. So, less is more with most of the poly's!

Essential Fatty Acids ("EFA's")

These are a type of polyunsaturated fat and are the very "good" fats that cannot be made by your body; so you need to get them from your food. We need these fats for greater energy, increased brain function, decreased blood pressure, and reducing risks of blood clotting. EFA's, although a fat, can also help decrease fat in the body as it burns body fat faster, slows down fat production, and increases energy which in turn burns more calories.

Omega-3 and Omega-6 are essential fatty acids (EFA's) that are polyunsaturated fats. Our bodies do not naturally make these either, but they are essential to our overall health: so we need to obtain them through our food or supplements. The problem with our Industrial Global Diet is that it is so high in bad-for-you Omega-6 that it severely damages our Omega-3 levels. The balance between the two is very important for long term health and wellness.[5]

What happens if we don't get enough? Well, recent research shows that Omega-3 deficiency is the 8th leading cause of preventable death in the United States among dietary, lifestyle, and metabolic risk factors and increases the risk of cardio vascular disease.[6] An EFA deficiency is associated not only with cardiovascular disease, but also diabetes and other degenerative conditions which are accountable for over 60% of the deaths in North Americans.[7] So, keep up your intake of food rich sources of Omega-3 and Omega-6, stay balanced and you can avoid the costly supplements while keeping optimally awesome!

Omega-3 Fatty Acids

These fats are found in high levels in chia seeds, hemp seed, oily fish, linseed oil, soybean oil, pumpkin seeds, and at lower levels in walnuts and dark green vegetables like seaweed, broccoli, spinach and kale. These EFA's can deliver super health benefits and can increase energy levels and brain memory/function while decreasing blood pressure and inflammation. Research shows that Omega-3 fatty acids may help lower your risk of chronic diseases such as heart disease, cancer, and arthritis too.

There are three important Omega-3 fatty acids to include in your diet:

ALA

These are short chain (18 carbon) Omega-3 fatty acid that if healthy, your body can make enough for its needs. It is a known anti-oxidant and is found in small amounts in animal meat and plant products, but in relatively large amounts in hemp seeds, chia, walnuts, canola oil, flaxseeds and camelina oil. Best to get it from foods, as the research on supplementing with it is inconclusive.

EPA

This is a long chain (20 carbon) Omega-3 fatty acid and our bodies can make this by naturally converting ALA and DHA. However, for many people this conversion process does not happen efficiently because of: (i) insufficient amounts of vitamins C, B6, B3, zinc or magnesium (which are all needed to convert ALA to DHA and EPA); (ii) if there is an imbalance in Omega-6 fats in comparison to ALA (as is usually the case in the Industrial Global Diet), the conversion rate slows down; or (iii) high insulin levels slows conversion as well.

EPA is also found mostly in fatty fish, in small amounts in eggs, and in very small amounts in seaweed. Some EPA is converted into DHA and studies on both have found that daily ingestion can help to reduce blood clotting, inflammation, blood pressure, and bad cholesterol.[8]

DHA

This is a long chain (22 carbon) Omega-3 fatty acid which our bodies can also make by converting EPA into DHA. It is also found mostly in fatty fish, in small amounts in eggs, and in seaweed. It is a major component of the gray matter of the brain, and also found in the retina, testis, sperm, and cell membranes. DHA has been associated with a decreased risk of mental decline associated with aging and better memory.[9]

Additionally, if you have limited or no meat and fish in your diet, it is important to supplement with high DHA and EPA products (my preference is spirulina, or microalgae, capsules — 200mg micro pills). A long term DHA deficiency can result in depression, fatigue, skin disorders, mental fog and joint inflammation.

Omega-6 Fatty Acids

Omega-6s are found in hemp seed, chia, safflower oil, corn oil, sesame oil and sunflower oils. Omega-6's are also EFAs but are not all the same in terms of health benefits. They are best described as the "make-sure-you-make-the-right-choice" Omega-6. Some Omega-6's don't have many benefits such as canola or corn oil which are found in most processed foods: these are very inflammatory and compete for the absorption of its nutritional-rich cousin Omega-3! Best choice is hemp seeds that are rich in the Omega-6: Gamma-Linolenic Acid (GLA), which is a natural anti-inflammatory and assists in cell fluidity. Hemp seeds also have healthy Omega-6 stearidonic acid which allows for faster metabolization of the short chain Omega-3's ALA's to longer form EPA's (see above)... AWESOME!

Omega-7 and Omega-9

These are NOT essential fatty acids and are monounsaturated fats. Omega-7 is found naturally in high amounts in sea buckthorn and is an excellent aid in improving the conditions of mucous membranes and assisting in great skin. Although a nice to have "Diva-Demand", Omega-7 is not essential. Omega-9 is naturally found in avocados, olives, peanuts and some vegetable oils (hemp, olive, canola, almond, hazelnut, and peanut). Omega-9 is not an essential fatty acid as your body can produce a limited amount, provided you are getting your proper amounts of Omega-3's and Omega-6's. It can help to reduce insulin resistance, cholesterol levels, and hardening of the arteries; so it is good to have. But many Omega-3 and Omega-6 rich foods also include Omega 9 in them... so don't fall prey to marketing as your body naturally makes this when you have your "essentials" in place.

Monounsaturated Fats

Monounsaturated Fat rich foods include: vegetable oils such as olive oil, canola oil, peanut oil, sunflower oil, and sesame oil and foods such as avocados, peanuts, and other nuts and seeds. These fats help reduce bad cholesterol levels in your blood and can lower your risk of heart disease and stroke. Monounsaturated fat is also typically high in vitamin E, which is a known antioxidant, so another "good" fat.

Saturated Fat

Foods high in saturated fat include animal based foods (meat, butter, tallow, lard, cream, meat, cheese). This fat raises the bad cholesterol levels LDL in your blood which over time can increase your risk of heart disease and stroke. To make matters worse, saturated fat rich animal based foods are often already high in cholesterol. So these heart heavy fats should be eaten in limited quantity and frequency. The one exception to this rule is coconut oil that has high levels of saturated fats, but acts like a fiber due to the length of its composition (more on this in the Superfoods section).

Trans Fatty Acid

This fat naturally occurs in small amounts in some dairy products, and cow and sheep meat. Unnatural in its composition, it is a man-made fat found in partially hydrogenated vegetable oils which are used in most prepared baked goods, cereals, chips, fried foods (both packaged food and in restaurants), cake mixes, ramen noodles, soup cups, dips, salad dressings, breakfast cereals, potato chips, crackers, cookie, candies, international coffee blends, microwave popcorn, vegetable shortening and some margarine. As an ingredient it is often referred to as "partially-hydrogenated vegetable oils", "hydrogenated vegetable oils" or "shortening"… just because you need to be even more confused while grocery shopping.

To make this mutant fat, through a chemical process, the vegetable Monounsaturated Fats and Polyunsaturated Fats are chemically and physically altered. This is done by injecting hydrogen into them under high pressure and heat to become high in trans fatty acid. This is done for commercial purposes as it substantially extends the shelf life of food due to its mutated form. The effects of trans fatty acids are purely damaging as consuming it: (i) lowers good cholesterol levels (high-density lipoprotein "HDL", which helps to build hormones, repair wounds and fuel the brain and also assists in dragging out the bad cholesterol);[10] (ii) raises the bad cholesterol levels LDL (which causes blood vessel damage);[11] and (iii) reduces the body's ability to absorb EFA's. It is also increases risks of depression, liver damage, type 2 diabetes and infertility.[12] All in all — a nasty mutated avoid-it-at-all-costs critter.

Summary:

Choose your fats wisely and make your food fats work for you daily. Completely nix all trans fatty acids as these are evil toxic l'il beasts. Substantially reduce saturated fat intake as these won't work well in large amounts over time. Enjoy monounsaturated in small amounts and always opt for daily amounts of EFA's. NEXT!

Protein

Proteins are a vital part of healthy living as they make up every cell, tissue, and organ in your body. There are thousands of different types of protein combinations (like a massive color wheel) that are each made up of different kinds of building blocks called proteinogenic amino acids. These protein assisting amino acids each have a different and distinct function in the body — so to have a range of these becomes an important part of your food combinations.

When you consume foods with protein, the amino acids are singularly broken down in your stomach and intestines, and are then reused and put back together by your body to make the specific proteins that your body needs. Once reutilized, these new protein formations help to build, maintain, and replace the tissue required for your muscles, organs, bones and immune system and also make up 75% of your non-water body weight.

Amino Acids

There are 20 amino acids that assist in DNA replication and protein synthesis and which are classified into two main groups: essential amino acids and nonessential amino acids.

Nine are called Essential Amino Acids ("EAA's") which means that your body needs them but cannot produce them, so your body to get them solely through food sources: either animal or vegetable based.

Whole Protein — The Essentials

A food comprised of all EAAs becomes a "complete protein", which means that your body will automatically recognize this food as immediately useable. If you think of protein amino acids as jigsaw puzzle pieces, a "whole protein" is a jigsaw puzzle that has been completed and your body understands the whole picture easily and can use the amino acids.

Conversely, if some EAA's are missing, the body has to wait around for the missing pieces until it can be used. If the pieces never show up, these amino acids are wasted as they are deemed unusable by the body if not used that day.[13] Plant based whole proteins are easier for your body to utilize and absorb as compared to animal based ones.

Complete proteins can be found in animal based foods such as meat, fish, eggs, and dairy products like milk, yogurt, and cheese. For plant based food sources, you can find all of your EAA's in: goji berries, hemp seed, cacao, quinoa, amaranth, spirulina, buckwheat, and chia.

A list of these essential amino acids and their benefits is set out here:

ESSENTIAL AMINO ACIDS	BENEFITS
Histidine	Helps with the synthesis of red and white blood cells and improves blood flow.
Isoleucine	Necessary for the synthesis of hemoglobin, which is the major constituent of red blood cells.
Leucine	Beneficial for skin, bone, and tissue repair and helps to promote growth hormone synthesis.
Lycine	Vital to synthesize enzymes and hormones. Also acts as a precursor for L-carathine which is essential for healthy nervous system function.
Methionine	Helps to breakdown fats and aids in reducing muscle degeneration.
Phenylalanine	Helps the central nervous system and can boost brain health for memory and learning.
Threonine	Helps to enhance a positive mood and is also an antioxidant.
Trytophan	Needed to help with the synthesis of the neurotransmitter serotonin and can help relieve migraines and depression.
Valine	Essential for muscle development.

Note as well the use of protein amino acids in absorption rates for post workouts. In a study published in the "Journal of Applied Physiology" (An Oral Essential Amino Acid-Carbohydrate Supplement Enhances Muscle Protein Anabolism After Resistance Exercise; February 2000) it was found that by including the three essential amino acids called "branched chain aminos": leucine, isoleucine and valine, in a beverage consumed after the first hour and the third hour after resistance training, there was a substantial increased rate of protein synthesis than in those who took the placebo drink with no effects.

Incomplete Protein — the Non-Essentials

All other non-essential proteins are called "incomplete" as they lack one or more of the EAA's and include: nuts, seeds, grains, legumes and beans.

These non-essential amino acids ("NEAA") and their benefits are set out here:

NON ESSENTIAL AMINO ACIDS	BENEFITS
Alanine	Removes toxins and strengthens the immune system while helping to metabolize glucose.
Arginine*	Helps to keep the blood vessels open (vasodilatation) which is important for heart health. Also is "regenerative" in that it promotes growth hormone production and supports the immune system.
Asparagine	Helps to balance the central nervous system, promote Amino Acid conversions and remove toxins (ammonia).
Aspartic Acid	Helps to stimulate endurance and can remove toxins from the blood stream.
Cysteine*	Helps to remove toxins from the body and stimulate collagen production for younger looking skin.
Glutamic Acid	Helps to metabolize fat and sugars, and assist in brain function.
Glutamine	Acts as "brain fuel" and it is one of few compounds to pass through the brain barrier.
Glycine	Promotes better functioning of the central nervous system and assists in keeping the prostate healthy.
Proline	Helps to promote tissue repair and build cartilage and collagen.
Serine	Helps to improve brain function, central nervous system function, and strengthens the immune system.
Tyrosine*	Helps to reduce stress and assists in improved brain function.

*- Considered essential in young children and the aging.

So, the BEST option is to choose plant based foods that have all of your EAA's — this ensures that your body gets the best, as well as the fastest and most easily absorbable, protein sources. Second best is to mix other non-complete protein foods with EAA foods or other non-complete foods that complement each other to become complete.

For example, if you mix dried beans, lentils and peas with nuts, seeds and whole grains, they complement one another and when mixed, become a complete protein. Still need some convincing to move to the plant based side of the fence?

Plant or Animal Protein? Making the Best Choice

As a functioning vegetarian, I often get told by meat eaters (usually while seated at wedding tables with strangers) that I must be protein deficient due to my green grub. But the fact is that meat is not what it is cracked up to be. Why choose plant based protein over animal based? Well here are a few plant-based tidbits to make you stop and think:

- Meat contains no fiber.

- Red meat is high in saturated fats and is very difficult for the body to break down.

- Most prepared meats include sodium nitrate as an additive to stabilize the red color and prevent the growth of bacteria, these include: bacon, ham, hot dogs, luncheon meats, smoked fish, and corned beef. These additives have been shown to cause cancer in animals when consumed in large quantities. There has been no long term study of its effects upon humans over time.

- Fish and shellfish are high allergens and may be contaminated with high levels of mercury. In addition, shellfish is high in bad (LDL) cholesterol.

- Cow's milk and dairy products are high allergens and have a low protein content based upon volume; plus a lot of saturated fats.

- Protein powders and meal replacements, whether animal based or vegetable, based, are no longer whole foods as they have been processed to increase protein levels. But how our bodies absorb and metabolize these foods is another story. Better to stick with whole foods that deliver all three macronutrients than processed and isolated ones. Also, these powders are often isolated proteins by means of using the neurotoxin hexane in the processing which is used to increase the speed and commercial costs of the protein isolation process. They also often include artificial sweeteners like aspartame which is linked to neurological disorders. Many sweeteners used in these powders and replacements contain no nutritional value and trick your body into thinking it is eating something sweet and may have harmful side effects (see the section on simple sugars under carbohydrates).

- Diets that are very high in animal based protein can be a major stress to the body with dangerous side effects.

- Diets high in red meat increase risks of high cholesterol levels due to lowered carbohydrate/fiber intake; stress on the kidneys and liver as an overload of unusable protein has to be broken down in the liver to separate out the nitrogen waste that is hard to get rid of; calcium leeching from your bones reducing bone mass; or high uric acid levels in the bloodstream which will cause gout or arthritis if left unchecked.

Excellent Enzymes

Additionally, proteins obtained from plant based foods provide the highest sources of enzymes. At any given moment, all of the work being done inside any cell in your body is thanks to the busy little enzymes working on overtime. They act like chemical-reaction machines inside each of your cells and are made from various long formed chains of amino acids which then become their own unique shape. This unique shape then allows the enzyme to take on a particular job (or chemical reaction) needed in your body.

They have a myriad of functions which are based upon two specific actions: breaking down molecules (such as a type of sugar called glucose for usable energy) and pulling them together (like building cell walls). They literally create a required reaction and speed up the process at which your cells get things done — like an amazingly efficient administrative assistant that keeps you organized, focused and on track.

All living cells contain enzymes and we are each born with our own personal supply that the body draws on when needed. However, your body has a limited ability to produce enzymes so you need to source these high functioning energy balls from enzyme rich foods. Enzymes have different characteristics, but generally speaking enzymes can be destroyed by high heat, naturally occurring acids and some medications.

Once again, the richest source comes from raw and natural foods like fruits, vegetables, and Superfoods. Although animal based food has enzymes as well, to get the benefit it would have to remain fresh and raw or with very limited heat. That's taking a "rare" burger to an all time low!

Summary:

Make sure that you get enough protein daily and that the protein sources are, preferably, whole and complete in order to be easily utilized by your body. Alternately, you can mix and match different types of plant-based proteins to get all the aminos that you need. Avoid animal based protein as your main protein source as the long term side effects can create bad effects, and opt for sources of protein that are rich in enzymes and predominantly plant-based.

Carbohydrates

Carbohydrates (Carbs) have had a bad rap with the "low-carb diet" trends. The diet gurus will tell you that carbs cause sugar spikes that result in your insulin levels doing back-flips, which in turn makes your body grab on to fat and store it. What those diet marketers don't tell you is that GOOD carbs are necessary for the effective function of your kidneys, muscles, central nervous system, and your heart.

Carbs are natural compounds (sugars, starches, celluloses, and gums) that are originally produced by plants (i.e. fruits and veggies) while undergoing photosynthesis. Carbs are our body's preferred energy source as they are the easiest to recognize and use, and the only forms of energy used by the brain.

Once ingested, Carbs are either used right away or, if not used, they are stored for future energy. Carbs play an integral role in ensuring a healthy intestine and efficient waste elimination. Too few Carbs can result in the breakdown of muscle tissue, fatigue, and poor brain power with physical symptoms such as nausea, weakness, dizziness and mood swings.

Carbs come in two major sizes: the simple mini ones that are not good for you, or the complex mega ones that have huge beneficial effects. Basically, Carbs are your body's major building blocks so the biggest blocks are the best choice. Let's review these micro and mega options.

Simple Carbs:

Simple Carbs are simply small molecules of sugar (glucose (dextrose), fructose and galactose). As they are small and easy to digest, your body quickly absorbs them. They are often referred to as providing "empty" calories since there isn't much benefit to eating them. And if consumed in large amounts over time they cause weight gain. You can find Simple Carbs in white sugar, cane sugar, most baked goods, white bread and even whole wheat products that have been overly processed (i.e. puffed and processed cereals). Simple Carbs come in different shapes and sizes and get utilized and stored in our bodies differently.

Monosaccarides

Monosaccarides are the simplest of them all! They would be the silly court jester in the Kingdom of Food. They include three types: Glucose, Fructose and Galactose.

Glucose

Glucose, in small amounts, provides energy to your body and brain and is imperative for body function. Once glucose is consumed, it is then taken into our blood stream where it travels to the liver. Once in the liver, it is converted into a compound called glycogen and is then sent back into the blood stream for instant energy.

The pancreas then produces the hormone insulin to help regulate and slow down carbohydrate and fat metabolism in the body. Insulin causes the cells in the liver, skeletal muscles, and fat tissue to use up excess glucose in the blood and store it. Think of this as an internal balancing act: your body tries to remain in a constant state of balance and insulin is the mechanism for trying to constantly retain this internal horizontal see-saw.

When the insulin does its job, and removes excess sugar from your blood, your blood sugar levels fall. If they fall too much and too quickly, the result can make you feel hungry and in need of energy — which is what sugar cravings are. In addition, when the pancreas has to focus solely on insulin release due to an extreme overload, it stops producing another hormone called glucagon which is the only hormone that allows stored body fat to be released.

Fructose

Fructose is another Simple Carb that is found naturally in fruits and vegetables. It is highly valued as a sweetener due to its extremely sweet flavor. Although fructose was once touted as the best sweetener due to its association with fruits, we now know that this is not a great sugar to consume in an isolated form in high amounts.

Even though fructose is a sugar, the liver recognizes it and processes it like a fat so it does not get transformed like glucose to be re-released into your body. Instead, 100% of any unused fructose is metabolized and stored in your liver as fat — acting exactly like alcohol in your body. If the liver gets too fat (and note; you can be fat on the inside and skinny on the outside), the body creates inflammation and in the worst case scenario: liver disease.

In addition, over time the body may develop what is called "insulin resistance" which results in: weight gain, high blood pressure which increases your risk of all cardio vascular diseases, and also increases cell division which in turn increases the risk of cancer. If insulin resistance is left unchecked for too long, the pancreas is then unable to make enough insulin which is when type 2 diabetes kicks in.

In addition, unlike glucose, fructose does not suppress the release of the "I'm full" hormone known as grehlin. So, you don't have the "Off" switch that tells your body it is no longer hungry.[14] Bottom line? Consuming high levels of fructose-sweetened foods has the result of making you feel hungrier, and over time, will lead to weight gain.

This is not all bad news. If you consume more glucose than fructose, the glucose can help to transport the fructose out of your system through the gut wall. In addition, not all fructose is considered equal as most fruit has high levels of fructose compared to glucose levels. Yet, fruit is also high in fiber which allows for the body to release the sugars slowly overtime. This means that the body can use up this extra energy and lowers the chance for fructose to be converted to fat.

Fructose was touted as the better choice of sweetener for many years as it has a lower glycemic index (GI — meaning extent to which insulin levels spike) of a rate of 19GI versus glucose which weighs in at 100GI. Unfortunately, the mega-marketing dudes used this as a means to make ridiculous amounts of money using cheap modified and mutated forms of plant based fructose, including High Fructose Corn Syrup (from modified corn starch — see more details on this deadly sweetener in the Sweetener Chart under the Coconut Superfood section), as an "insulin friendly" sweetener.

What we now know is that high isolated fructose intake, without the fiber as found naturally in fruit, is a nightmare. High fructose levels have been linked to an increase in LDL;[15] high blood pressure, obesity; gout; heart disease; and raised levels of uric acid in the body.[16]

Galactose

Galactose is a sugar molecule that is used in the cells of the body and brain but the body is able to produce it on its own from glucose, so it is not essential to obtain it from foods. Galactose is found in dairy products, sugar beets, gums, and seaweed and in chia and flaxseed's mucilage.

Galactose is also one of the two simple sugars, together with glucose, that makes up the protein called lactose that is found in milk. It is not really useful as a sweetener, as it is only one third as sweet as glucose, but enjoys a low glycemic rating even lower than fructose. Like glucose, it is metabolized in the liver and must be converted first into glucose then secondly into glucagon before it can provide energy in the bloodstream. Research has been done and suggests that larger quantities of galactose can increase risks of memory loss[17] and ovarian cancer.[18]

Disaccharides:

The group of sugars known as disaccharides is basically one step up from their super simple court jester cousins. They are comprised of two Monosaccharides, so they take a wee bit longer to break down as they have to jump through a hoop to get processed by the body — but they are still on the simple side of things!

Lactose

Lactose is made up of two simple sugars Glucose and Galactose that are linked together. It is an important carbohydrate during infant development, and all milk including human milk contains it.

However, as we get older, lactose is not an essential or needed Simple Carb. In fact, intolerance is common among adults as the body stops producing the enzyme lactase which breaks down the lactose. Symptoms of lactose intolerance include queasiness, cramps, bloating and flatulence. We can chat more about this under the section on common allergens — milk being right up there!

Lactose can only be broken down into galactose and glucose using the enzyme lactase that is found in your small intestine. Lactose is not very sweet and is only 15% as sweet as sucrose with a surprisingly higher glycemic index of 45.

Maltose

Maltose is not a naturally occurring sugar in nature and is created by germinating grain. The structure is formed by bonding two units of glucose which provide the first link in a process that eventually results in the creation of starch. The body breaks it down into two glucose sugars making it a higher GI rate of 105 as compared to the solitary glucose level of 100GI.

Sucrose

Sucrose, or saccharose, is most commonly known as table sugar, but is also found in a natural form in fruits and vegetables. Table sugar is an isolated and condensed form of sucrose and is usually made from cane sugar or beet sugar. Sucrose has a glycemic load of 65GI and is made up of both 50% glucose linked to 50% fructose.

In order to be metabolized and used, sucrose must be broken down in the body into its component parts: fructose and glucose. Although it is 50% fructose, because the body must first break it down to use it, it does not present the same stresses on the body as a pure fructose does or its mutated version high fructose corn syrup.

Sucrose is safe enough if taken in moderate quantities. However, because of our culture's sweet tooth, sucrose is added to nearly all processed foods, so the safe daily quantity is easily exceeded. Excessive consumption of table sugar has been linked to tooth decay, diabetes, and obesity.

The FDA recommends no more than 10 spoons of added sugar per day for an adult (sorry, this seems like an extraordinary amount as is!). Can you believe that most people in the developed world are consuming about four times this amount? For example, a 500 ml bottle of soda typically contains about 60 grams of sugar which equals a whopping 15 teaspoons of sugar (each being 4 grams) or ⅓ of a cup. So, think of the ⅓ cup of pure sugar next time you reach for a soda (or worse, your child does)!

Complex Carbs

Complex Carbs are disaccharide and monosaccharide sugars that have bonded together to form a Big Momma of a sugar chain. Because they are bigger, your digestive enzymes have to work that much harder to break them down in order to be absorbed through your intestines.

This results in a slowdown of digestion so you can absorb the energy in a slow but steady supply, which limits the amount of sugar that is converted into fat for storage. By maintaining a steady flow of glucose through your blood stream (with no spikes), you will ensure optimal fat burning efficiency and have long-term appetite control with minimal food cravings.

Complex Carbs come in two versions: starch and fiber.

Starch

Starch is naturally produced by all green plants as an energy reserve and is a major food source for humans. Cereals, roots, and tubers of plants are the main source of dietary starch. Starch rich foods include: rice, wheat, corn, and potatoes. As starch can be difficult to digest, most starch rich foods need to be cooked. High in fiber in its natural state, starch can be a great source of body energy — but remember — unused energy is stored as fat. Also, watch out for the processed and refined starches (corn starch, potato starch) as these have had their fiber removed or are structurally compromised so they act like a Simple Carb not a Complex one.

Fiber

The Carbs that cannot be digested are referred to as fiber. Fiber can only be found in plant-related foods, especially the outer layers of cereal grains and the fibrous parts of fruits, legumes, and other vegetables. Fiber has many benefits as it helps to promote bowel regularity, decreases risks for heart disease and obesity, and can help to lower LDL.[19]

A high fiber diet can also assist in weight loss and weight management as it makes you feel "full" longer.[20] Diets that are low in fiber (like a high meat diet) can cause problems such as constipation and hemorrhoids and can increase the risk for certain types of cancers especially colon cancer. Non-allergenic fiber rich foods include: chia, hemp seeds, oats, quinoa, goji berries, whole-grains, seeds, fruits (with edible skin and edible seeds), beans and legumes.

There are two kinds of fiber: soluble and insoluble. We need both of these for optimum digestive health.

Soluble Fiber

This attracts water and forms a gel which helps to slow down the absorption rate of glucose (sugar) in your blood, and helps to stabilize your blood sugar levels by reducing the sugar spikes. As you now know, when you have a sugar "high" your pancreas stimulates the production of insulin, which if left unchecked can contribute to Type 2 Diabetes and increase the risk of heart disease and strokes.

Soluble fiber binds with fatty acids and can also help to reduce bad cholesterol as it impedes cholesterol absorption. Appetite control is another added benefit, as soluble fiber allows for the glucose to be slowly brought in to your system; making you feel fuller for longer. It is found mainly in: oats, hemp seeds, lentils, fruits, veggies, beans and seeds.

Insoluble Fiber

This helps you to maintain a healthy digestive system as it moves through the intestines intact; adding bulk to your diet and getting rid of the toxic compounds lurking about in your intestinal tubes! It also helps to balance acidity in the intestines, keep the pH balance optimum, and reduce the risk for microbes to grow. Insoluble fiber also helps to prevent constipation with the added bulk and can protect against diseases such as colon cancer and diverticulitis. Food sources include: chia, vegetables such as green beans and dark green leafy vegetables, fruit skins and root vegetable skins, grains, seeds and nuts.

Summary:

Like protein and fat, it is important to make conscious and informed choices about what kind of carbohydrate to eat. Put down the bagels and the doughnuts, give up the sweet treats as a daily dose, and instead look for fiber rich foods that will keep you squeaky clean and super skinny from the inside and out.

Micronutrients

These tiny little micronutrients are made up of many compounds including the well known and studied anti-oxidants, vitamins, minerals, and the lesser known (and less essential) phytochemicals (plant chemicals). While all foods are comprised of some element of fat, protein or carbohydrate, not all foods contain micronutrients.

Although we only need small amounts of micronutrients on a daily basis, poor food choices can result in a major deficiency which can have catastrophic effects upon the body. Unfortunately, with our poor and confusing labeling laws, these important wee wonders are not highlighted as having the important role that they have. Deficiencies can have huge effects including: premature aging, birth defects, mental impairment, lowered immune system and susceptibility to diseases.

The great news is that all plant based foods include these edible wonders in various capacities and combinations. The super news is that Superfoods float to the very top of the good food pyramid as they are chock full of not only the great kinds of macronutrients but also are super sources of the micronutrients.

So, let's learn about these small sources of super sustenance!

Antioxidants

Simply put, an antioxidant is a kind of molecule that prevents damaging chemical reactions from taking place to other molecules. Oxidation reactions are the cause and result of disease and are believed to be a major cause of free radical production — a precursor to cancer growth. Antioxidants are used to treat cancer, heart disease, and neurodegenerative diseases. These fabulous fighting machines include: beta-carotene, glutathione, vitamin C, vitamin A, and vitamin E as well as enzymes.

Vitamins

Vitamins are compounds that our bodies need to reap the benefits of our macronutrients. They are like wonderful assistants who help the macros to be the best that they can be. They work in perfect harmony and are an integral part of building a good U-home.

So, when you eat food that is both rich in vitamins and macronutrients, you are providing your body with a big boost and allowing it to function both efficiently and effectively. If you hired a builder to build you a house and he only provided the foundation and roughed in structure, you would be left with a house that was unfinished and unusable. Vitamins act as the "finisher" to the house-of-you and are an imperative part of the process. Choosing vitamin rich foods, like those found in Superfoods, are an important part of the macronutrient process to make them effectively work for you.

Unlike our macronutrients of protein, carbohydrates, and fats, vitamins do not yield usable energy when broken down. Instead, vitamins help to support the enzymes that are used to release energy from carbohydrates, proteins, and fats, but they do not provide energy themselves.

For these reasons, it is important to avoid marketing claims that suggest that they are providing "energy vitamins" or diets that claim to replace foods with vitamin supplements. Macronutrients are macronutrients and vitamins are vitamins. The two need each other to be the best that they can be!

Let's take a peek at what all of these vitamins do and why you need each and every wonderful one of them. As well, we will look at where you can find these lovely entities to ensure that you are feeding your body in the best way possible!

Vitamin A — This vitamin is essential for reproduction; growth and development in children; keeping the linings of organs such as the lungs and digestive tract healthy; and helping the body to fight infections. Vitamin A also includes beta-carotene (which the body uses to make vitamin A) which is also a powerful antioxidant and may help to protect against diseases such as cancer and heart disease.

- **Superfoods:** Cacao, goji berries, hemp seeds

- **Other:**[21] Fortified cereals, darkly colored orange or green vegetables, orange fruits (cantaloupe, apricots, peaches, papayas, and mangos)

Vitamin B1 (Thiamin) — Vitamin B1 is needed to release the energy from fats, proteins, and carbohydrates so that it can be used by the body. It's also essential for the nervous system and to keep the heart healthy. This vitamin is also essential for growth in children and for fertility in adults.

- **Superfoods**: Cacao, coconut, goji berries, hemp seeds, oats

- **Other**: Fortified breads and cereals, dried beans, whole grains (wheat germ).

Vitamin B2: (Riboflavin) — This also helps to release the energy from carbohydrates, fats, and proteins; is necessary for growth; and needed for healthy eyes, skin, hair and nails. Because this vitamin forms part of the enzymes that are needed for energy metabolism, you may need more if you are highly active.

- **Superfoods**: Cacao, coconut flour, coconut sugar, goji berries, hemp seeds, oats, quinoa

- **Other**: Fortified breakfast cereals, legumes, yeast extract, green leafy vegetables

Vitamin B3 (Niacin) — This also aids in the release the energy from carbohydrates, fats, and proteins so they can be used by the body. This vitamin is also involved in controlling blood sugar levels, keeping skin healthy, and maintaining the proper functioning of the nervous and digestive systems. The body is also able to make niacin from an amino acid (protein building block) called tryptophan.

- **Superfoods**: Cacao, chia, coconut flour, coconut sugar, hemp seeds, oats, quinoa

- **Other**: Crimini mushrooms, shiitake mushrooms, asparagus

Vitamin B5 — This vitamin performs a wide variety of functions in the body; starting from production of neurotransmitters in the brain to fabrication to helping to release energy from food. It keeps the nervous system and skin healthy, and it is also needed to form certain stress hormones.

- **Superfoods:** Cacao, coconut flour, coconut sugar, goji berries, oats

- **Other:** Whole grains, beans, yeast extract

Vitamin B6 — Helps in the metabolism of protein, especially the conversion of tryptophan into niacin (see Vitamin B3). This vitamin is essential for the formation of red blood cells, antibodies, and brain chemicals called neurotransmitters and it provides relief from the symptoms of premenstrual syndrome (PMS).

- **Super food:** Cacao , coconut flour, coconut sugar, goji berries, hemp seeds, oats, quinoa

- **Other:** Yeast extract, brown rice, oats, whole grains, avocado.

Vitamin B12 — This vitamin is needed for the formation of red blood cells and is essential for normal nerve function, growth, and the production of energy. Meat is a great source of B12.

- **Superfoods:** coconut sugar (trace)

- **Other:** Fortified rice beverages, nutritional yeast flakes

Biotin — Biotin belongs to the B vitamin group and is needed for energy production and to metabolize proteins, carbohydrates and fats. It's also needed for healthy skin and hair.

- **Superfoods:** Oats

- **Other:** Yeast extract, Swiss chard, beans, whole grains, brown rice

Folate/Folic Acid — This B vitamin is essential for the formation of red blood cells. It also works with Vitamin 12 to protect the nervous system and is needed for growth and the reproduction of cells.

- **Superfoods:** Chia, coconut sugar, oats, quinoa

- **Other:** Dried beans and other legumes, sprouts, green leafy vegetables, asparagus, fortified products such as orange juice, rice, cereals

Vitamin C — Vitamin C is essential for the formation of collagen; which constitutes a major part of the connective tissue: important for healthy skin, bones, cartilage and teeth and helps to heal wounds. It helps to prevent anemia by assisting the absorption of iron, and is a powerful antioxidant which can help to protect the body against the harmful effects of cell-damaging free radicals.

- **Superfoods:** Cacao, chia, coconut flour, coconut sugar, goji berries

- **Other:** Red berries, kiwi, red and green bell peppers, tomatoes, broccoli, spinach, guava, grapefruit, orange

Vitamin D — This vitamin helps to strengthen bones as it helps the body absorb bone-building calcium. The best way to get it is to bask in the sun! If you live in the northern hemisphere you may want to supplement with a Vitamin D3 through the dark winter months.

- **Superfoods:** none

- **Other:** Fortified cereals, orange juice, shitake and button mushrooms.

Vitamin E — Vitamin E is a powerful antioxidant and may have benefits in helping to protect against diseases such as cancer and heart disease. Vitamin E is an essential part of the cell membranes, helps wounds to heal and prevents scarring. It is also needed for healthy red blood cells and nerves.

- **Superfoods:** Cacao, goji berries, hemp seeds, oats

- **Other:** Avocado, seeds, some green leafy vegetables, whole grains.

Vitamin K — Vitamin K helps the blood to clot after an injury. Unlike most of the other vitamins, which need to be provided by diet, about half of the vitamin K we get is made in the large intestine by bacteria. So good gut flora is key!

- **Superfoods:** Oats, cacao

- **Other:** Green leafy vegetables, thyme, romaine lettuce, sage, oregano, cabbage, celery, sea vegetables, cucumber, leeks, cauliflower, tomatoes, blueberries

Minerals

Minerals are true gifts from Mama-Nature. They literally only come from the earth, from plants and water, and are not made in our bodies. They are essential nutrients and have vital functions and are necessary to sustain life and maintain a healthy body.

Minerals are vital for metabolic processes and are needed for many processes including: bone and teeth development, hormone production, building protein, development of blood, and creating energy. There are major-nutrients (meaning you need higher quantities like 100mg per day or more including: sodium, calcium, potassium, chloride, magnesium, phosphorus and sulfur) and there are "trace-minerals" that are equally as important but are less needed on a daily basis.

Because minerals come from the ground, the importance of the type of food grown, how it is grown, and where it is grown become incredibly important for the mineral content of food. Additionally, with commercial farming practices that rely so heavily on chemicals for soil conditioning and the overuse of the soil (i.e. they do not give the land a break as traditional farming practices vehemently dictated) the mineral content of the soil, and the plants it produces, are seriously de-mineralized.

The Industrial Global Diet's high reliance upon processed foods and fast foods, results in striping our bodies of minerals and amounts to greater demineralization. Unfortunately, like vitamins, our North American labeling laws do not require all minerals to be disclosed (Grrrrr). As vital as minerals are to our bodies, they have become mostly a mystery for the average, and often de-mineralized, consumer.

The good news is that minerals can be pumped up when combined with vitamin rich foods. The combo of vitamins and minerals also often allows for better mineral absorption. For example, vitamin C allows for better iron absorption and vitamin D allows for better absorption of calcium, phosphorus, and magnesium.

So, let's get busy and review these magnificent minerals!

Calcium — Vital for building strong bones and teeth.

- **Superfoods:** Chia, cacao, coconut flour, coconut sugar, goji berries, hemp seeds, oats, quinoa

- **Other:** Green leafy vegetables, calcium-fortified foods (orange juice to cereals and crackers)

Chromium — Enhances the action of insulin and helps to metabolize fat, carbohydrates and protein.

- **Superfoods:** Cacao

- **Other:** Potatoes, peas, thyme, whole grains

Copper — Needed for growth, utilization of iron, enzymatic reactions, connective tissues, hair, eyes, ageing, and energy production.

- **Superfoods:** Cacao, chia , coconut sugar, goji berries, hemp seeds, oats, quinoa

- **Other:** Sunflower seeds, pumpkin seeds, garbanzo beans, lima beans, lentils.

Germanium — Germanium is an anti-viral mineral that helps to enhance oxygen supply to the tissues and increases the ability of the body to produce g-interferon (interferon has been linked to actions that can help to fight cancer). It is a powerful analgesic which enhances the effects of the body's own endorphins.

- **Superfoods:** Goji berries

- **Other:** Ginseng, garlic, shitake mushrooms

Iodine — Is needed for healthy thyroid function which regulates metabolism

- **Superfoods:** Chia, hemp seeds

- **Other:** Navy beans, baked potato skin, dried seaweed

Iron — Helps to promote the formation of hemoglobin (the oxygen-carrying pigment which is part of the red blood cells). It also helps to transport oxygen from your lungs to the rest of your body.

- **Superfoods:** Cacao, chia, coconut, goji berries, hemp seeds, oats, quinoa

- **Other:** Green leafy vegetables, beans, dried fruits, potato skins, whole grains

Magnesium — Assists with energy production, and heart, artery and muscle function. Helps with blood circulation.

- **Superfoods:** Cacao , chia, coconut, goji berries, hemp seeds, oats, quinoa

- **Other:** Green leafy vegetables, pumpkin seeds, sea vegetables, green beans, cucumber, bell peppers, celery, kale, cantaloupe, sunflower seeds

Manganese — Needed for bone formation, thyroid function, formation of connective tissues, sex hormone function (yippee!), calcium absorption, blood sugar regulation, immune function, and in fat and carbohydrate metabolism.

- **Superfoods:** Cacao, chia, coconut, goji berries, hemp seeds, oats, quinoa

- **Other:** Rice bran, pumpkin seeds, sunflower seeds

Phosphorus — Supports proper digestion of riboflavin and niacin, aids in transmission of nerve impulses, helps your kidney to effectively excrete waste, provides stable and plentiful energy, forms the proteins that aid in reproduction, and may help block cancer.

- **Superfoods:** Cacao, chia, coconut, goji berries, hemp seeds, oats

- **Other:** Rice bran, pumpkin seeds, sunflower seeds, toasted wheat germ

Potassium — Balances water within the body and is important for muscle and nervous system function.

- **Superfoods:** Cacao, coconut, goji berries, hemp seeds, oats, quinoa

- **Other:** Green leafy vegetables, legumes, tomatoes, potatoes, citrus fruits, dried fruits

Selenium — Is required by the body for proper functioning of the thyroid gland, and may help protect against free radical damage and cancer.

- **Superfoods:** Goji berries, quinoa, oats

- **Other:** Sunflower seeds, brown rice, bran

Sulphur — It is necessary for the proper functioning of all living cells, reduces heavy metals, supports liver function, promotes cardiac health, and may help prevent cancer.

- **Superfoods:** Cacao, coconut sugar, hemp seeds

- **Other:** Cruciferous vegetables (i.e., broccoli, cauliflower, bok choy, cabbage, etc), legumes

Zinc — Supports your immune system, cell growth, and wound healing.

- **Superfoods:** Cacao, chia, coconut flour, coconut sugar, goji berries, hemp seeds, oats, quinoa

- **Other:** Legumes

Phytochemicals

Phytochemicals, pronounced "fight-o-chemicals," are complex chemicals found in plants that work with nutrients and dietary fiber to protect against disease. Phytochemicals are found in fruits, vegetables, beans, and grains. Scientists have identified thousands of phytochemicals, although only a small fraction have been studied closely.

These little rascals are believed to have huge benefits as they can help to S-L-O-W down the aging process and reduce the risk of cancer, heart disease, stroke, high blood pressure, cataracts and osteoporosis. They are very numerous and are grouped into many families that all share similar characteristics. We won't get through all of these wonderful compounds, as that would just be its own book, but let's take a look at what some of them can do.

Alkaloids

Alkaloid-containing plants tend to be bitter in taste and have pharmacological effects that have been used by humans since ancient times for therapeutic and recreational purposes. Many alkaloids are so potent that they continue to be used today for common medicines.

Foods rich in alkaloids include: coffee, cacao, potatoes, tomatoes, eggplant, peppers, and goji berries.

Hydroxycinnamic Acids

These compounds are immune-boosting and disease fighting. They include the compound coumarin, which has blood-thinning, anti-fungicidal, and anti-tumor qualities.

Foods include: licorice, strawberries, apricots, cherries, cinnamon, sweet clover, and goji berries.

Carotenoids

Carotenoids are the pigments that make up the brightly colored fruits and vegetables. Fruits and vegetables that are brightly colored (like dark green, purple, blue, yellow, orange, red), generally contain the most phytochemicals and the most nutrients.

Cartenoids help to slow down aging; reduce diabetic complications; reduce the risk of heart disease, stroke, and blindness; and can help keep certain types of cancer at bay.

This family of phytochemicals includes: alpha-carotene, beta-carotene, lutein, lycopene, cryptoxanthin, canthaxanthin and zeaxanthin.

Foods that are high in Carotenoids include: carrots, mangoes, watermelon, cantaloupe, apricots, papaya, kiwifruit, carrots, pumpkins, sweet potatoes, winter squash, tomatoes and green vegetables, such as broccoli, spinach, collard greens, Brussels sprouts, Swiss chard, romaine lettuce and goji berries.

Flavonoids

Flavonoids, also called bioflavonoids, act as antioxidants which as you recall act to neutralize or destroy free radical mutant cells. Flavonoids include: resveratrol, anthocyanins, quercetin, hesperidin, tangeritin, kaempferol, myricetin, and apigenin.

Foods that are high in flavonoids include: red grapes, red wine (happy!), broccoli, onions, oranges, tangerines, berries, apples, kiwifruit, grapefruit, green tea, goji berries, cacao and quinoa.

Phenolic Compounds

Phenolic compounds may reduce the risk of heart disease, bad cholesterol, and certain types of cancer.

Foods high in phenolic compounds include: prunes, red grapes, kiwifruit, currants, apples, tomatoes, blueberries, raspberries, strawberries, blackberries, currants, cacao and goji berries.

Organosulfides

Organosulfides include many compounds; two of which are my favorites! Sulphoraphane is an anti-oxidant and may reduce the risk of colon cancer and is found in cruciferous vegetables: broccoli sprouts, broccoli, cauliflower, kale, turnips, Brussels sprouts, cabbage, bok choy and collard greens.

Allium compounds are antibacterial and antimicrobial and may reduce the risk of certain types of cancer and lower cholesterol and blood pressure. These include the "bad date" foods such as: garlic, onions, chives, leeks and scallions. Can you say "Vichyssoise Soup" anyone?

I have only touched on a few of these natural wonders to give you an idea of how bountiful fruits and vegetables can be. There are so many wonderful compounds in the fruit and veggies that we eat that science is discovering more and more about them each day. I truly find it amazing that Mother Earth has provided us with such miraculous foods that are naturally rich in flavor with incredible healing compounds!

Summary:

The micro-nutrients all work in conjunction with each other to allow for more efficient body function and greater nutritional and protective properties. By ensuring that you get enough micro-nutrients in, you are also guaranteeing that your body can defend itself against disease and the aging process. Plants are the best means to obtain all of these wonderful compounds. Although on the small side, these micro-nutrients deliver BIG on the benefits!

Part Two: Allergen Alert(ness)

I want to be clear on something from the get-go: I am no specialist in allergies, nor am I an "Allergist". There are excellent books with greater detail than this one and of course, always see a medical practitioner for detailed information, treatment and diagnosis. But what I am is passionate about choosing foods that are right for your body.

What led me to research and explore allergies and food intolerances was my own discovery of my extreme gluten intolerance along with the harrowing stories of food reactions by so many lovely people that I have had the privilege to meet.

It can be a very lonely world when you cannot eat major food groups — one can often feel "freakish" or "high-maintenance" around well-intentioned family and friends and especially when ordering at restaurants!

So, this book is not an allergen bible, but rather intended to provide simple information for those with issues: to help identify a potential allergy or food sensitivity; know what to look out for; and provide some rays of hope! So, let's get going.

Allergies to foods, and food intolerance, are on the increase, and nobody really knows why, although there is some speculation that it may due to:

- Our changing environment;

- The fact that we have engineered the removal of historical bacteria and viruses making us so striped down that our immune systems are compromised;

- Genetically modified and chemically treated food;[22] and

- Our highly processed diets that also deplete our immune functions.

But even though the root cause is unknown, the numbers don't lie — According to the Centers for Disease Control and Prevention, from 1997 to 2007 the number of children with food allergies rose 18 percent and the predictions for future allergen growth are high.[23]

Allergens are not the only thing on the rise. Specific food intolerances are as well, and although they have less severe effects than allergies and are not based upon the immune system's response mechanism, they are still very serious and uncomfortable.

Food intolerance symptoms can be numerous and may include: vomiting, diarrhea, blood in the stool, eczema, urticaria (hives), skin rashes, wheezing and runny noses, fatigue, gas, bloating, mood swings, nervousness and migraines.

Food intolerances have a big variety of causes, ranging from a lack of certain digestive enzymes (like an intolerance to a natural sugar lactose that is found in milk), abnormalities in the structure and working of the bowel or intestines (as in irritable bowel syndrome), chemical sensitivities (such as caffeine or alcohol) and inherited conditions.

To be allergic to something means that your immune system has become highly sensitized to it. Your blood contains antibodies, which are cells that form part of your immune system. On a daily basis, these fight off invading organisms such as bacteria or viruses. One antibody, called IgE, identifies what should be attacked. Usually, when working well, it looks for parasites, free radicals, or viruses. But for some unknown reason, IgE sometimes becomes programmed to identify and attack a specific protein from a specific food. As a result, the body releases certain chemicals to ward off a wrongly perceived invasion, and this causes allergy symptoms. Because the body thinks it is being massively attacked, the results of consuming an allergenic food can be swift and life threatening.

With a true allergy, an adverse reaction to a food occurs more quickly than one from intolerance; symptoms can start within minutes or even seconds. A food allergy reaction often includes the following symptoms:

Allergy Symptoms:

- Itching in the mouth;

- Tongue or throat swelling;

- Flushed face, hives or a rash, red and itchy skin;

- Swelling of the eyes, face, and lips;

- Trouble breathing, speaking, or swallowing;

- Anxiety, distress, faintness, paleness;

- Sense of doom;

- Weakness;

- Cramps, diarrhea;

- Vomiting;

- A drop in blood pressure, rapid heartbeat;

- Loss of consciousness; and/or

- In the most serious cases it can cause an anaphylaxis reaction that can be fatal.

Diagnosis:

Get tested by an allergist to find out whether or not the problem is an allergy.

Allergists commonly do skin tests, which involve placing a small drop of allergen on the skin and then pricking the skin through it to see if there is a reaction, such as a hive and surrounding redness.

Tests can also be done through blood work to measure IgE levels in the blood.

Another test is the oral food allergy challenge done in a medically controlled environment, where you are given increasing amounts of suspect foods to see if and how you react to them.

High Allergen Foods

Just a handful of foods are to blame for 90% of allergic reactions to food. These common foods are known as the "big eight", and include:

1. Milk
2. Eggs
3. Peanuts (groundnuts)
4. Tree nuts

5. Shellfish
6. Fish
7. Soy
8. Wheat

Let's go through each of these and see where the problem lies and what to look out for. Some of the allergen food sources will likely surprise you!

Milk

Cows' milk allergy is caused by a reaction to types of protein in cows' milk, such as casein and a whey protein called beta-lactoglobulin (BLG). Although pasteurization alters the whey structure, it does nothing to casein.

Allergy to cows' milk is the most common food allergy in childhood and affects 2-7% of babies. Children usually grow out of milk allergy by the age of three, but about a fifth of children who have an allergy to cows' milk will still be allergic to it as adults. Luckily the symptoms of milk allergy are usually mild, and only in rare cases can be severe.

Lactose is a sugar found in cow, goat, sheep and human milk and is what many people are intolerant to. People with low levels of the enzyme lactase cannot properly metabolize lactose, and consuming it can result in diarrhea, cramps, gas and bloating.

Watch Out For Food Sources of Milk:

- Ammonium, calcium, magnesium, potassium, sodium caseinate;

- Casein, caseinate, rennet casein;

- Curds;

- Delactosed, demineralized whey;

- Dry milk, milk, sour cream, sour milk solids;

- Hydrolyzed casein, hydrolyzed milk protein;

- Lactalbumin, lactalbumin phosphate;

- Lactate, lactose;

- Lactoferrin;

- Lactoglobulin;

- Milk derivative, fat, protein;

- Modified milk ingredients;

- Optatm, simplesse® (fat replacers); and

- Whey, whey protein concentrate.

Watch Out For Possible Food Sources of Milk:

- Artificial butter, butter fat/flavor/oil, ghee, margarine;

- Baked goods and baking mixes;

- Brown sugar, high protein flour;

- Buttermilk, cream, dips, salad dressings, sour cream, spreads;

- Caramel coloring/flavoring;

- Casein in wax used on fresh fruits and vegetables;

- Casseroles, frozen prepared foods;

- Cereals, cookies, crackers;

- Cheese, cheese curds, cottage/soy cheese;

- Chocolate;

- Desserts;

- Egg/fat substitutes;

- Flavored coffee, coffee whitener, non-dairy creamer;

- Glazes, nougat;

- Gravy, sauces;

- Kefir (milk drink), kurniss (fermented milk drink) and malt drink mixes;

- Meats such as deli meats, hot dogs, patés and sausages;

- Pizza;

- Instant/mashed/scalloped potatoes;

- Seasonings;

- Snack foods;

- Soups, soup mixes; and

- Soy cheese.

Watch Out For Non-Food Sources of Milk:

- Cosmetics;

- Medications; and

- Pet foods.

What to Eat Instead:

- For creams in soups and sauces, blend in cooked quinoa and hemp seeds. See my recipes for inspiration on how easy this is.

- Make your own hemp milk: 3-4 tablespoons hemp mixed with one cup of water (add in a pinch of: cinnamon, nutmeg, cardamom, etc) and blended on high, makes a delicious milk-like drink with higher protein, EFA and great fiber!

- For non-dairy milks, buyer be (a)ware! Look for ones with no CARRAGEENAN, a common thickening agent that has very dangerous effects:

  → It causes inflammation in tissues.[24]

  → Mice exposed to low concentrations of carrageenan for 18 days, developed "profound" glucose intolerance and impaired insulin action, both of which can lead to diabetes.[25]

  → It is hard on the intestine so avoid it if you suffer from any inflammatory bowel disease.

- For cheese, opt for:

  → Nutritional yeast flakes as a parmesan cheese replacement. It is high in protein and B12. It is made from yeast culture in glucose, often from either sugarcane or beet molasses. When the yeast is ready, it is deactivated with heat and then harvested, washed, dried, and packaged.

  → Daiya Cheese — a non-soy based and easy to melt cheese made from tapioca and arrowroot.

Eggs

An egg allergy is caused by various proteins found in either the egg white or the egg yolk. Good news is that more than 50% of people grow out of their allergy in adult life. Cooking can destroy some of these allergens, but not others.

So, some people might react to both cooked eggs and raw eggs. Occasionally someone might react to egg because they have an allergy to chicken, quail or turkey meat, or to bird feathers (bird-egg syndrome).

Watch Out For Food Sources of Eggs:

- Albumin/albumen;
- Conalbumin;
- Egg substitutes;
- Eggnog;
- Glovulin;
- Livetin;
- Lysozyme;

- Meringue;
- Ovalbumin;
- Ovoglobulin;
- Ovolactohydrolyze proteins;
- Ovomacroglobulin;
- Ovomucin, ovomucoid;
- Ovotransferrin;

- Ovovitellin;
- Silico-albuminate;
- Simplesse® (egg replacement); and
- Vitellin.

Watch Out For Possible Food Sources of Eggs:

- Alcoholic cocktails/drinks;
- Baby food;
- Baked goods and baking mixes;
- Battered/fried foods;
- Candy, chocolate;
- Cream-filled pies;
- Creamy dressings, salad dressings, spreads;
- Desserts;
- Egg/fat substitutes;
- Fish mixtures;

- Foam topping on coffee;
- Homemade root beer, malt drink mixes;
- Icing, glazes such as egg washes;
- Lecithin, is a food additive that acts to emulsify foods or keep them from spoiling. Lecithin can be made from eggs, egg yolk, soybeans, or corn. When reading a food label, it is often not explained what food source the lecithin is made from, and it becomes important to call the manufacturer to find out. Yet, another example of the need to know where your food comes from!
- Meat mixtures such as hamburgers, hot dogs, meatballs and meatloaf;

- Pasta;

- Quiche, soufflé;

- Béarnaise, hollandaise sauces; and

- Soups, broths and bouillons

Watch Out For Non-Food Sources of Eggs:

- Anesthetics;

- Certain vaccines;

- Craft materials;

- Hair care products; and

- Medications.

What to Eat Instead:

- For baking, make an egg replacement from chia by mixing 1 tablespoon of chia with 3 tablespoons of water (let this mixture sit for 10 minutes and then stir). This combination equals one egg in recipes.

- For replacement of scrambled eggs, mix cooked and chopped cauliflower, with a little coconut flour and soaked chia and season with salt and pepper.

Peanuts and Nuts

Every Mom in North America knows the stress of nut allergies. Not only the moms who have children with the allergy but the ones that must ensure no allergen-risk food goes to school in lunches. Peanut allergy is one of the most common food allergy in children, adolescents, and adults. The number of children with nut allergies has skyrocketed.

According to the results of a study led by Dr. Scott H. Sicherer of the Mount Sinai School of Medicine, the number of cases of peanut allergies tripled between 1997 and 2008. In addition, the allergenic responses, especially to peanuts, can be extremely severe.

Even small amounts of peanuts can have a major effect, so it is important to take this one especially seriously!

Peanuts are a member of the legume family and not botanically related to tree nuts. Some people with a peanut allergy might also react to other nuts and legumes (such as soya, green beans, kidney beans and pea family foods) as these foods contain similar allergens to peanuts.

Watch Out For Sources of Nuts

- Almonds, brazil nuts, cashews, hazelnuts (filberts), macadamia nuts, pecans, pine nuts (pignoli), pistachio nuts and walnuts; and

- Peanuts are also known as: anacardium nuts, nut meats, pinon, arachide, beer nuts, cacahouète/cacahouette/cachuète, goober nuts, goober peas, kernels, mandelonas, Nu-Nuts,^{tm} nut meats and valencias.

Watch Out For Possible Sources of Nuts:

- Baked goods;

- Salads ;

- Chocolate bars and bars;

- Trail mix;

- Flavored coffee;

- Almond and hazelnut paste (found in icing, glazes, marzipan, nougat);

- Nut substitutes;

- Baked goods, i.e., cakes, cookies, donuts, energy bars, granola bars, pastries;

- Cereals;

- Chili;

- Ice cream and flavored ice water treats, frozen desserts, frozen yogurts, sundae toppings;

- Dried salad dressings and soup mixes;

- Ethnic foods i.e., Thai, Vietnamese, Chinese, curries, egg rolls, satays, Szechuan and other sauces, gravy, soups;

- Hydrolyzed plant protein (HPP), hydrolyzed soy protein (HSP), or hydrolyzed vegetable protein (HVP), which may contain soy, wheat, corn, or peanut as the source of protein;

- Peanut oil;

- Snack foods such as candy, candy bars, chocolate, dried fruits, chewy fruit snacks, trail mixes, popcorn, chips;

- Vegetarian meat substitutes; and

- Edible fruit arrangements.

Watch Out For Non-Food Sources of Nuts:

- Ant baits, bird feed, mouse traps, pet food;

- Cosmetics, hair and skin care products, soap, sunscreen;

- Craft materials;

- Bean bags; and

- Medications and vitamins.

What to Eat Instead:

- For a peanut taste and flavor, opt for the hemp seed product slow roasted hemp seeds. They are a terrific taste that is very similar to peanuts and can be used in a similar fashion in baking, trail mixes, butters and sauces.

- For a creamy cashew kind of flavor, opt for Delores variety of hemp seeds" recipe that can be used in a similar manner. With a sweet and creamy consistency they are an excellent way to boost the nutritionals of any recipe from a cashew level to a Superfood level.

Shell Fish/ Fish

Fish allergies tend to be on the more severe side allergic responses. Adults tend to have higher allergic responses to shellfish and fish than children. More than 2.7% of the population has it! Unfortunately, this allergy can just creep up on you as an adult, so it is sometimes difficult to diagnose or prepare for. Surprisingly, there are many foods to watch out for that may have fish as an ingredient that are usually not disclosed on labels.

Watch Out For Food Sources of Shellfish:

- Abalone;
- Clam;
- Crab;
- Crayfish (crawfish, écrivisse);
- Cockle;

- Conch;
- Limpets;
- Lobster (langouste, langoustine, coral, tomalley);
- Mussels;

- Octopus;
- Oysters;
- Periwinkle;
- Prawns;
- Quahaugs;

- Scallops;
- Shrimp (crevette);
- Snails (escargot);
- Squid (calamari); and
- Whelks.

Watch Out For Food Sources of Fish:

- Anchovy;
- Bass;
- Bluefish;
- Bream;
- Carp;
- Catfish (channel cat, mud cat);
- Char;
- Chub;
- Cisco;
- Cod;
- Eel;
- Flounder;
- Grouper;
- Haddock;
- Hake;
- Halibut;
- Herring;
- Mackerel;
- Mahi-mahi;
- Marlin;
- Monkfish (angler fish, lotte);
- Orange roughy;
- Perch;
- Pickerel
- (dore, walleye);
- Pike;
- Plaice;
- Pollock;
- Pompano;
- Porgy;
- Rockfish;
- Salmon;
- Sardine;
- Shark;
- Smelt;
- Snapper;
- Sole;
- Sturgeon;
- Swordfish;
- Tilapia (St. Peter's fish);
- Trout;
- Tuna (albacore, bonito);
- Turbot;
- White fish; and
- Whiting.

Watch Out For Possible Food Sources of Shellfish and Fish:

- Coffee;
- Deli meats;
- Dips, spreads, imitation crab/lobster meat;
- Ethnic foods such as fried rice, paella, spring rolls;
- Fish mixtures;
- Garnishes;
- Gelatin, marshmallows;
- Hot dogs;
- Pizza toppings;
- Salad dressings;
- Sauces;
- Soups;
- Sushi;
- Tarama (roe); and
- Wine and beer (used as a fining agent).

Watch Out For Non-Food Sources of Shellfish and Fish:

- Lip balm/lip gloss;

- Pet food; and

- Compost or fertilizers.

What to Eat Instead:

- Get your protein from better sources that are NOT bottom feeders (aka: poo eatin' crustaceans), and which also have no saturated fats. For better protein opt for: hemp seeds, quinoa, buckwheat and amaranth, and for essential fatty acids use sources such as: chia, hemp, spirulina and microalgae.

Soya

As a vegetarian, I used to rely heavily upon soy for my veggie protein source. But, like anything in life, the devil is in the details.

Soy is used in most processed foods and fast foods. In fact most people eat it without even knowing it. A soy allergy is most common in infants and typically develops around three months of age. While for most children, a soy allergy will disappear within a few years, a severe soy allergy can be a lifelong condition. Soy is a common allergy and often misdiagnosed.

If you are eating soy it is REALLY important to eat non-GMO soy as research on animals has identified that GMO soy consumption showed:

- Disturbed liver, pancreas, and testes function;[26]

- More acute signs of ageing in the liver than the control group fed non-GMO soy;[27]

- Enzyme function disturbances in kidney and heart;[28] and

- In female rabbits it showed changes in uterus and ovaries compared with controls fed organic non-GM soy or a non-soy diet.[29]

In addition, a review of 19 studies (including industry's own studies submitted to regulators in support of applications to commercialize GM crops) on mammals fed with commercialized GM soy and maize, and that are already in our food and feed chains, found consistent toxic effects on the liver and kidneys.[30] Strangely, long-term feeding trials on GMOs are not required by regulators anywhere in the world. Ummm, why?

Additionally, try to avoid soy and any soy products that are not made in North America; as many overseas soy processors use aluminum drums to process the soy which is then transferred to the food. High aluminum exposure has been associated with the potential (although unproven) increased risks for Alzheimer's.[31] Proven or unproven, we know that aluminum accumulates in nerve cells that are particularly vulnerable in Alzheimer's disease.

Also opt for ONLY Organic soy protein as soy manufacturers opt for the cheapest means of separating the soy protein (and grain oil extractors do the same thing) from the soy beans by submerging soybeans in a chemical bath with hexane — a byproduct of gasoline refining.

Hexane is a known neurotoxin recognized by the Center for Disease Control which is also recognized by the EPA as an air pollutant. The addition of hexane substantially speeds up the separation process of the oil from the protein or grain and results in a hexane residue (which does not have to be identified on any packaging or labeling).[32]

Unlike the European Union, North American regulators do not have any standards for accepted food production "residue" amounts. Soybean processors use it as a solvent—a cheap and efficient way of extracting oil from soybeans, a necessary step to making most conventional soy oil and protein ingredients.

Any non-organic product that contains a soy protein isolate, soy protein concentrate, or texturized vegetable protein, will likely have hexane in the processing. Surprisingly, although hexane is a neurotoxin, the FDA and CFIA do not monitor or regulate hexane residue in foods. To add fuel to this toxic fire, almost every major ingredient in conventional soy-based infant formula is hexane extracted. It makes me SOY mad!

If you need even more reasons not to eat this sloppy soya sop, soy is also: high in lignans (a phytoestrogen) which can mess with your estrogen levels and endocrine function; high in phytic acid which reduces assimilation of calcium, magnesium, copper, iron and zinc (the phytic acid can only be removed with long fermentation (not soaking or cooking)); and is the highest food source of trypsin inhibitors, (an enzyme that aids digestion by breaking down proteins and reduce risk of pancreatic cancer) — so basically soy's protein claims actually cause you to not absorb it (duh!).

Watch Out For Soy Based Foods:

- Edamame;
- Kinako;
- Kouridofu;

- Miso;
- Mono-diglyceride;
- Natto;

- Nimame;
- Okara;
- Soya, soja, soybean, soyabeans;

- Soy protein (isolate/ concentrate), vegetable protein;

- Tempeh;

- Textured soy flour (TSF), textured soy protein (TSP), textured vegetable protein (TVP):

- Tofu (soybean curds): and

- Yuba.

Watch Out For Possible Sources of Soy:

- Baby formula;

- Baked goods and baking mixes (including bread, cookies, cake mixes, doughnuts, or pancakes);

- Bean sprouts;

- Bread crumbs, cereals, or crackers;

- Breaded foods;

- Canned tuna and minced ham;

- Chewing gum;

- Cooking spray, margarine, and vegetable shortening/ oil;

- Dressings, gravies, and marinades;

- Frozen desserts;

- Hydrolyzed plant protein (HPP), hydrolyzed soy protein (HSP), or hydrolyzed vegetable protein (HVP), which may contain soy, wheat, corn, or peanut as the source of protein;

- Lecithin, is a food additive that acts to emulsify foods or keep them from spoiling. Lecithin can be made from eggs, egg yolk, soybeans, or corn. When reading a food label, it is often not clearly stated which food sources the lecithin is made from, and it becomes important to call the manufacturer to find out. Another example of the need to know where your food comes from!

- Meal replacements and meat filler;

- Monosodium glutamate (MSG);

- Sauces (soy, teriyaki, or Worcestershire);

- Seafood based products;

- Seasonings, spices;

- Snack foods (candy, chocolate, fudge, popcorn, or potato chips);

- Soups, broths, soup mixes, stews, or stock;

- Soybean oil (highly refined soybean oil is considered safe because it contains no soy protein; however, it may be best to avoid all types of soy oil, especially if it is a main ingredient, because of the possibility of soy proteins being present);

- Spreads, dips, mayonnaise, or peanut butter; and

- Vegetarian dishes.

Watch Out For Non-Food Sources of Soy:

- Cosmetics and soaps;
- Craft materials;
- Glycerine;

- Milk substitutes for young animals;
- Pet food; and
- Vitamins.

What to Eat Instead:

- Get protein from better plant based sources such as hemp seeds, quinoa, buckwheat and amaranth.

- Like all foods, source the best stuff to eat and know how and where it is made. When eating soy, know how much you are consuming by reading the labels, be aware of any allergic responses and ensure that you are eating good quality non-GMO soy. It is also possible to lead a very healthy and happy vegetarian life without soy — so reach for your whole food Superfoods instead.

Gluten / Wheat

What is a Wheat Allergy?

When someone has a wheat allergy it means the immune system has an abnormal reaction to one of four proteins from wheat (albumi, globulin, algliadin and gluten), with symptoms similar to that of other allergic food reactions.

What is Gluten Intolerance?

Gluten sensitivity affects roughly 15% of the population, and is a non-allergic and non-autoimmune condition in which the consumption of gluten can lead to symptoms that are similar to those who suffer from celiac disease or a wheat allergy. Gluten sensitivity might be diagnosed by determining elevated levels of IgE in the blood, or more effectively, when symptoms go away after going on a gluten free diet. It is also important to rule out allergens found in many wheat based processed products such as yeast or amylase, as these allergies or intolerance can have similar effects.

What is Celiac Disease?

Celiac disease is a lifelong autoimmune intestinal disorder that cannot be cured. To develop celiac disease, a person must have one or both of two genes known as HLA-DQ2 and HLA-DQ8.

The major environmental factor is gluten ingestion, and the sensitivity to gluten is very high. Gluten proteins interact with the celiac disease genes to trigger an abnormal immune response that damages the lining of the small intestine. More than 97% of patients with celiac disease have at least one of the two genes. Most patients (more than 90%) carry the DQ2 gene. Fewer than 10% carry the DQ8 genes. It can be genetic and may affect several family members.

Common Wheat Allergy, Gluten Intolerance and Celiac Symptoms:

- Many can live symptom free.

- It can be triggered initially by pregnancy or childbirth, severe emotional stress, or even surgery.

- Symptoms are extremely varied and a number of bodily systems may be affected.

- Mimics other intestinal disorders, such as irritable bowel syndrome, gastric ulcers, and anemia.

- Look for: weight loss/gain. chronic diarrhea and/or constipation, abdominal pain, gas, bloating, weakness, inadequate growth in children, anemia, pale skin, lack of fat under the skin, fatigue, arthritis, depression, brain fog, and fibromyalgia, attention-deficit disorder and hyperactivity, schizophrenia, muscular or bone or joint pain.

Celiac Diagnosis:

- Recent studies show that this disease affects about one in every 100 people, with 97 percent of those remaining undiagnosed.

- In the U.S., it takes an average of nine years for diagnosis (Ahemmmm: why 8 years too late?).

- It is often dismissed by physicians as psycho-somatic, depression, or attributed to a number of other "unknown" conditions (like IBS or fibromyalgia).

- Higher risk people are those with a family history of celiac disease, anyone with Type 1 Diabetes, people with multiple endocrine disorders (thyroid, and Addison's diseases), both women and men with fertility problems, and people with other auto-immune disorders (lupus, rheumatoid arthritis, and Sjogren's syndrome).

- To diagnose, blood tests are usually the first step and measure levels of certain autoantibodies which attack the body's own tissues. The autoantibodies that doctors usually measure to test for celiac disease are called immunoglobulin A (IgA), anti-tissue transglutaminase (tTGA), and IgA anti-endomysium antibodies (AEA). Unfortunately there can be false negative results so repeat tests become important.

- A small-bowel biopsy can also be used to determine intestinal damage and, later, monitor the healing progress. Ordinarily, the lining of the small intestine (the mucosa) is covered with hair like projections called villi that are responsible for absorbing nutrients. In patients with untreated celiac disease, the inflammation that develops in response to gluten causes these villi to shrink and flatten making it hard for the body to absorb nutrients. This can often lead to malnourishment or stunted growth in children.

- Since the body may be trying to cope with long-term malnourishment, it's also important to measure blood levels of iron, folic acid, vitamin B12, and calcium.

- DNA test: A positive test would increase the likelihood that the symptoms were caused by celiac disease, but would not prove it (the only way to prove the diagnosis would be to resume eating gluten and then undergo a biopsy.) Unlike a blood test, a negative genetic test, however, would not irrevocably confirm that there is no celiac disease.

What the #@$!& does "Gluten Free" Mean?

Let's just be REALLLLLLLY clear on this one: Gluten Free, from a labeling and manufacturing perspective, does not mean "has no gluten in it".

In the US in 2007, the FDA determined that a "Gluten Free" claim means that the food has no wheat, rye, barley, or any crossbreeds of these grains (unless gluten removed), and does not contain 20 or more parts per million (ppm) of gluten.[33]

The FDA is currently reviewing this 2007 "proposal" and has had input from many gluten organizations to take the 20ppm down to 10ppm. This level of 20 ppm is also recognized internationally in the Codex Alimentarius Standard for Foods for Special Dietary Use for Persons Intolerant to Gluten (Codex Stan 118-1979).

Likewise, in Canada the government has accepted the 20 parts per million on the basis that: (a) those affected by Celiac disease have been shown to be capable of tolerating a small amount of gluten in their diet (or threshold level); and, (b) studies found signs of damage to the intestinal villi were found in Celiacs given 50 mg/day of gluten while those who consumed 10mg/day appeared safe and would be "unlikely to cause significant histological abnormalities".[34]

The Canadian government also stipulated that the food cannot contain gluten proteins from barley, rye, triticale, wheat, kamut, spelt or oats.[35] To clarify, barley, rye, triticale, wheat, kamut, and spelt all contain gluten naturally. Oats are often identified, misleadingly, as being full of gluten — which is unfortunate as naturally they are gluten free. Not sure why the Canadian Government did not take the high road on this one and use this as an opportunity to educate. It would have been nice if they identified that oats, and other grains and seeds ARE naturally gluten free but becomes cross contaminated due to the lack of consideration and good practices by growers and processers. This leads us to the important issue of cross contamination.

Cross contamination means that a food naturally gluten or wheat free, has become contaminated as a result of either:

- Crop contamination, where a gluten free crop is close to a gluten crop resulting in airborne gluten residue;

- Storage of naturally gluten free grains, seeds, or flours in facilities or silos that have stored gluten food and have not been properly decontaminated;

- Processing (dehulling, cleaning, grinding, sorting) of many different crops in one facility so that residue results due to airborne or equipment contamination; or

- Packaging in a facility that is not a gluten free facility resulting in airborne or equipment contamination.

So, the potential of any food, even if naturally gluten free like oats, to be contaminated is quite high if the manufactures, on ALL levels of the food manufacturing process, are not consistent with clear quality control issues.

If you are a Celiac, the next time you reach for the bulk bin of amaranth, think again. Just because it is naturally gluten free does not mean that it is. A lot of companies have jumped on the gluten free band wagon so choose carefully. Buy your food from conscious companies that actually care. They are out there.

Watch Out For Sources Of Wheat:

- Atta;

- Bulgur;

- Couscous;

- Durum;

- Einkorn;

- Emmer;

- Enriched flour, white flour, whole-wheat flour;

- Farina;

- Gluten;

- Graham flour, high gluten flour, high protein flour;

- Kamut;

- Seitan;

- Semolina;

- Spelt (dinkel, farro);

- Triticale (a cross between wheat and rye);

- Titicum aestivom; and

- Wheat bran, wheat flour, wheat germ, wheat starch.

Watch out For Possible Sources of Wheat:

- Baking powder;

- Most baked goods e.g., breads, bread crumbs, cakes, cereals, cookies, crackers, donuts, muffins, pasta, baking mixes;

- Batter fried foods;

- Binders and fillers in processed meat, poultry and fish products;

- Beer;

- Coffee substitutes made from cereal;

- Chicken and beef broth;

- Falafel;

- Gelatinized starch, modified starch, modified food starch;

- Gravy mixes, bouillon cubes;

- Communion/altar bread and wafers;

- Hydrolyzed plant protein (HPP), hydrolyzed soy protein (HSP), or hydrolyzed vegetable protein (HVP), which may contain soy, wheat, corn, or peanut as the source of protein;

- Ice cream;

- Imitation bacon;

- Pie fillings, puddings, and snack foods;

- Prepared ketchup and mustard;

- Salad dressings;

- Sauces i.e., chutney, soy sauce and tamari;

- Seasonings, natural flavoring (from malt, wheat);

- Candy, candy bars; and

- Pie fillings and puddings.

Watch Out For Non-Food Sources Of Wheat:

- Cosmetics, hair care products;

- Medications, vitamins;

- Modeling compounds such as Play-Doh; and

- Pet food.

What to Eat Instead of Wheat:

- Other vegetarian foods to look for are: all Superfoods, buckwheat, amaranth, teff, montina, sorghum, millet, beans, rice, potatoes, and seeds; and

- For flours choose: coconut flour, arrowroot flour, cassava flour, buckwheat flour, masa flour, potato flour, rice flour, tapioca flour, pea flour, yam flour, sorghum flour and mesquite flour.

Also, many people with Celiac disease are also lactose intolerant at the time of diagnosis. BUT After sticking to a gluten-free diet and allowing the intestinal lining to heal, you may be able to tolerate dairy products over time. A good chance though to lay off the dairy in the meantime!

Buyer Be (A)Ware

Food allergies and intolerance are definitely here to stay. Hopefully, this growth in issues will also translate into a growth in knowledge and proper diagnosis.

But dealing with food allergies can be a very difficult hurdle. I have literally spoken with 100's of individuals who had just received their allergy diagnosis and were in complete shock and trauma. It can be pretty overwhelming when someone in your household is diagnosed with an allergy, or food sensitivity, as the whole household will have to morph and meals will never be the same. But, this seemingly traumatic moment can become an excellent opportunity for a super change for the entire family. So, with the bad comes an incredibly good opportunity for all to get healthier... if you make the right choices.

But be(a)ware, as many allergen-free prepared foods share the same properties of poorly prepared food choices. Because allergies and intolerance are such a personal issue, many companies will market to this fear and tout the "gluten free", "nut free" or "dairy free" aspect of a food. In reality, there are often very little nutritional benefits in many of these "free" grocery options.

My personal belief is that it is not a good choice to trade off one health issue for another. So, for example, if you are celiac, and your bodily system is already taxed and functioning in a state of high or semi-alert trauma, why eat foods that have little to no nutritional benefits like tapioca or rice?

So what to do?

Well, simply put: it is "Superfoods to the rescue". All Superfoods are naturally gluten and wheat free, nut and peanut free, soy free and vegan (meaning: dairy, milk, animal and shellfish/fish free). In addition, the huge nutritional benefits mean that you obtain all of the great fats, fiber, and whole protein that you need!

Superfoods' composition of high levels of minerals allows us to re-mineralize our bodies and counteract the environmental damages and commercial farming practices that both contribute to stripping our bodies and food sources of minerals.

But as law school taught me, "Buyer Be(a)ware".

Like all food purchases and decisions, it is important to know where your food comes from. As we discussed above, make sure that you source it from reliable sources. Though, you should also know how the Superfoods are stored and packaged too, as this can make a difference in terms cross contamination. For example, even though hemp seeds are naturally gluten/wheat free, if a non-conscientious farmer stores their hemp in a silo that housed wheat, you now have gluten contaminated hemp. So, who you buy from can become as important as what you are buying.

An additional aspect of allergy-related eating is to start making more things in the safety of your own home. This can be an excellent opportunity to roll up your sleeves, put on the apron and start making super great meals that are allergen free, and which nourish and delight the whole family.

How We Experience Food

It is not only important WHAT we eat, and HOW it is grown, but HOW we eat it. They say that the eyes are the mirror to the soul, but I think it can also be said that the soul can be reflected by how you view and experience food. I believe that there are three fundamentally different approaches to it.

The first is the "drive-by-while-on-the-fly" experience. This is less of an experience than a fast flash of a bad memory. Any sort of fast food is simply that: food that is gulped down with no appreciation of its content nor care taken in its preparation. It is also usually eaten in the car, or inhaled while en route to someplace else.

In addition, the ingredients in these fast foods would shock even the most Mickey-D lovin' dude. When you take the time to find out what is in these fast foods, and what negative effects they have on your body, it is astonishing that most fast food is even legal. But it is possible to make healthy foods that are quick and simple, yet delicious, by incorporating Superfoods into your daily routine.

On the second tier is the "meal". A meal requires some level of thought and care, even if cobbled together before a soccer game or a big meeting. It requires you to think, prepare and then sit and eat. Meals have some level of interaction in their preparation, as there is the social element of eating and taking some time to experience the food. Meals can either be one tiny titch of a level up from fast food or a great choice of homemade delights.

A sit down meal is only a little bit better than fast food if the nutritional composition is poor, which includes most prepared and frozen foods as these foods are commonly high in additives, saturated fats, low fiber, devoid of any enzymes along with limited vitamins and minerals.

Conversely, an at home meal prepared with care and thought along with nutritional benefits can make the belly and soul do a happy-hum. We also know that eating together, with communal bowls to choose from, and serve oneself, is the best way for children to develop excellent healthy eating habits.[36]

Then there are the "real deal meals". These are eating experiences that are well prepared and thought out — usually experienced at a dinner party or a night out at a great restaurant. They are meant to be a myriad of textures, tastes, and flavors and can be the "real deal" if done properly.

They are the true "foodie" experiences, where your mouth waters and you think — how did they do this? But these dining experiences don't have to be exclusive nor infrequent as they can be done in the comfort of your own home with a little bit of work and with great results. By adding incredible Superfoods to the menu, these "real deal meals" can go from great to truly Superfoody.

Realistically, we should all strive daily for the healthy version of Eating #2. We know through studies that family style eating produces a healthier result. This adds the communal aspect of eating, which is an important part of the experience, and keeps us out of the drive-thrus — which should be renamed drive-backs.

The real-deal-meals are hard to accomplish on a daily level given the amount of time it takes to prepare, but should always be savored for the flavor. If you can strive to have a more consistent communal eating experience, by simply adding in Superfoods to your daily routine, you can take your food from drabby to fabby.

Now, What Kind of Diet?

There are a lot of people, with a lot of published books and a list of credentials and publications, who profess to be experts on the perfect types of foods to eat and have the perfect SYSTEM of eating. So, we should be just like them, right? Some of these "systems" come and go, just like any trend, and some are here to stay for a while. But at the end of the day, it is always a personal choice. Let's review a few of these common food schools of system-eating-thought.

Omnivore

An omnivore is one who eats some or all of foods in a plant based diet and also eats some or all animals, fish, shellfish and their by-products.

Paleo

A Paleo diet is based upon eating modern foods that emulate the foods available to our pre-agricultural ancestors and include: meat, fish, fowl, vegetables, fruits, roots, tubers and nuts with an omission of all grains, legumes, and dairy.

Grains are defined as small edible fruit that is hard on the outside and which originates from the grass family (versus a seed that is a small embryonic plant covered in a seed coat with stored food). The most typical grains are the ones harvested from the grass family and include: barley, bulgur wheat, corn, durum wheat, kamut, millet, rice, rye, semolina wheat, sorghum, spelt, teff, triticale, wheat, and wild rice. Seeds from buckwheat, amaranth, quinoa, chia, and acai can be used like grains but are actually seeds that are eaten on a paleo diet.

Plant Based Diet

Thanks to a number of high profile television personalities, a plant based diet has become a household term. This type of eating means that a person eats predominately plant based foods which would include, vegetables, fruits, seeds, nuts, and grains. It is not meant to be a purely vegetarian or plant-based diet but is more of a conscious way of eating mostly plant based whole foods.

Raw Food

A raw food diet consists of unprocessed raw plant-based foods that have (usually) not been heated above 115 degrees Fahrenheit (46 degrees Celsius). Raw food proponents generally believe that foods cooked above this temperature lose their enzymes and thus a significant amount of their nutritional value and are harmful to the body.

The problem with this regimented diet is that new research suggests that different foods have different temperatures at which they should be eaten for most nutritional benefits. I think we will see more and more research in this area during the next few years. Raw foodists can range from fruit only, vegetables only, to those that eat raw meat and fish as well.

Vegan

A vegan is someone who does not eat (and usually does not use) any food or by-products from any animal, bug or insect (bees), fish or shellfish.

Vegetarian

Vegetarian diets can range from those that eat vegetables, fruit, grains, and no animal meat to those who include some fish, shellfish, insect or bug products or by-products including: fish, shellfish, honey, bee pollen, dairy or eggs.

Listen to Your Body and Get the Best

I have seen and spoke with many speakers and individuals who follow strict diets, or who have a particular food routine that they believe in and which works for them. I personally love being a vegetarian/vegan (I fluctuate) and it works well for me. I also live in a northern climate so when it is 10 below zero, I really want to eat a hot steaming very un-raw soup!

But, having said that, I think that everyone has to take responsibility for what they eat and how their body responds to the food. Like allergies or food intolerance, your body will tell you what you need or are deficient in. You just need to listen to it while it is tapping on the door and definitely pay attention before it starts pounding on it!

Regardless of whether you choose to be an omnivore, raw, vegan, veggie, paleo or anything else, plant based foods make a huge difference in adding in daily nutrients. But even these plant based choices on their own are not enough. By including Superfoods daily, you get incredibly rich and high nutrients so that your body needs less of any other food. Luckily, Superfoods (but for a few paleo issues on grains), fit into all food routines!

The one thing that I am a stickler for is to buy as much of my food (or meat for meat eating family members) from non-commercialized farms. I am less obsessed by organic certification as I am about knowing how the food is grown and good growing practices.

Many small farms cannot afford the expense, or suffer the politics, of getting certification. With the exception of food grown in a green-thumb's summer backyard, there is nothing that compares to a chemical-free fruit or veggie. The main differences between naturally grown /organic and that of a conventional fruit, veggie, or grain is no GMO's, improved taste, and chemical free food (since they are grown with no toxins nor covered in carcinogenic pesticides, herbicides or fertilizer).

Basically, organic or naturally grown are what used to be considered NORMAL. Now, the UNNORMAL (genetically modified, grown in chemicals, and processed with only the bottom line in thought) is "normal" and the "used-to-be-normal–until-the-last-30-years" has a new chi-chi "weirdo" and expensive tagline of: ORGANIC.

I personally believe that long term research and conscious thought arrives at the very simple truth that non-commercial organic and natural food:

- Nourishes our bodies and mind;

- Forces commercial farming to have greater care over the food chain and food processing;

- Supports consumer efforts to eat and buy less food because they need less as nutrient-rich foods give greater sustenance with less caloric intake required;

- Promotes locally-grown and family-run farms; and

- Has an overall effect upon the health and safety of our planet by encouraging non-mutated food, clean water sources, healthy soil, and improved human health by reducing exposure to man-made chemicals.

With the new economy, price is always an issue. So, a cheap alternative to organic and free-range foods at the grocery store is to go direct to the farmers and buy in bulk — this will cut out the middleman costs.

Another cost-effective means of opting for organic alternatives is to join a cooperative food group that focuses on natural and organic options. You can also source local organic farms, go to local farmers' markets in season, freeze produce for winter wants, and look into organic produce delivery services in your area. The best option of all is to start a garden in your own backyard and grow it yourself!

Avoid If You Can

If you cannot afford all organics at your table, ensure you choose organic produce for the now-famous, or infamous, "Dirty Dozen" (meaning highest in toxins when NOT organic):

- Apples
- Celery
- Sweet bell peppers
- Strawberries

- Peaches
- Nectarines
- Grapes
- Spinach

- Lettuce
- Cucumbers
- Potatoes
- Blueberries

On a Budget

To save some money, you can buy the following conventional foods in a non-organic form as they tend to have less toxins as part of conventional farming practice:

- Onions
- Sweet corn
- Pineapples
- Avocado
- Cabbage

- Sweet peas
- Asparagus
- Mangoes
- Eggplant
- Kiwi

- Domestic cantaloupe
- Sweet potatoes
- Grapefruit
- Watermelon
- Mushrooms

Regardless of what kind of food routine you have, choose foods that give you the greatest "bang for the buck"! Opt for plant based foods, organic, and natural when it really counts, and choose Superfoods for the biggest bang for your buck.

Part Three: Superfoods —
WHAT, WHY, AND HOW?

Superfoods are just awesome and they fit into all of our required needs, as we have discussed above:

- They have an incredible source of nutrients including our macro and micro nutrients, along with phytochemicals;

- They are not one of our high allergen triggers and are naturally gluten free;

- They can be easily incorporated into family meals or eaten quickly as a super snack;

- They are plant based;

- If you choose well, Superfoods can be sourced from conscious growers that use sustainable agronomics; equal trade; heirloom seed programs; organic or natural farming methods; and traditional harvesting and processing techniques.

So which ones do we pick?

There are a lot of people who are great educators on the benefits of many nutrient rich foods. Let's face it; the world is such a wonderful place: there are so many foods, especially fruits and vegetables that are equally as wonderful to eat as they are good for us. But a Superfood should go above and beyond the food call of duty.

What distinguishes a great food from a Superfood, for me, is four fold:

- First, a Superfood should include tri-balanced nutrient-rich foods. This means that it contains a portion of macro-nutrients: protein, good fats, and carbohydrates

- Secondly, a Superfood should include a myriad of micro-nutrients such as: vitamins, minerals, enzymes, antioxidants, and phyto-nutrients.

- There must be proven health benefits above and beyond the macro-nutrients and micro-nutrients.

  True Superfoods can assist in disease prevention and reduction in health risks, including: allergies, arthritis, asthma, depression, diabetes, fibromyalgia no hyper, heart disease, high blood pressure, skin disorders, stroke, and cancer. Amongst other benefits, Superfoods may also assist in promoting: metabolism, immunity, longevity, anti-aging through cell regeneration, increased mental performance and memory improvement, higher energy levels, increased sex drive (yup!), and physical stamina.

  - It has to taste SUPER!

I have chosen my top favorites that meet with my criteria. I have left out some foods that may seem surprising,[37] but the following are the super-loves of my foodie life!

Quinoa

History

Quinoa (pronounced KEEN-wah) is an amazingly versatile and nutrient rich little seed. It is native to the Andes Mountains of Bolivia, Chile, and Peru and has been eaten for over 5,000 years. It was a staple of the Incans and their current rural descendants.

Quinoa means "mother grain" in the Incan language and is cooked and prepared like many other grains but is, in fact, not botanically a grain but a tiny seed. It comes from the same botanical family as sugar beet, table beet, and spinach and is most similar to the other "pseudo cereals" like buckwheat and amaranth.

Quinoa was, and still is, a staple food for the South American people all living in the high altitudes of the Andes Mountains. Very few crops can survive in the harsh weather found in the Andes: high altitudes (10,000–20,000 feet above sea level) with its severe fluctuations in heat and cold, frost, intense sun, and drought-like conditions.

Quinoa is a hardy crop and successfully grows in the harsh conditions in the Andes, so has been historically highly esteemed and valued by indigenous people as an excellent and reliable food source. In fact, the Incan's respect for such a nutrient rich crop was incorporated into many traditions and ceremonies that surrounded the cultivation, harvest, and consumption of quinoa.

During the 16th century, the Spanish conquest of South America resulted in the invasion of the Andes, and the Incas were forced into Spanish rule. The Spanish scorned quinoa as "food for Indians", and banned the cultivation and consumption of quinoa due to its status with non-Christian ceremonies.

Quinoa, see p. 60

The Incas were forced to grow the nutritionally inferior crops of wheat, corn, and potatoes; with quinoa only existing as a sparse weed like plant. Luckily, enough of these "weeds" survived and the quinoa crops have been successfully re-cultivated with a resurgence in popularity in South America and now worldwide.

As indicative of its popularity, recently the Food and Agricultural Organization of the United Nations (FAO) has officially declared that the year 2013 be recognized as "The International Year of the Quinoa." Quinoa has now been singled out by the FAO as a food with "high nutritive value," impressive biodiversity, and an important role to play in the achievement of food security worldwide.

Plant

The plants grow from 1 ½ to 6 ½ feet in height, and come in a range of colors that vary from white, yellow, pink and red, to purple and black. A thick stalk grows at the center of the plant and produces the tiny quinoa seeds that grow in clusters towards the top of the plant stalk. High elevation with short day lengths and cool temperatures ensure its healthy growth.

Gluten Free

Quinoa can be included on a gluten-free diet, as it lacks gluten and does not belong to the same botanical plant family as wheat, barley, or rye. In addition, some studies also show quinoa flour to have higher-than-expected digestibility allowing the nutrients to be easily absorbed into your system.

Nutritional Benefits

Quinoa is jam-packed with nutrient rich benefits. This Superfood is considered one of the most complete whole foods found in nature. Although it is often cooked and treated much like a grain, it boasts higher vital nutrients compared to grains such as wheat, barley, and corn.

Fiber

Quinoa has almost two times the soluble fiber of wheat, rice, or rye, making it a super fiber choice. Its intestine-healthy, low cholesterol fiber helps clear your digestive tract and keep it in tip-top condition by nourishing the good intestinal bacteria. The high fiber acts as a prebiotic that feeds the micro flora (good bacteria) in your intestines, helps with elimination, eases bloating, and helps to tone your colon. So start your toning exercises from the inside out!

Good Fats

Quinoa is low in fat and calories. One cooked cup has about 222k with 3.4g of fat. The fat is comprised of 25% oleic acid (a heart-healthy monounsaturated fat) and approximately 8% in the form of the Omega-3 EFA (associated with decreased risk of inflammation-related disease).

Surprisingly, recent studies have shown that quinoa does not get oxidized as rapidly as might be expected given its higher fat content than other grains. The end result is that cooking with quinoa does not appear to significantly compromise the quality of its fatty acids, and this explains many antioxidants that help in the oxidative protection.[38]

Protein

Quinoa has almost 14-16% protein and includes all of the essential amino acids, making it a whole protein. It is also rich in the amino acid lysine which plays an important role in the absorption of calcium and the formation of collagen, and it can help prevent breakouts of cold sores in some people.

Anti-oxidants

Quinoa has a number of antioxidant phytonutrients, and two concentrations of flavonoids (quercetin and kaempferol) even higher that that found in high-flavonoid berries like cranberries or lingonberries.

Vitamins/Minerals

Quinoa is unique to any other grain as it is higher in manganese and copper; which both act as antioxidants. It also includes high levels of magnesium; which help to relax your muscles and blood vessels, and which can also help to reduce blood pressure. Compared to other grains, quinoa is higher in calcium, phosphorous, magnesium, potassium, iron, and zinc and is a source of folate, thiamine, riboflavin, and vitamin B6.

Heart/Cholesterol

Animal studies identify that daily intake of quinoa can help to reduce bad cholesterol and help maintain levels of good cholesterol while also reducing blood sugar levels.[39]

Anti-Inflammatory

Recent studies are providing us with a greatly expanded list of anti-inflammatory phytonutrients in quinoa. This unique combination of anti-inflammatory compounds may be the key to understanding preliminary animal studies that show decreased risk of inflammation when animals are fed quinoa on a daily basis, and that it is also an anti-obesity food.[40]

The list of anti-inflammatory phytonutrients in quinoa is now known to include: polysaccharides like arabinans and rhamnogalacturonans; hydroxycinnamic and hydroxybenzoic acids; and flavonoids like quercetin and kaempferol. Small amounts of the anti-inflammatory Omega-3 fatty acid, alpha-linolenic acid (ALA), are also provided by quinoa.

Other Benefits

Unfortunately, the research on quinoa is pretty limited even though it has been around for a very long time. However, other studies on other foods that are similar to quinoa in fiber and protein content suggest that quinoa would help reduce blood sugar levels, risk of diabetes, and that quinoa's antioxidant and anti-inflammatory phytonutrients may help to reduce cancer risks in humans. Its low glycemic load also makes it a great option for diabetics.

How to Use it

- Replace foods such as rice and pasta with quinoa as a side dish or in main dishes such as lasagna, stews, or sushi.

- Use it when making homemade vegetarian burgers for super protein.

- Toss into cookies for a healthy boost to a sweet treat.

- Add it to salads for an extra boost of delicious nutrients.

- Eat it for breakfast with fruit for a whole and hearty start to your day.

- Use in sauces as a naturally nutritious thickener.

- Add a tablespoon to smoothies for great fiber, anti-oxidants, and protein.

Cooking and Storing

To cook quinoa, add 1 part quinoa to 2 parts liquid in a saucepan. Cover and bring to a boil, then reduce the heat to simmer for 18-20 minutes (check that water has absorbed into quinoa) then remove from heat and remain covered for 10 minutes. Then fluff with a fork and season.

If you desire the quinoa to have a nuttier flavor, roast it first by placing the desired amount in a skillet over medium-low heat and stir constantly for five minutes, and then prepare as described above.

Store quinoa in an airtight container for up to 3-6 months, or an airtight container in the fridge for up to 12 months.

Daily Serving

According to the USDA, a cup of cooked quinoa provides:

- 8 grams (or 16% daily) of protein;
- 58% of your daily recommended manganese;
- 30% of your daily magnesium;
- 28% of your daily phosphorus;
- 21% of your daily fiber;

- 19% of your daily folate;
- 18% of your daily copper;
- 12% of your daily Thiamin and Riboflavin; and
- 11% of your daily Vitamin B6.

So just eat it!

What to look for

Look for unpolished pre-washed quinoa (not mechanically polished). This means that the outer layer of the quinoa seed is still entirely intact. Some commercial producers strip quinoa's outer layer off using mechanized processes (centrifuge) to cheaply remove the naturally occurring sour tasting Sapotin which forms on the seeds exterior.

Instead, an unpolished previously washed version preserves the dietary fiber content found in the outer germ layer, provides a better taste, and can be immediately cooked with no rinsing required. Need more reasons? Unpolished quinoa contains up to 50% more fiber!

Also, like all food, look for ethically farmed. Buy from reputable sources to ensure that those making your food can also afford to eat it! Cooperative farms are the best source to ensure that everyone can enjoy the benefits of this wonderful seed.

Chia

History

I am just going to start out by saying that chia that you eat is NOT part of the Ch-Ch-Ch Chia Pet. This constant media reference to the chia food and Chia Pets being one and the same is one of my "pet" peeves as it identifies that the person does not understand what "food chia" really is. Chia food and the Chia Pet come from the same family of food — much like broccoli and cauliflower, but are completely different plants. The Chia Pet is a plant variety called Salvia Columbariae (which looks like a chive) and has little nutritional value.

The chia that we are chatting about is the variety called Salvia hispanica L. which is an ancient grain indigenous to South America. It was used as a food source as early as 3500 B.C., and served as a cash crop in central Mexico between 1500 and 900 B.C. Chia was used in a myriad of ways including on its own, in beverages, as a flour, pressed for oil, in medicine, and even as offerings to the gods as part of religious ceremonies.

Chia was a main dietary staple of the Mayans, who developed advanced societies and cities from 250 AD and continuing in influences up until the 16th century Spanish conquest. The Aztecs, who flourished in Mexico from 1400AD on used the chia seed as a running food, and messengers were provided small pouches to take as a main food staple while running with messages from one city to another. The Aztecs also relied heavily on chia as one of the four staples that sustained them.[41] Interestingly, the ancient Aztecs relied solely from these four grains, which ironically meet today's dietary requirements as set out by the Food and Agriculture Organization-World Health Organization!

Unfortunately, the Spanish conquest of South America was very aggressive, resulting in the suppression of native traditions and even banned the traditional staple food crops due to their close association with native religious ceremonies. As a result, the chia crops were almost lost and were limited to small areas of growth. In the 1990's a group of South American growers developed a chia growing project in order to promote and develop the reemergence of the chia crops, which is great news for us!

Plant

Chia is a very pretty plant. It produces a long stem that grows up through the center of long thin leaves. The stem then produces, at the top tip, a cluster of flowers with small seeds at their center. The black chia plant produces purple flowers with black seeds, while the white chia plant produces white flowers with white seeds at their center that spike up to 6 inches long. At the peak of its maturity, a chia plant can grow as high as 4-5 feet high.

The hardy plant can adapt to a wide range of soils, climates and minimal rainfall, but thrives in desert like conditions with warm humid days and colder nights. It requires a long period of growth between 110-114 days.

Chia, see p. 66

Gluten Free

Chia is naturally gluten free and can be included on a gluten-free diet, as it lacks gluten and does not belong to the same botanical plant family as wheat, barley, or rye. In fact, the absorption of chia, and the gentle insoluble fiber, along with whole protein makes this an excellent addition for anyone who has any intestinal or gluten sensitivity. Its high nutritionals along with anti-inflammatory properties can help anyone gets a rockin' good intestinal tract back. Hypoallergenic and gluten-free, chia is ideal for those with gluten sensitivity, carbohydrate intolerance, hypoglycemia, celiac and intestinal disorders.

Nutritional Benefits

Chia is one of nature's tiniest wonders. Smaller than a sesame, this li'l seed includes excellent fiber, incredible fats, whole protein and filled with micronutrients. Chia proves that the best things come in the smallest packages!

Fiber

The incredible rich amounts of insoluble fiber allow for beneficial digestive health and improved intestinal function. Chia is an excellent source of insoluble fiber with some soluble thrown in for good measure (8:1 ratio). A high level of insoluble fiber ensures healthy elimination to gently clean you out and keep you regular. But this fiber is a very gentle one as compared to other insoluble fibers that can be harsh (like psyllium husk, whole flax, seeds, and nuts). The benefit is that the toxins in the intestinal tract are removed, keeping you squeaky clean!

Highly hydrophilic, chia holds 14 times in weight in water (looking like tapioca pudding when water added) to keep you well hydrated internally. It also expands in the body upon digestion; helping you to reduce blood sugar spikes and making you feel full for longer while maintaining a great electrolyte balance.

Good Fats

Chia seeds are the best plant source of Omega-3's known, and they contain over 60% essential fatty acids. Chia is extremely rich in the Omega-3 alpha-linolenic acid with an impressive ratio of Omega-3 to Omega-6 as 3:1. This high Omega-3 level can help to balance out the North American over-consumption of "bad" Omega-6's such as corn oil and safflower oil (which can lead to inflammation).

Protein

Chia contains more than 20% whole protein, which is quickly and efficiently used by the body for energy.

Anti-oxidants

This little seed is jammed with antioxidants including: Vitamin E, caffeic acid, chlorogenic acid and flavinoids: miricetin, quercetin and kaempferol. The high anti-oxidants allow this super seed to build the immune system and ward off infection and illness. It is an excellent way to keep the doctor at bay!

Vitamins/Minerals

Chia is an excellent source of many minerals including: phosphorous, potassium, iron, folate, zinc, and copper. Chia also provides an abundance of calcium and magnesium (allowing the calcium to be absorbed), important for the health and strength of bones and teeth and is also rich in boron, which helps the body assimilate and use the calcium. Its high levels of minerals all work together to ensure that all of the benefits of this Superfood are absorbed and utilized by the body.

Heart/ Cholesterol

Chia's extremely high fiber makes it a perfect go to for anyone who wants to reduce cholesterol levels. Research has found that by simply eating chia, it decreased the C-reactive protein levels by 21% (a measurement for determining heart inflammation).[42]

Anti-Inflammatory

The high amounts of Omega-3 help to reduce the effects of a diet high in bad Omega-6, which if left unchecked leads to inflammation. So, chia can help to limit the breeding ground for diet induced inflammation.

Other Benefits

Research has found that by simply eating chia there was a: doubling of ALA and EPA levels; substantial reduction in blood sugar levels of 40% by slowing down the body's conversion of carbohydrates to simple sugars (this is especially important for those with hypoglycemia and diabetes); reduced systolic blood pressure by 6.3 ± 4 mmHg with a natural blood thinning effect (22%) so your heart doesn't have to pump as hard; and decreased the C-reactive protein levels by 21% (a measurement for determining heart inflammation). These findings provide a potential explanation for improvements in blood pressure, coagulation, and inflammatory markers especially for those with risks of type II diabetes.[43]

Likely due to its high fiber and goopy consistency when exposed to water, research on chia also found that appetite cravings decreased after eating chia which may play a role in decreasing food consumption and assist in weight loss.[44] Chia also extends out the period of digestion which provides your body more time to absorb all of the nutrients that chia has to offer.

How to Use it

Due to its lack of taste, it can be used in pretty much anything to pack in lots of nutritional punch without affecting flavors. By just adding it in to your daily routine you can help reduce snacking, improve heart function, reduce the risk of/conditions of Type 2 Diabetes, and greatly assist your digestive system and intestinal tract.

- Simply add into yogurt, cereal, and oatmeal.

- Thicken naturally by adding to soups, stews, and sauces.

- Add to salads, dressings, stir fries, and smoothies.

- Make into puddings by mixing with your choice of milk or water.

- Toss into pancakes, cookies, and other baked goods for an added nutritional boost.

- Mix with water to use as an egg substitute in baking — excellent for vegans! (1T Chia to 3T water).

- Add to fruit juices and freeze for a healthy summer treat.

- Toss into your favorite homemade trail mix for an amazing quick, healthy snack.

- Sprinkle on bad choices (like pizza) or take a shot of it before you indulge in the red wine: it will help to keep blood glucose levels balanced by making a GOOD choice.

Cooking and Storing

We know from the research done (where chia was baked into bread) that the temperature of 350F for 45 minutes does not negatively affect the nutritional composition. So this is a great Superfood to bake with.

For storage, you can't get much easier: whole seed can last many years when kept in a cool dry place. For ground seed, because the outer shell has been broken, there is some level of oxidization which can lead to spoilage if heated. However, unlike flax seed that has little anti-oxidants, the high levels in chia allow for the oxidization to occur slowly. So, the ground chia will be shelf stable in its package for a year. But when opened should be put in the fridge to slow down the oxidization process, and should last 6-8 weeks. If Chia is rancid, it will smell and taste slightly fishy. Also if the grounds stick together in clumps it is also a sign that this one should be composted ASAP!

Daily Serving

For best results, use 3-4 tablespoons a day. Two in the morning with breakfast, and then one each at lunch and dinner is preferred as this ensures that our blood glucose levels remain low, while allowing your nutrients in chia and food to be slowly and efficiently absorbed. Increase water intake if you do not drink a lot of water.

What to look for

The white chia seed has a more porous exterior and is bioavailable and absorbable as is with research to identify its benefits. The black seed has a harder outer shell and has not been studied for nutrients or absorption. But for the difference in exterior and research studies, the white and black have the same nutritionals if grown with the best agronomics.

Most importantly, buy chia from a reliable source! With a conscientious grower, the crop is harvested at the best possible time, without sacrificing the nutritional composition of the chia.

Hemp Seeds

History

Hemp was grown in China as early as 4000 BC and was used for paper, food, cloth and fishing nets. Hemp has enjoyed a long history of use for fiber including the use of it for canvas and for sails on boats (canvas comes from the root of its name "cannabis"). Hemp has also been used historically for ceremonials: as incense, for heightened awareness, or for special ceremonial clothing. It was even left in the tombs of pharaohs to identify its importance for medicine, oil and fiber. As long ago as 3000 BC, the Chinese emperor and herbalist, Chen-Nung wrote about hemp's medicinal and beneficial effects on malaria, female "issues", and other illnesses.

Integral to European life in the first millennium, hemp was transported across the ocean and quickly became a vital crop for North Americans. In the 1700's and 1800's American and Canadian farmers were required by law and/or encouraged to grow hemp as a staple crop. In fact, in 1776 The Declaration of Independence was drafted on hemp paper and the founding fathers George Washington, Thomas Jefferson, and John Adams were hemp farmers.

In the 1930's, the Federal Bureau of Narcotics, Dupont, and William Randolph Hearst created propaganda campaigns against hemp, as they threatened the new petroleum-based synthetic textiles of which Hearst and Dupont lead the pack. In addition, there was a growing fear (racism?) of relocated racial minorities who accepted the recreational use of Marijuana — as a result, the hemp crops for food and industrial use became associated with such racial fear (the word Marijuana comes from the combo of the Spanish and South American Mexican names: 'Maria and Juan').

By 1937 The Marijuana Tax Act was passed in the United States which made hemp growing prohibitive. Following along in Uncle Sam's footsteps, in 1938 Canada prohibited marijuana and all hemp production under the Opium and Narcotics Control Act.

Hemp was reintroduced to North Americans as a result of Canada's recognition of hemp as a crop for food and industrial use over a decade ago. It is still banned as a crop in the United States but is allowed to be imported into the United States for food sources from Canada or China.

Plant

Hemp plants have a variety of different uses which include fiber, food, medicinal purposes, and recreational uses. The vast numbers of hemp varieties available reflect that. For food crops, the hemp plant strains are bred for low their low psychoactive content (tetrahydrocannabinol (THC)) and high nutritional content.

Hemp is a very green crop as it cleans the soil, and feeds it with lots of natural nitrates. In addition, because it is so hearty it can grow without the use of weed control and needs little fertilizer compared to other crops. The seeds are planted March and May in the northern hemisphere, between September and November in the southern hemisphere and matures in about three to four months. At its full height, hemp can grow up to 7-8 feet high!

Gluten Free

Hemp is naturally gluten free and can be part of a gluten-free diet, as it lacks gluten and does not belong to the same botanical plant family as wheat, barley, or rye. Hemp has an exceptional amount of whole protein along with anti-inflammatory compounds that assist in getting a healthier intestinal tract going. Hypoallergenic and gluten-free, hemp is ideal for all.

Nutritional Benefits

Hemp is one of the tastiest superfoods and has so many high powered benefits. With lots of protein, anti-oxidants and great healthy fats, it is a tasty way to pump up any meal or snack.

Fiber

Hemp seeds are comprised of approximately 25 percent Carbs, almost all of which is in the form of soluble and insoluble fiber (a ratio of 4-to-1). The soluble fiber helps to reduce the LDL while the insoluble gets the junk out of the trunk!

Delores Hemp Seeds and Slow Roasted Hemp Seeds, see p. 71

Good Fats

Hemp seeds are packed with Omega-6, Omega-3 in the ratio of approximately 4:1 — the ratios recommended by the World Health Organization. The Omega-3s in hemp are more readily converted as a result of the presence of the Omega-6 stearidonic acid which helps to transition the Omega-3 plant based ALA to EPA. Win — win!

One of the best Omega-6's that hemp has to offer is its high gamma linolenic acid (GLA). GLA is highly anti-inflammatory and helps inhibit the release of histamine (the excess of which causes allergies). Most importantly, the GLA in hemp benefits the entire endocrine system by building hormones and brain tissue. GLA is not found in any other food source except for spirulina and Mother's milk (although evening primrose oil and borage oil supplements have GLA). As important as GLA is, our bodies do not naturally make it so to get it in through food is vital to overall health.

Those with premenstrual syndrome, diabetes, scleroderma, eczema and other skin conditions can have a metabolic block that interferes with the body's ability to make GLA. In addition, Western societies may be partially GLA-deficient as a result of aging, glucose intolerance, and high dietary fat intake. So, the importance of getting it in is even greater.

Protein

Hemp seeds contain more than 33% whole protein, which is quickly and efficiently used by the body for energy. Of the highly digestible protein, over 65% of it is Edestin (a globulin protein). Edestin is very similar to the globulin that is present in human blood plasma which means that the protein is easily digested and absorbed. The body uses globulin proteins to make antibodies which attack infecting agents.

The other important protein in hemp seed is Albumin, which helps destroy free radicals. These little lovelies together are absolutely essential to maintaining a healthy immune system as they help to neutralize alien microorganisms and toxins. Hemp protein can help kick these little monsters to the back door — good riddance!

Anti-oxidants

Hemp seed also has great antioxidants including: Vitamin E, carotene and the unique element of chlorophyll. This green antioxidant (responsible for the green color in all green plants) is one of nature's best detoxifiers and alkalizing compounds. So a tasty way to fight free radicals!

Vitamins/Minerals

Hemp seeds are a rich source of minerals as they draw many from the soil (which is why it is important where it is grown). These minerals include: phosphorus, calcium, potassium, silica, magnesium, iron, sodium, sulphur, chlorine, manganese, zinc, copper, platinum, boron, nickel, germanium, iodine and chromium.

Heart/Cholesterol

More GLA cheerleading here. GLAs, again, help to not only reduce bad cholesterol but increase the good — so the bad ones remaining get kicked to the curb — and GLA's have been found to reduce plaque buildup in arterial walls.[45] There is also some research that suggests that the EFA's can help to reduce rheumatoid arthritis.[46]

Anti-Inflammatory

It is GLAs to the rescue again! As discussed above, GLAs help to reduce inflammation which is imperative for overall health.

Other Benefits

Old wives tales tell a long-standing story that GLA is good for allergies. Not surprisingly, it is fact that women and children who are prone to allergies appear to have lower levels of GLA in breast milk and blood. The catch is that there is no good scientific evidence that taking GLA helps reduce allergy symptoms.[47] So, if you decide to try GLA for allergies, speak with your health care provider to determine if it is safe for you and track your allergy symptoms for signs of improvement.

GLAs, as found in hemp, have potential benefits for breast cancer treatment as one study found that women with breast cancer who took GLA had a better response to tamoxifen (a drug used to treat estrogen sensitive breast cancer) than those who took only tamoxifen.[48]

How to Use it

- Sprinkle onto salads, cereal, yogurt, and oatmeal.

- Add into home baked goods and recipes such as cookies and brownies.

- Blend with water to make a creamy hemp milk (one measurement of hemp seeds to 2 measurements of water — then blend on high until mixed — you can strain for an even smoother version)

- Use as a healthy coating in lieu of bread crumbs.

- Add into salad dressings.

- Add into dinners such as lasagna or your favorite salad.

- Add to smoothies and your favorite blended beverages.

- Use as milk or cream replacement in dips, soups, and sauces.

Cooking and Storing

Hemp seed cooked at a temperature of 350F, or less, for 25 minutes, or less, does not experience any negative effects to their nutritional composition. For soups and stews, I recommend adding the hemp seeds at the end and blend them in without boiling.

For storage, you can store unopened containers in a cool dark place. If opened, and you will not use up within a couple of weeks (which you should!), I would either store it in the fridge or, better yet, freeze it and draw down on it as you need it.

Daily Serving

For best results, use 2-4 tablespoons a day. Two in the morning with breakfast, and then one each at lunch and dinner is preferred as this ensures that you get the pure protein power at all of your meals. Many people forget protein in the mornings so this is an easy way to start the day super powered up!

What to look for

Look for hemp that is fresh with large seeds (they taste better). You can identify great fresh hemp by the smell and taste: the fresh stuff should have a nutty taste with a pleasant finish. If it tastes bitter or smells fishy dump it! Also look for high GLA counts as this is such a beneficial aspect of hemp seeds and different varieties have more GLA's than others.

Cacao

History

No magical mystery here. Cacao is the root of all chocolate and is not only a super healthy food to eat but it also has been used by indigenous cultures for centuries: they knew the benefits of cacao in a big way. It is interesting as modern science is now confirming how beneficial cacao is (with over 300 compounds in it!), which is exactly what the indigenous cultures already knew. Mystery solved.

The origin of cacao beans start in northern areas of what is now South America. Cacao beans have been traded and consumed as early as 600 B.C. Later, the Mayans used cacao beans in daily life as mood enhancers, as gifts, and as part of sacred marriage and succession ceremonies. It is even referenced as part of the creation of man itself![49]

Later on the Aztecs, like the Mayans, had a high regard for cacao. They revered it as well and it became a part of their currency. They took great pains to protect cacao crops and to grow cacao, even in the courtyard of Montezuma II's palace. Talk about sweet revenge!

In the 1500s, the Spanish conquest resulted in European introduction, and eventual love, of cacao. Cacao in Europe was viewed as a rich man's pleasure and was used for a variety of ailments and maladies, and as an aphrodisiac — and was even the love drug of choice by Casanova!

It was not until cacao went industrial that it really became known and used by all levels of society. In 1828, a Dutch chemist named Conrad Van Houten patented a process, now known as the cocoa press, which separated the cocoa butter from the chocolate liquor and created cocoa powder. He then added alkali to the powder to make it easier to mix and giving it a milder, less-intense flavor. It also allowed easy mixing of the cacao powder to water, and it could be boxed and packaged for use. Chocolate was born, followed shortly by the creation of the chocolate candy bar.

Plant

The cacao fruit tree grows in acidic soils with a lot of compost to boost it. It enjoys tropical weather and likes to be close to the Equator with temperatures around 80F with humidity. The cacao trees like to be protected from the elements which are why it works well with other plants surrounding it such as coconut, avocado and bananas. It takes about 4 years to produce fruit which, once matured, it does all year long. A ripened pod takes about a half a year to develop and is just over half a foot long when ready to be picked. Within each pod the cacao nuts (beans) develop and number upwards of 50 per pod.

The pods are gently taken down from the trees and then manually opened to remove the beans within a week to 10 days after harvesting. They then undergo a fermentation process (which also removes the naturally occurring phytic acid) which should take a day for the Criollo variety. This also brings out the chocolate flavor. The beans and pulp are placed in a box with coconut or banana leaves placed on top. This will allow micro-organisms to develop and initiate the fermentation of the pulp surrounding the beans. These chemical reactions cause the chocolate flavor and color to develop while maximizing the anti-oxidants.

The beans are then dried to reduce the moisture content so that they do not spoil. For the best taste and most nutrient density, drying should take place slowly (in the sun preferably) but not too slowly. If dried too quickly, the beans become bitter, and if done too slowly they may develop mold with off flavors.

Gluten Free

All natural cacao products are naturally gluten free. Most cacao products are harvested in countries where no wheat is grown making it unlikely for cross contamination to take place.

Nutritional Benefits

Cacao is one of the most mineral rich and powerful foods to eat. With over 300 compounds in it, it offers up all of the macronutrients and tons of the micro's as well. Plus it tastes incredible and can be used in sweet and savory dishes.

Fiber

Cacao is a surprisingly good source of dietary fiber. For a 1 tablespoon serving: cocoa powder contains 1.5 grams dietary fiber (7 percent of the daily value); and for nibs, 1 tablespoon provides 9 grams of fiber (42% of daily value!). The fiber in cocoa is mainly insoluble fiber — so a tasty way to keep the toxins flowing OUT!

Good Fats

Approximately 36% of the fat in the cacao bean is healthy fat made up of either mono- or polyunsaturated fat, of which, oleic acid (the fatty acid high in olive oil) makes up the largest proportion. Of the saturated fat content in cocoa butter, over half comes from stearic acid which has been shown to have a neutral impact on blood cholesterol.[50]

Protein

Another surprise is that this tasty treat has whole protein in it. Cacao nibs and beans boast about 15% protein. Most importantly, cacao contains the essential amino acid tryptophan. Tryptophan, along with B3 and 6 and magnesium, is critical in order for the body to make serotonin — our happy anti-stress transmitter! So this protein helps us to feel super!

Cacao Beans Nibs and Powder, see p. 77

Anti-oxidants

Cacao is exceptionally high in concentrated antioxidants — the highest food source in the world! Unlike processed dark chocolate, antioxidants are preserved in raw cacao. Cacao beans contain polyphenols (similar to those found in wine) with antioxidant properties which are health beneficial. These compounds are called flavonoids and include catechins, resveratrol, epicatechins, and procyandins. The antioxidant flavonoids are found in the nonfat portions of the cacao bean. The flavonoids also reduce the blood's ability to clot and thus reduce the risk of stroke and heart attacks.

Vitamins/Minerals

Cacao enjoys high vitamin C and A. Cacao also has an incredible array of minerals including: calcium, chromium, iron, zinc, copper, potassium and manganese. It is one of the richest sources of magnesium which we know is vital for heart and brain health.

Heart/Cholesterol

Cacao is heart health in a small delicious delivery system, as evidenced by the long term use of it by indigenous people. In a research released in 1997, researchers from the Harvard Medical School studied the effects of cocoa and flavanols on Panama's island dwelling Kuna people, who are heavy consumers of cocoa. They found that the Kunas had significantly lower rates of heart disease and cancer compared to the mainlanders who do not drink cocoa. The researchers concluded that the improved blood flow after consumption of flavonol-rich cocoa may help to achieve healthy heart benefits and may assist the brain to improve learning and memory.[51]

Recent research also shows the beneficial cardiovascular effects of cacao, likely due to the polyphenols/flavonoids which improved: blood vessel strength, blood pressure, insulin resistance, and lowered blood sugar levels.[52] Other research indicated cacao's properties can help: reduce bad cholesterol and increase the good,[53] increase the dilation of blood vessels;[54] reduce DNA oxidation;[55] increase overall antioxidant capacity,[56] and decrease the risks for blood clots.[57] A study done on people with congestive heart failure concluded that Flavonol-rich chocolate acutely improves vascular function in such patients.[58]

An important point to note is that raw cacao beans give you the biggest bang for the buck as the processing from cacao to chocolate bars markedly reduces the concentration of flavonols.[59] So the raw whole food wins again!

Other Benefits

Cacao is also a rich source of serotonin which is a neurotransmitter that helps us to feel happy and content. So happy, happy, joy, joy! In addition, phenylethylamine (I don't even TRY to say this so let's go with PEA's) are a bunch of compounds that are found in cacao. This is what our bodies naturally produce when we fall in love... is Valentine's Day making more sense?

These compounds, along with magnesium, also help to suppress appetite so a great and tasty way to shed some weight naturally (and pssst: remember long ago when you fell in love and had no appetite? Well, it was REAL!). Cacao also is a good source of chromium, an important mineral that helps to stabilize blood sugar levels and reduce appetite. So a double whammy.

Cacao's source of theobromine, an alkaloid, is another big plus when using this wonderful bean. With 1% theobromine, you get the benefits of caffeine like stimulant (which stimulates the cardio system) without taxing the nervous system or elevating blood sugar like caffeine does. Did you know that cacao's theobromine can also help in the prevention of cavities? The compound theobromine actually helps to kill streptococci mutans which is one of the strains of bacteria that cause tooth decay. So munch away on nibs and say adios to Dr. Dentist!

How to Use It

Beans:

- Simply eat them on their own!

Powder:

- Use daily as a super anti-oxidant supplement.

- Add a ½–1 tablespoon into smoothies for a nutrient boost.

- Sprinkle on yogurt, oatmeal or cereal for fabulous taste.

- Add to sauces and soups for a smoky finish.

- Add into baked goods and desserts to improve nutritional value.

- Swap out up to 20% of other flours in recipes with cacao powder instead.

Nibs:

- Eat alone for a boost of energy.

- Simply top your morning cereal or oatmeal with them for a heart healthy breakfast.

- Add into healthy baked goods, puddings, and desserts.

- Mix into smoothies for a delightful and crunchy surprise.

- Add as a salad topper.

- Add into healthy trail mixes for super source of anti-oxidants and energy.

Cooking and Storing

Keep stored in a cool, dry place with no exposure to extreme heat in tightly sealed bags. Cocoa powder can typically be stored for 2 years.

Daily Serving

Beans: for adults: eat 8-10 a day (better yet, one bean for 20 pounds of weight) OR nibs should be enjoyed in 2 tablespoons a day. Cacao powder is a wonderful anti-oxidant boost with a ½ tablespoon a day.

What to look for

Make sure you are getting the best — opt for Criollo Arriba beans not the cross breeds that are Forastero and Trinitario. Criollo is the rarest and most nutrient dense so make sure you are getting what you think you are buying. Raw cacao has a very strong taste but it should not be super bitter, nor should it have a white film on it — this indicates improper drying.

Also avoid ANY cacao or chocolate product that does not state the origins. Most of the world's chocolate (can you say NESTLE?[60]) is sourced from Southern Africa (especially, Cote D'Ivoire, Nigeria, Ghana and Somalia). Child labor camps have been set up with forced labor, outright abuse and often time's child trafficking. The crazy irony is this: we feed our kids chocolate every Christmas and Easter to make them feel happy and good, but it has been made by kids in Africa that have been taken from their homes and forced into labor at a young age. We need to rethink this as a culture (my gentle way of saying: "please stop buying this karmic krap").

For cacao powder look for a light brown color as a very dark color indicated a high heat in the processing — done usually as a fast and easy way to process the powder. The powder should have a strong chocolate flavor but not be bitter in taste. Avoid dutched or processed cacao powder, as the high heat diminishes the beneficial phytochemicals. Harvard researcher Dr. Hollenberg even identifies the myths surrounding the "benefits" of dark chocolate — it is the real raw cacao that is the real deal, not chocolate bars (no matter how 'dark').[61]

Goji Berries

History

Holy history Batman! These lovely little berries, filled with taste like a cross between a cranberry and a raisin, have been around a LONG time! They have been used for over 2000 years in many traditional Asian medicine systems. One of the oldest references to goji is a poem from Liu Yuxi during the Tang Dynasty where he says: "the goji nourishes body and soul, drink of the well and enjoy long life".

The plant is highly prized by Tibetan healers, who treat liver, kidney, eye, and skin problems; tuberculosis, diabetes, anxiety, and insomnia. This powerful berry has been used to lower blood pressure for thousands of years. One Chinese Medica dating back 2,000 years cites the use of these berries in treatments ranging from replenishing vital essences to strengthening and restoring major organs.[62]

Folklore has it that the goji berry was "discovered" by people who drank from a certain well for water that had beneficial youthful effects — the fountain of youth perhaps? It just so happens that a goji tree grew over the well, dropping its ripened fruit into it. Although unproven, we do know that Tibetan doctors have used the Goji berry as a curative and "functional food" for thousands of years.

Plant

Goji is a perennial shrub. With so many years behind it, the goji has developed over 80 varieties (the most popular being the Lycium barbarum, also known as the "goji berry" or "wolfberry"). Once pollinated, the goji bush develops small fruit that can range from the color yellow to orange or dark red, and they are usually oblong in shape and resemble cranberries in size.

The goji bush is very adaptable and can grow in various temperatures. Goji berry plants can survive winter temperatures as low as — 40 Celsius (-40 F) and summer temperatures as high as 38 Celsius (100 F). Although the berries can grow in any kind of soil, rich quality soil allows for better flowering and fruit. The one thing goji berries demand is well drained soil as they don't do well in wet or soggy conditions. With their aggressive root systems they are uniquely drought tolerant after they are up and running! The plant can grow from 6-10 feet high.

Gluten Free

Goji berries are naturally gluten free. Again, these are unlikely to be at high risk for contamination as they grow in areas that do not process high allergen foods like wheat.

Goji Berries, see p. 83

Nutritional Benefits

Goji berries boost so many benefits, it often sounds too good to be true — but they are for real! Deliciously nutritious, these are a must have in the pantry and your daily diet.

Fiber

Goji berries are made up of over 65% carbohydrates with 10% being fiber, 36% being polysaccharides (very complex long chain sugars) and only 21.7% being simple sugars(making this a low-glycemic fruit).

Good Fats

The goji berry is made up of over 8% essential fatty acids half of which are the healthy polyunsaturated fats.

Protein

More protein than whole wheat (13% more), the goji berry displays an insulin-like action that is effective in fat decomposition. With its whole protein, and 18 amino acids, this berry packs a powerful protein punch!

Anti-oxidants

Goji berries also have a very high ORAC (Oxygen Radical Absorbance Capacity) level to prevent free radical oxidation — they measure 25,000 with antioxidant levels more than ten times higher than blueberries and about three times higher than pomegranates. Goji berries have been studied for their huge immune boosting effect.[63]

Vitamins/Minerals

Goji berries are packed with micronutrients including 21 trace minerals, such as: zinc, iron, selenium, copper, calcium, phosphorus, and vitamins A, B1, B2, B6, E and vitamin C. Not only rich in vitamins and minerals, goji berries are the richest food and plant source of carotenoids (beta carotene, lutein, lycopene, cryptoxanthin and zeaxanthin). Cartenoids help to protect the retina of the eye and improve eye sight.[64] A study of elderly adults published in 2001 in Optometry and Vision Science found that goji juice protected the macula from damage[65] which is a common ailment of diabetics.

Heart/Cholesterol

Goji contains cyperone, a substance that promotes a healthy heart and regulates blood pressure. Use of goji berries has shown a reduction in blood pressure, bad cholesterol and improving the good. In fact, a recent study found that the antioxidants in goji juice can reduce the risk of cardiovascular conditions.[66]

Other Benefits

Goji berries are the "memory berry" and can assist in improving memory and mental agility.[67] Goji berries have also been shown to promote liver health and to remove the toxins.[68]

Likely due to the excellent source of selenium and germanium, cyperone, anthocyanins, and betain (a nerve tonic), physalin (which is an active compound against all major kinds of leukemia) goji berries have been used to treat cancer patients and improve cancer treatments.[69]

Goji contain special polysaccharides which are long chain sugar molecules that feed the white blood cells in the gut. They strengthen the defense system and are responsible for controlling your body's most important immune systems and have been linked to reducing human leukemia cell growth and increasing the white cell count.[70] The unique polysaccharide content in goji berries also stimulates the pituitary glands to increase the secretion of Human Growth Hormone which is linked to anti-aging, muscle, and tissue repair, reducing body fat, improved memory and sleep.

Note though that goji berries contains betaine, an aborticide substance, so pregnant women should avoid them.

How to Use It

- Eat alone for a chewy boost of energy.

- Add when baking your favorite cookies, muffins and energy bars.

- Add into teas and eat the goji berries after — they expand will and become plump and juicy!

- Simply top your morning cereal, yogurt, or oatmeal with them for a heart healthy and immune boosting breakfast.

- Mix into smoothies for a delightful colorful surprise.

- Add into pancakes for greater health.

- Add into trail mixes for a super source of anti-oxidants and energy.

Cooking and Storing

Like any dried fruit, goji berries are best stored in a sealed container at or below 30C. They do not need to be refrigerated but may be if not consumed within a few weeks of opening package.

Daily Serving

For best results, use 2-4 tablespoons a day (grab a handful). Try to spread it out over the day with at least one tablespoon in the morning with breakfast, and another one at lunch and dinner is preferred.

What to look for

Like all food, the proof is in the proverbial processing pudding. Avoid goji berries that are dry: they should be slightly moist and chewy. Also avoid those that have a salty or strong aftertaste as these may have been sprayed with chemical pesticides or sulfur dioxide. Opt for berries that have a rich red color but not a bright red (avoid cheap and dyed ones). Avoid any goji that looks like it could pass for a large rodent's calling card.

Coconut

History

Exactly where coconuts originated is not known although we know they go WAAAAAAY back: the oldest fossils known of the modern coconut date from the Eocene period from around 37 to 55 million years ago and were found in Australia and India.[71]

More recently, the coconut was first written about was in India over 2,000 years ago. Coconut is referenced in the 4th century BC, as well as in the Tamil literature dating from the 1st-4th century AD. Coconuts were featured throughout the Hindu epic stories of the Ramayana and Mahabharata (from the ancient Indian text of the Puranas). As a result of its history of use in India, the coconut enjoyed a prominent role in Indian ritual and mythology. Maybe because it resembles a human head, or maybe because it is so delicious, it was known as sriphala (or "fruit of the gods").

Coconut plant has a myriad of uses. The roots are used for dyes and medicine. The trunk may be used for buildings parts, furniture, novelty items and paper pulp. The shell is used for charcoal for cooking. The husk is used for rope, matting, and coarse cloth such as floor mats, doormats, brushes and mattresses. The coconut leaves can even be used for roofing (for thatch).

But best of all, coconut is used for culinary purposes including: oil, milk, water, meat, nectar, and

Coconut Flour and Coconut Sugar, see p. 87

sugar — which is made from making an incision on the stem leading to the fruit, with the nectar dripping out and cooking the nectar until it becomes a sugar. Coconut nectar can even be fermented into vinegar and booze! No wonder in Sanskrit, the name of coconut is "kalpa vriksha", translated it means "the tree which provides all the necessities of life". Uh-huh!

Plant

Although the origin of coconut is one tough nut to crack, coconuts, regardless of their name, are fruits not nuts — so nut allergy sufferers can relax.

Coconut is part of the palm family and can grow up to a 100 feet! The plants thrive on sandy soils and are highly tolerant of salinity soaked soil, making them great for by-the-seaside shade! They like to have steady sunlight (mean annual temperature of 27F), regular rainfall and enjoy high humidity (70–80%+) for optimum growth. They are truly tropical.

Gluten Free

All natural coconut products are gluten free. The great thing as well, is most harvested coconut is made in countries where no wheat is grown making it unlikely for cross contamination to take place.

Nutritional Benefits

The nutritional benefits of coconut are very high. In fact there are many products that come from the coconut tree which are so good to eat and good for you — these include: coconut oil, coconut meat, coconut flour (fiber), coconut sugar and coconut water. I will discuss some of their benefits below, but just know that whatever you choose to use it is a good choice!

Fiber

Coconut meat is high in fiber and is a filling and tasty way to keep the bad LDL down. Is soothing anti-inflammatory compounds along with great fiber help to gently keep the intestinal tract clean and calm.

Good Fat

Simply put, coconut oil is a saturated fat that acts like a fiber. Fats come in a bunch of sizes and their size determines how they work in our bodies. So they can be short-chain fatty acids (SCFA), medium-chain fatty acids (MCFA), and long-chain fatty acids (LCFA).

Most fats and oils in our diets (a whopping 98%), whether they are saturated or unsaturated or come from animals or plants, are made up of long-chain fatty acids. By comparison, coconut oil is composed predominately of medium-chain fatty acids, also known as medium-chain triglycerides or "MCT".

The length of the fatty acid is very important as our bodies respond to and metabolize each length of fatty acid differently. Unlike its taller brother, the MCFAs do not have a negative effect on cholesterol and help to protect against heart disease. MCFA helps to lower the risk of both atherosclerosis and heart disease.

MCFAs also support the immune system and are anti-viral, anti-bacterial and anti-microbial which helps to fight off invaders (even herpes) and help to keep you strong.[72] They also help to speed up the metabolism by increasing the thyroid's effectiveness. Also, because MCFA is not able to be stored in the body and needs to be burned up, it helps to shred those pounds and to provide fast and usable energy. Combining coconut oil with EFA's also doubles their effectiveness in the body.

Protein

Coconuts have 18 amino acids making them an incredible fruit based protein. So this sweet treat is also the building blocks for strength and endurance.

Anti-oxidants

Ferulic acid, as found in coconut and other seeds, fruits and some vegetables, has many benefits and is a known anti-oxidant, helps to decrease inflammation and has anti-tumor properties. It also protects the liver during alcohol ingestion by warding off free radicals.

The second anti-oxidant in coconuts is p-Coumaric acid which is found widely found in fruits, vegetables, and tea. Together these two compounds work synergistically and are responsible for over 80% of the antioxidant capacity of coconut oil.

Vitamins/Minerals

Coconut is a good source of vitamins: C, B1, B2, B6, and B9. It also has many minerals including: potassium, phosphorus, calcium, magnesium, iron, sodium, manganese, zinc, copper and selenium.

Heart / Cholesterol

Coconut has very little cholesterol, but can help to stimulate the HDL, healthy cholesterol, in the liver. Ferulic acid also serves to lower blood pressure by causing dilation of the blood vessels and inhibits plaque buildup in arteries and increases HDL while kicking LDL in the behind! p-Coumaric acid in coconut also effectively lowers LDL cholesterol and helps to prevent plaque buildup.

Coconut, especially the MCFA has been studied for its anti-oxidant effects to zap free radicals and for its anti-carcinogen properties to assist treating some cancers and cancer treatment side effects.[73] In addition, coconut oil MCFA has been found to help reduce the risk of coronary heart disease (CD) by killing off bacterial and viral infections: as studies are showing a direct correlation between CD and chronic low-grade bacterial and viral infections (Chlamydia pneumoniae, CytOmegalovirus, and Helicobacter pylori).[74] Its anti-inflammatory effects also help to reduce risks.[75]

Other Benefits

The MCFA in coconut also helps to reduce blood glucose levels and assist in weight loss[76] and reduce the risks of aging (like ALS, Alzheimer's and dementia).[77] Coconut has dramatic effects and benefits on healing damaged kidney and liver organs and can provide ongoing protection to keep these organs healthy.[78]

On a glam note, coconut oil may also reduce symptoms associated with psoriasis, eczema, and dermatitis and help to soften skin while preventing wrinkles, sagging skin, and age spots.[79] So go ahead and slather it ON!

How to Use It

Coconut sugar:

With its great nutritional values, no adverse effects, and low glycemic index (35 GI), and low fructose levels (10%) it is unique to its other sweet competitors. Cane sugars (white and brown sugar), dates, maple syrup, and molasses are all high glycemic foods creating insulin levels to fluctuate and are hard on the pancreas.

Coconut sugar is a far better choice (see chart below) than low glycemic sweeteners such as agave (55GI) that have very high levels of fructose which is stored in the liver and produces fat making it harder to burn as an energy source. In addition, coconut sugar is nutrient dense with no side effects unlike sugar alcohol based sweeteners such as xylitol and sorbitol and plant based stevia.

Oil:

- Use it to fry with, oil pans, and swap out butter in recipes (use 25% less oil than butter). The flash point on coconut is much higher (375F) so it is a great oil to fry with.

- Add to toast for a healthy morning boost.

- Use it to make popcorn for added flavor and health.

- Add a tablespoon to your smoothies daily for great immune boosting elements.

- Make icings out of it.

- Use it as a natural body softener externally and as a hair oil treatment.

Flour:

- Use daily as a super fiber supplement.

- Add a tablespoon into smoothies for a nutrient boost.

- Sprinkle on yogurt, oatmeal or cereal for fabulous fiber.

- Use as a nutritious thickener in sauces and soups.

- Swap out your breadcrumbs for coconut flour for breading.

- Add into baked goods and desserts to improve texture, and nutritional value.

- Swap out up to 20% of other flours in recipes with coconut flour instead.

Sugar:

- Use in cocoa, tea, and coffee.

- Use in baked goods with a one-to-one ratio of white sugar to coconut sugar.

- Use it for syrups and sauces for pies and crumbles.

- Sweeten your morning cereal, oatmeal or granola with it.

- Cook with it, and use as a sweet finish for soups, and sauces.

Milk:

- Use in baking and cooking instead of dairy milk

- Add to cereal, oatmeal and smoothies.

Cooking and Storing

Coconut oil, sugar, unopened flour, and dried meat can be stored well sealed in a cool dry place for a year. If your coconut flour is opened, best to keep it in a mason jar in the fridge as it will last up to 6 months. Discard the oil if any signs of mold on top or a strange smell.

Daily Serving

Try for a tablespoon of coconut oil daily to keep the viruses and bacteria at bay. Also opt for a tablespoon or two of coconut flour to keep excellent fiber flowing through your internal faucet to keep squeaky clean. Coconut sugar can be used anytime you need a sweet reminder of how super life is!

What to look for

Coconut oil is the oil extracted from the meat of the coconut. It can be done by wet milling, dry milling, enzymes added, a manual press or centrifuge. Using one of these processes makes it virgin oil. Refined, bleached, and deodorized oil, or RBD oil is usually made from copra (dried coconut kernel) which is placed in a hydraulic press with added heat and the oil is extracted. This provides a high yield "crude" coconut oil that is not suitable for consumption because it contains contaminants. You would know a RBD coconut oil as it has no coconut taste or aroma. RBD oil is used for industrial and pharmaceutical purposes. It is the RBD oil that they use to hydrogenate to create the mutated trans-fatty acid (TFA) — this is a fat that is used to preserve many junky foods and is a definite NO-NO!

So when buying oil, look for:

- Virgin oil

- Color: look for a snow white color when solid and perfectly clear when liquid. Any shades of yellow or gray scream inferior quality (mold from old coconuts or smoke residue form gas or wood heating to obtain oil).

- Taste and Smell: the best a coconut oil should retain a soft coconut smell and taste: it should be a light aroma. A strong smell or taste indicates high heat processing and potential contaminants. If they have no flavor they are essentially RBD oil, even if they did come from fresh coconut.

When buying coconut flour and sugar, look for a white colored flour and a light brown or tan colored sugar. If the flour is yellow tinted or the sugar a dark brown it indicates that a high heat processing has taken place that will denature and "burn" the food. The high heat speeds up the processing time making it more lucrative for the producer but with less nutrients for you! So choose wisely.

With coconut sugar, life can be sweet! Coconut sugar is such a lovely gift and is truly a better sweetener than all else out there — including palm sugar. In the interests of clarifying the benefits of coconut sugar as compared to other sweeteners in the market, the following chart is an excellent summary.[80]

NAME	GI	FRUCTOSE %	CAL. / TBSP	MINERALS	VITAMINS	AMINO ACIDS
Coconut Sugar	35	10%	10	Potassium, magnesium, zinc & iron	B1, B2, B3, B6	16/20 AA (High Glutamine)
Honey	30/Raw 75/Proc.	38-50%	60	Calcium, copper, magnesium, manganese, phosphorous, iron, sodium, zinc, potassium	B2, B3, B5, B6, B9, Vitamin C	Small Amounts 18 AA
Maple Syrup	54	50%	50	Great source of magnesium, calcium, potassium, sodium, copper & zinc	Trace of B1, B2 and B5	0
Palm Sugar	35	38–48%	45	Potassium, magnesium, phosphorous, iron, zinc	B1, B2, B3, B6	12
Stevia	0	0	0	Stevia leaf has been found to contain iron, phosphorous, calcium, potassium, copper manganese & zinc	Vitamin A and Vitamin C	9 EAA / 8 NEAA
Agave	30	55–90%	45	Trace amounts only of calcium, potassium, manganese, magnesium & iron	Trace amounts of Vitamin C, K, B1, B2 and B6	0
Brown Rice Syrup	20	0	45	0	0	Trace AA
Maltodextrin	105–136	0	56	Trace amounts, if any	Trace amounts of Vitamin C, K, B1, B2 and B6	0

BENEFITS	SIDE EFFECTS
Safe & excellent sugar option for diabetics & hypoglycemic due to low GI level. Helps to regulate blood sugar levels. Look for Coconut Sugar that is a yellow-brown color which indicates chemical free and minimally processed. Will not give you an energy 'crash'. Glutamine helps support the immune, digestive, and nervous system as well as removing excess ammonia from the body. May reduce chances of developing breast cancer. Minerals contained in this sugar help to prevent cardiovascular disease, are necessary for proper nerve & brain function, blood health, strong immune system, kidney function and cell health.	Avoid if allergy to coconut or tree nuts. Otherwise, no bad side effects have been found.
Raw: alkaline, anti-viral, antibacterial, anti-fungal and anti-inflammatory. Stabilizes blood pressure and blood sugar. Soothes coughs, asthma, hay fever and throat irritations. Treats diarrhea/stomach ulcers. Topical use for healing wounds.	Avoid giving to children under 1 yr (botulism).
Antioxidant properties effective in slowing down the aging process, and fighting off free radicals therefore protecting the body from nasty disease causing invaders. Helps with digestive problems such as gas and bloating. Can aid in muscle repair and cell damage.	Maple syrup can tend to be high in calories, and therefore may be connected with weight gain if consumed often and in large quantities. Make sure when buying maple syrup, purchase from a valuable source, make sure it does not contain aluminum from processing.
Can assist with healing the body and preventing illness. May reduce chances of developing breast cancer. Helps with preventing diabetes due to low GI level. Minerals contained in this sugar help to prevent cardiovascular disease, are necessary for proper nerve & brain function, blood health, strong immune system, kidney function and cell health.	Higher fructose level that is not too far from HFCS fructose level creating stress on the liver. Not suitable for those with tree nut allergies.
Decreases sugar cravings. Can kill off yeast and certain microbes. Inhibits growth & reproduction of harmful bacteria. Can aid with diabetes, high blood pressure, heart disease, skin problems, gum disease & tooth decay.	Few studies have examined long term use of stevia. May compound effect of diabetes medication & cause low blood sugar. Can act as a diuretic, & can cause allergic reactions in people sensitive to plants such as marigolds, daisies & ragweed. Banned in several countries in Europe.
Does not cause sharp rises or falls in blood sugar. Can aid with healing of wounds due to antibacterial properties.	Depletion of body's minerals, inflammation of the liver, hardening of arteries, insulin resistance, heart disease, weight gain & obesity. Contains high levels of toxic saponins which disrupt red blood cells.
Low glycemic index does not cause spikes in blood sugar levels.	Brown rice fields are grown in the old cotton fields in the USA. A study showed that infant formulas containing brown rice syrup contained 20-30 times more arsenic than formulas without it. The natural arsenic is taken up from the soil and into the brown rice. Inorganic arsenic exposure through ingestion has been shown to cause cancer in the skin, bladder, liver and lung. Babies are especially vulnerable to these toxic chemicals.
Cannot induce allergies due to no protein.	May contain gluten. Increases blood sugar levels, which increases insulin secretion causing stress on the pancreas. Causes tooth decay. Has shown to cause liver and kidney enlargement in rodents.

NAME	GI	FRUCTOSE %	CAL. / TBSP	MINERALS	VITAMINS	AMINO ACIDS
Xylitol	8	0	29	Trace amounts only. Aids in absorption of calcium		0
Brown Sugar	64	0	52	Calcium, iron, copper, potassium, phosphorous, manganese & magnesium	Trace amounts of B3, B6 and B9	0
White Sugar	64	0	50	Very little traces of zinc, copper, iron, selenium & manganese	Extremely small trace of B2	0
Corn Syrup	100	0	65	Trace amounts sodium, copper, magnesium & selenium	Small traces of B1, B2 & pantothenic acid	0
Splenda	80	0	0	0	0	0
Aspartame	0	0	0	0	0	0 / Chemically created
High Fructose Corn Syrup	89	55–80%	53	None. Actually causes mineral deficiencies by driving them out of the body.	Extremely small trace of B2	0

BENEFITS	SIDE EFFECTS
Reduces plaque formation and dental caries due to increased salivary flow	Has been known to cause diarrhea, bloating and flatulence. Can cause low blood sugar. Intake of high doses of xylitol has also shown to cause liver failure in dogs, which can be fatal as well as elevated levels of liver enzymes associated with liver damage.
Contains less calories than refined white sugar, and therefore slightly more effective (but not by much) in preventing weight gain. Raw and brown sugars maintain some of the natural minerals that has shown to prevent growths/abnormalities in mice, although this hasn't been studied yet on humans.	Although slightly better than refined white sugar, too much can still cause dental health problems such as erosions of tooth enamel, decay and cavities. Can cause obesity, diabetes, hypertension, heart disease, osteoporosis and vitamin and mineral deficiencies. Speeds up signs of aging. Suppresses your immune system. Addictive and can cause side effects such as mood swings, depression and anxiety when these cravings aren't met.
No known health benefits of white sugar due to high processing, added chemicals, bleaching, additives and other bad substances. Processing of this 'sugar' strips it entirely of any naturally occurring minerals and vitamins.	Too much can cause dental health problems such as erosions of tooth enamel, decay and cavities. Can cause obesity, diabetes, hypertension, heart disease, osteoporosis and vitamin and mineral deficiencies. Speeds up signs of aging. Suppresses your immune system. Addictive and can cause side effects such as mood swings, depression and anxiety when these cravings aren't met.
No health benefits found. Only 'benefit' to your body is that it acts as a food preservative and protects food from water activity that generally allow microorganisms to grow, extended shelf life of processed foods.	Can cause similar health issues as HFCS can including obesity, declined heart health, high blood pressure, diabetes and tooth decay.
No calories, but side effects and high GI counteract any benefits.	An indigestible substance. A short term study in rats showed they suffered from shrunken thymus glands, as well as enlarged livers & kidneys. No long term studies were done before the FDA approved it. Contains chlorine which is harmful to the body in large amounts. Can cause headaches, stomach / digestive problems, anxiety, skin rashes, muscle aches, weakened immune systems, liver/kidney damage, birth defects and cancer as well as numerous other problems when eaten in large amounts due to sucralose content. Studies also indicate you eat more artificial sweeteners as they stimulate appetite and produce carbohydrate cravings.
No calories, but side effects outweigh any benefits.	Can cause seizures, dizziness, tremors, migraines, memory loss, slurring of speech, confusion, fatigue, depression, & nausea . Aggravates hypoglycemia. Can deteriate stomach lining and cause stomach ulcers and some research indicates Aspartame may be involved in formation of cancers. Some doctors have suggested that Aspartame should not be given to children. Children lack a barrier of protection that prevents the wrong nutrients from entering the brain (which adults have). Aspartame should not be consumed by people who have a disease called phenylketonuria, because their body's cannot metabolize phenylaline.Studies also indicate you eat more artificial sweeteners as they stimulate appetite and produce carbohydrate cravings.
No health benefits found. Only 'benefit' to your body is that it acts as a food preservative and protects food from water activity that generally allow microorganisms to grow, which extends shelf life of processed foods.	Genetically modified, interferes with Thyroid function, high blood pressure, diabetes, causes weight gain/obesity & many other health problems.. Found in fast food, processed meals and pop and can cause people to overeat. Promotes fat production. Studies also indicate you eat more artificial sweeteners as they stimulate appetite and produce carbohydrate cravings.

The following are foods I think are awesome, but for reasons described below, fell a little short of my criteria for Superfood. But these foods are incredible to get in.

Algae

This stuff is powerful. It is incredible as a super source of minerals, vitamins, high chlorophyll, anti-oxidants, and detoxification (heavy metals and liver). It supports the immune system and can boost white blood cells. It has also been studied to measure results. It is a great thing to get in every day but I prefer to use as a supplement than cook with it (maybe a few salad dressings).

Quite frankly, there is very little you can do to make this stuff taste good, so pop your supplement pills and be done with it. Chlorella can help rebuild tissue and beneficial gut bacteria or you can also opt for blue-green spirulina which has excellent protein, vitamin A and GLA. E3 Live is another great source of algae and tastes pretty harmless in smoothies.

Bee Pollen/Honey

I kept this out as I wanted a complete non-animal and plant-based book. But bee pollen is LOADED with minerals, has all your B vitamins, along with vitamin C, D, E and K and good fats and amino acids. The pollen as well can be good for allergies as it produces histamine and can neutralize allergies. Honey has been long used as a natural healing agent as it has antibiotic effects.

Goldenberry

These berries are so tasty and delicious and are sour and sweet and chewy and tasty at the same time. I love to eat them on their own, as my mouth bursts with flavor. They are filled with high vitamin A and C, bioflavinoids and protein. They are lovely in a trail mix, on a salad, or on an early morning oatmeal or cereal. For me, their benefits are so far surpassed by goji berries (except for protein) that they are a second berry fiddle — but a super tasty one all the same!

Maca

This root from the Peruvian Andes is an adaptogen, meaning it can adapt to your bodies chemical physical or biological sources of stress. This can help to re-stabilize the cardiovascular and nervous system and hormonal system. It helps to support the adrenals, thyroid and libido. It has great minerals, good fats and vitamin B1, B2, C and E!

The reason I have not highlighted it as not as much as a –wow- as some of the other Superfoods, is that it has a malty and pasty powdery texture. It is great in smoothies and as a smoky finish to sauces or stews/soups, but it not something you want as a flavor up front. It is great to get in everyday as a supplement or to plop the powdered version in your smoothie. Don't eat a tablespoon on its own as you will need a spoon to jar open your jaw — this stuff sticks!

Oats

I love oats!

They are naturally gluten free and full of goodness. Unfortunately, as I noted above, many people think that oats are full of gluten and are an unhealthy grain to eat. Some people, including some Celiacs, have allergic responses to oats. It is important to note that many suffer from the cross contamination aspect of them rather than from oats themselves. Real oats are gluten free, so make sure you get them from a reliable source that states they are gluten free (less than 20ppms).

In fact, for Celiacs oats have actually been found to assist those with the disease to enhance the nutritional values of their diets, particularly for vitamins and minerals, as well as increasing antioxidant levels, which helps the body to eliminate free radicals as well as protect the brain from oxidative damage.[81]

In addition, oats are high in fiber and protein (1 cup of oats = 6 g of protein and 4 g of fiber) which allows for a long digestion and a reduction in blood glucose levels. It is also very high in manganese, a mineral that helps enzymes in bone formation and a cup of oatmeal give you 70% of your daily requirement. Oats are a great addition, if you obtain the best kind!

Sea Veggies

These veggies have been used for thousands of years for their nutrients and are such a rich source of fiber, protein, beta carotene, enzymes, vitamins (A, D, E and K) and minerals. Look for dulse, nori, kelp, and wakame. They can be sweet, fishy, and salty — at a minimum. They have a distinctive taste and may take a little of getting used to.

Not Included — and Why?

It is such a personal decision what food to eat so I don't want anyone to get upset with what I have to say next. I just feel that there is a lot of info out there about "amazing Superfoods" that is bordering on misinformation. So, I want to be clear why a couple of the foods that are often identified as Superfoods are not my personal choices. That is not to say that the food is not nutritious — most of them are. But I want to be clear why I did not reference it.

Acai

Acai is bitter with a strong after taste and a "choke it down" for me — but some love it. It is touted as a huge anti-oxidant source (especially by multi-level-marketing companies that can say anything that they want with no recourse) but it has limited research done on it to substantiate many of the marketing claims made. The evidence on it is that it has high anti-oxidants (a little less than goji berries) and not much else. I am sure it is good for many, but it is not in my useable pantry: it tastes bad, is expensive and there are other better options.

Camu Camu

Blah — I have to say I just don't like the way it tastes. Basically it is exceptionally high in vitamin C. Yup. And that's it. Again, I don't think that qualifies (for me anyway) as a Superfood. Plus the benefits of the high vitamin C can be obtained in an even greater nutrient rich way through goji berries (which taste a whole lot better), so my feeling is why bother buying this expensive vitamin C when you can get it elsewhere with greater nutritional benefits?

Flax

Uh-Ohhh. Yes, I said F-L-A-X. Saying a bad word about flax in North America is comparable to blasphemy. North Americans use a lot of flax for a healthy food source and many depend upon flax for fiber and EFAs. It is important to note that there is some research out there that identifies that there are some risks with consuming it. By educating yourself about all of the information, you can make a more informed decision about choosing to eat it and how much you choose to eat. So, here are some facts (along with the sources of research) that I discovered in my review:

- Canada is one of the world's biggest flaxseed growers: so it is heavily promoted as a North American crop.

- Flaxseed contains the cyanogenic glycosides which naturally defends flaxseed against micro-organisms and herbivores. But in the body these build up as poison as they are converted into thiocyanate in the intestinal tract. The body can detoxify cyanide to up to 50 g flaxseed/day (6 tbsp) but high blood levels of thiocyanate for prolonged time may have adverse effects on the thyroid function.[82]

- Linatine is a vitamin B6 antagonist in flaxseed.[83] Low vitamin B6 status has been associated with increased homocystein levels, and plaque formation, which increases the risk for heart disease.

- Lignans are present in many plant foods; including seeds, whole grains, flaxseed, sesame seed, beans, fruits, and some vegetables. Flaxseed is by far the highest source of lignans found in nature, with 100-800 times more lignans than other foods.[84] Lignan glycosides from food are converted into enterodiol and enterolactone by bacteria in the colon. These lignans have been found to bind to proteins called estrogen receptors, and to exert either estrogen-like or anti estrogen-like effects.

It is suggested that if there is little estrogen in the body, e.g. after menopause, lignans may act like weak estrogens. When estrogen is abundant in the body, they reduce estrogen's effects by displacing it from cells. The problem is that you don't really know how your body will respond. Interference with estrogen functioning may either prevent or promote cancers, such as breast cancer, that depend on estrogen to start and develop. Studies on the safety of lignans in animals and humans have shown inconsistent results.[85]

- Since phytoestrogen supplements have been shown to cause growth of breast tissue in animals and healthy women, and lignans are a type of phytoestrogens, use of lignan supplements for a long time could increase breast cancer risk.

- Since cadmium is a heavy metal that can bind to estrogen receptors, it is speculated that tumor growth induced by flaxseed, may be due to its high cadmium content. Cadmium from flaxseed was found to significantly accumulate in the liver and kidney of rats.[86] It was previously shown that cadmium doses higher than 7ug/kg/weight activate estrogen receptors, induce early puberty onset, and alter breast development, predicting increased breast cancer risk.[87]

- Most studies on the effect of flaxseed on blood glucose levels and insulin resistance have shown no effect.[88] Although one study found that flaxseed improved insulin sensitivity in adults with elevated lipid levels.[89]

- The effect of flaxseed and flaxseed oil on blood lipid values, inflammation (lower CRP), and blood pressure levels has been found in several studies, although results are inconsistent.[90]

Lilian Thompson, PhD, an internationally known flaxseed researcher from the University of Toronto, says she wouldn't call any of the health benefits of flax "conclusively established," and that the contribution of whole flax seeds to the nutrient intake of humans is not known because no clinical studies of their digestibility has been conducted.

Flax has been touted as an ancient crop, and it IS: but as a crop for its fiber. Throughout the ages, flax was used predominantly for its fiber not as a food source. It was used for linen production and for its oil (linseed oil) which was used for wood conditioning and for oil paints — this aspect of its historical use is well documented. But for food, most of the references that I could find indicated that flax was used for ingestion for diuretic uses only. Flax was not used as an historical nutritional food source throughout the ages. It was not until the 20th century that flax became used as a daily food source. So to sum it all up — given the facts above, we have not seen the long term effects of daily flax use. So going out on a limb here, I am just sayin' be careful.

Bottom line, all of the benefits of flax (Omega-3, fiber, protein) are found in chia. But chia has none of the negative as set out above. So, if I had to choose (being aware that my Mom died of breast cancer at 56 and my Dad is a prostate cancer survivor and I stay far away from any foods that has an estrogen effect), I will always choose chia.

Super Power Sour Kreem and Rockin Red Super Salsa, see p. 143

Part Four: Cookin'

GET WHAT YOU NEED

Like anything, when you take up a hobby or craft you need the right tools. Cooking and baking are no different. Ironically though, many people who spend time in the kitchen do not invest in the tools that they need to make life easier and simpler. I am the perfect example of that.

It took me a good 15 years of my adult cooking life to invest in Henkel knives due to their perceived prohibitive expense. But by making an earlier investment in good knives, over the many pairs of swanky svelte boots bought in my twenties, it would have saved me a lot of time, frustration, and band-aids.

To get started in the kitchen, you will need a few things for the best results. You don't have to run out and buy them right away, but it is not a bad idea to keep a running list and to have the list on hand for Christmas, birthdays, or special events where loved ones may be inclined to make a purchase on your behalf… especially if promised some savory samples!

Also, don't shy away from sourcing good reused kitchen tools. Try secondhand stores, eBay, Kijiji, Craigslist, and local newspapers for items that you are looking for. You can often get incredible deals with great quality.

One of the best food processors I have ever used is my sister's and she got it at a local garage sale. It is from the 1980's and has 2 speeds: on and off. I think the motor in it could be swapped out for a lawn mower, it is that powerful. So, keep your eyes peeled for deals and help save the planet at the same time — reuse!

For the purposes of this book, there are a number of kitchen gadgets that are a good foundation upon which to build:

Blender

I use a high powered blender for smoothies and liquid based soups. I do not use it to blend anything thick as it is easier to pour and clean in a food processor. But for smoothies and blended soups, my Vitamix is my new best friend. You don't have to splurge on an expensive version like mine, but make sure the blender that you get has a good motor with a secure lid! My ceiling has been blasted with a myriad of colored soups due to cheapo blenders with bad lids.

Bowls

Bowls are important. You need different sized for different purposes. Try to get glass ones as they last longer and are more stable on the busy kitchen counter. For maximizing kitchen space, try to get a multiple set that can stack easily and be tucked away when not in use.

Cast Iron Fry Pans, Wok

I use cast iron as they actually provide iron back into foods, and have no toxic coating. Stay clear of coated pans as their chemical base leaches into foods. As well, once scratched the coated pans become ever more toxic so toss them immediately. Instead, cast iron survives the test of time and can be reused over and over again.

I like to rescue them from the dump and at garage sales. If rusty, simply use steel wool on them with hot water until shiny and new again. Coat with a trusted oil (coconut oil is my choice) and heat in a low oven for 20-30 minutes to "season'" before initial use and by means of cleaning it thereafter. Never use soap on it as it will strip it — to clean just scrub under hot water, recoat, and reheat.

Cook Pots — Aluminum Free

Aluminum is a cheap metal that is often used in cookware. It leaches into the food it is cooking and is known to be a contributing factor to Alzheimer's Disease. So keep your pots aluminum free, look for a good base with copper bottoms which will ensure a more consistent base heat.

Also, lids are key. I personally like the glass tops so I can see what is going on and do not have to lift the lid and release heat; forcing me to catch up on cooking. They should also have lids that fit really securely and have an easy to grab handle. I like ones that can fit my hand with an oven mitt as any kitchen witch (or wizard) knows, you sometimes have to multi-task while on the move.

Food Processor

I have burned through so many of these it is not funny — to keep less out of the landfill I finally invested in a good one with a strong motor. Look for one with high volume for the big dinner parties you will now host, and one with a powerful motor. They do go on sale (usually near the Christmas holidays and post Boxing Day deals) so stay on the lookout. These are great for blending larger liquid quantities, and for fast slicing and grating.

Hand Wand Blender

These handy gadgets are a great way to cream a soup or a blend up a sauce or gravy right in the pan. Easy to use, they are a good way to do fast blending jobs with little mess. They cannot blend up big jobs or really chunky projects, but for small blends it is a great tool to have. Plus, they are fun to use.

Knives

The key to great prepping is in the knives. Watch for sales and just make the investment. Your fingers will thank you. I personally like Henkel for their weight and shape but it is a personal preference. The straight edges can be easily sharpened with a great knife sharpener (get one of these too), but the serrated ones (usually used for cutting breads) should never be sharpened.

Magic Bullet/Mini-blender

These contraptions are not expensive and are the best things on hand to whip up a fast sauce or blend in some items into soups and stews. As a plant-based cook, the best way to get creamy consistency without the cream and butters is to use hemp seeds and quinoa as a blend in. You will notice that I am the queen of blending. It is a little bit more work, but it allows the dishes to have the added Superfood component and taste similar to the not-so-good-for-you version. So, in my world, a small blender is an important part of any Superfoody kitchen!

Measuring Cups

You will need teaspoon measurements (⅛, ¼, ½ and 1) along with tablespoons (¼, ½, 1, 2) and cups (¼, ½, ⅓, ⅔, ¾ and 1, and 2). I like to keep them in a big basket on my counter for fast fetches. I also have larger measuring glass cups up to 4 cups for the bigger jobs.

Oven and Stove Top:

If you don't have one already, you will need to buy one… just seeing if you are paying attention!

Nice To Haves:

Keep these on the birthday and big holiday lists for the "I really want this but won't buy it for myself!"

- Cookie dough dropper,
- Mandolin,
- Melon baller,
- Hand food dicer,
- Superlative grater, and
- Garlic press.

Now, with all of your kitchen tools and food you are very well equipped to start making healthy superfoody meals. So let's get started!

Breakfast literally means "breaking the fast": as last's night's dinner is a distant memory for your body. During sleep, your body is in a state of fasting, so nourishing your body first thing in the morning is an important part of a healthy daily routine. Yet studies show that fewer than half of us are eating breakfast — this poor choice can result in long term adverse health effects.

Without nourishment, the body releases insulin and blood glucose levels rise in an attempt to rebalance things. Without nourishment for long periods, the body "stockpiles" food in fear of more fasts once it finally is fed. The end result is that the body then starts to store food as fat which creates stress and over the long term can result in hard to beat weight gain.

By comparison, research[91] shows that a healthy breakfast can help initiate weight loss and keep it off. It helps to jump start the metabolism, and helps you to feel fuller for longer. In addition, a healthy start to the day will decrease bad snack desires.

Research on children also identified that children who ate healthy breakfasts made better food choices throughout the day and had improved attendance, memory, concentration, problem-solving ability and test scores. Results also showed that adults, who regularly ate breakfast, lowered the rates and risks of developing Type 2 diabetes and heart failure over their lifetime.

Additionally, most grocery store breakfast choices are high in simple carbs, have little or no protein and are teeming with bad sugars. The processed cereals, pre-made waffles, and hot cereal packages are great examples of what NOT to eat to get your body humming. These are usually so unhealthy that they have to "fortify" them — meaning that the manufacturer has to add vitamins just to be able to make some positive marketing claim: like "Lucky Charms" are "part of nutritious breakfast" (only because the neon colored cereal is shown with an orange and glass of milk beside it).

Instead of these sugary, dye infused bowls of type 2 Diabetes triggers, opt for a healthy breakfast that is high in protein and fiber with good fats. Opt for quality over quantity: the more nutrient rich foods you eat the less you will need.

Bottom line? It's a no-brainer: eat a Superfood breakfast daily!

Super Start Oatmeal, see p. 110

Perfect Pancakes with Decadent Drizzle

Nothing screams Saturday morning like pancakes. But instead of reaching for that premade bad mix filled with sugar and bad flours, this recipe offers up a simple and super solution.

Ingredients:

Pancakes:

- 1 ½ cups non-dairy milk (plus more if needed)

- ¾ teaspoon vanilla

- 1 ½ cup gluten free oat flour (or GF quinoa flour and all-purpose)

- 3 tablespoons white whole seed chia

- 1 tablespoon baking powder

- 1 tablespoon coconut sugar

- ½ teaspoon of cinnamon

- ⅛ teaspoon rock salt

- Coconut oil for frying

Directions:

1. In a small bowl, mix vanilla and non-dairy milk.

2. In another large bowl, sift in the flour, add chia, baking powder, coconut sugar, cinnamon and rock salt.

3. Mix wet mixture into the dry mixture and stir until combined. Let sit 3 minutes. Batter always should be thick but not gooey nor runny.

4. In a fry pan, turn heat to high. Once heated turn to medium, and cook pancakes in batches. Add ½ a tablespoon of coconut oil and add scoops of ¼ cup of batter into pan, spreading each out a little (so not too thick) to form pancakes. When small bubbles form on top of pancake, flip and cook 1-2 minutes until nicely browned. Add 1-2 tablespoons of non-dairy milk to batter if it gets too thick while waiting for 1st batch of pancakes to cook.

5. Cook in batches until done. Pour drizzle on top. Garnish with orange zest.

Makes about 10 pancakes.

Drizzle:

- 1 cup coconut sugar
- ¼ teaspoon ground cinnamon
- ½ cup orange juice
- 1 teaspoon coconut oil
- 1 teaspoon cacao powder

Directions:

1. For the drizzle, place all ingredients in a small pot.

2. Combine and bring to a low boil on medium/high heat, stirring occasionally.

3. Reduce heat to medium, and let low boil for 5-10 minutes, until it thickens, stirring occasionally. Set aside.

Super Start Oatmeal

This recipe is fast and easy. Rich in fiber, vitamins, and minerals; the combination of oats, coconut oil, chia, hemp, goji, and coconut sugar help boost immunity and energy, decrease inflammation, provide whole protein and EFA's, lower blood sugar levels, and ensure great digestive health. This can be made as quickly as it takes to boil your kettle — so no excuses here!

Ingredients:

- ½ cup water boiled
- ⅓ cup quick flake oats (Gluten Free)
- 1 tablespoon coconut oil
- 1 tablespoon white whole seed chia
- 1 tablespoon slow roasted hemp seeds
- 1 teaspoon cacao nibs
- 1 teaspoon goji berries
- ½ teaspoon coconut sugar
- ¼ teaspoon cinnamon

Directions:

1. Boil water.
2. Assemble dry ingredients and place in a bowl.
3. Pour water on top, stir and let sit for a minute.
4. Top with rice milk.

Makes one serving.

Ola Granola

Granola has a reputation of being a little on the boring side. But this recipe brings the "ola" back to granola.
It is super easy to do and is such a powerful breakfast punch — you will begin your day with a super charged start.

Ingredients:

- 2 tablespoons coconut oil
- 1 cup gluten free quick flake oats
- ½ cup unsweetened coconut flakes
- ⅓ cup raw pumpkin seeds
- ⅓ cup raw sunflower seeds
- ¼ cup goji berries

- 4 tablespoons coconut sugar
- 3 tablespoons cacao nibs
- 2 tablespoons whole seed chia
- 2 tablespoons Delores hemp seeds
- ¼ teaspoon ground cinnamon

Directions:

1. In a medium sized saucepan melt coconut oil at med/high heat.

2. Once melted, turn heat to medium add in all ingredients and cook for 7-10 minutes, mixing frequently.

3. Spoon mixture into a bowl and allow to cool.

4. Once cooled keep in a tightly sealed container.

Makes about 2 ½ cups.

Marvelous Goji Muffins

Muffins are one of the easiest make-ahead breakies you can manage.
They are easy to bake and even easier to bring out of the freezer for nutrition on the go!

Ingredients:

- 2 cups gluten free oat flour or GF all-purpose flour

- 2 teaspoons baking powder

- 1 teaspoon baking soda

- ½ teaspoon rock salt

- ⅔ cup white whole seed chia

- 2 tablespoons coconut oil, melted

- 1 teaspoon vanilla

- 1 cup unsweetened apple sauce

- 2 teaspoons grated lemon rind

- ⅓ cup maple syrup

- ½ cup goji berries, coarsely chopped

- ¼ cup slow roasted hemp seeds

Directions:

1. Preheat oven to 300F.

2. Grease 24 muffin tins with coconut oil, (or use cupcake papers to make it really easy!).

3. In a medium sized mixing bowl, mix flours, baking powder, baking soda, rock salt and chia.

4. In a second bowl, mix together coconut oil, vanilla, apple sauce, lemon rind, maple syrup and goji berries.

5. Mix goji mixture into dry mix quickly and place into muffin tins.

6. Bake for 25 minutes, remove and let cool before removing from tin.

Go-Mango-Go Porridge

This porridge is really easy to make and can be done the night before for an even easier early morning rise. Filled with protein, anti-oxidants, and healing benefits, this is such a dynamic way to start the day. With rich flavors and sweet fresh mango this dish is also a great before bed snack. Whenever you choose to eat it, this recipe is a keeper!

Ingredients:

- 1 can light coconut milk
- 1 ½ cups mango juice
- 1 cup unpolished quinoa
- ¼ cup goji berries

- ¼ teaspoon rock salt
- 1 cup mango fruit diced (about ½ a ripe mango)
- ½ tablespoon lime juice

Directions:

1. Place coconut milk, mango juice, quinoa, goji and rock salt in a pot with secure lid on.

2. Bring to a boil then turn to low heat and cook for 30 minutes with lid on.

3. Take off heat with lid still on, and let sit for 5 minutes.

4. Remove lid and fluff quinoa with a fork,

5. Add in fresh mango and lime juice and gently stir. Serve hot or cold.

Makes 4 cups.

Apple of My Eye Pudding

This is an easy to make ahead super healthy breakfast. If you make enough you can also enjoy as a midday snack or after dinner dessert. Feel free to add more flavors and play with the spice measurements.

Ingredients:

- ¼ cup white ground chia
- 2 cups unsweetened apple sauce
- 2 tablespoons coconut sugar
- 2 tablespoons Delores hemp seeds
- 2 tablespoons coconut oil, melted
- ½ teaspoon vanilla
- ⅛ teaspoon cinnamon
- Pinch of ginger and nutmeg

Directions:

1. Add all ingredients to blender and blend on high until creamy.

2. Place in serving cups and chill in fridge for a couple of hours.

3. Top with "Not-a-Nut Crunch" and serve.

Makes 4-6 servings.

Hempstir Butter

This butter is one of the best ways that you can start your day.
Easy to make and even more easy to use it is a busy person's hemp dream come true.

Ingredients:

- ½ cup Delores hemp seeds
- 1 tablespoon coconut oil, melted
- ¼ cup non-dairy milk
- 1 ½ tablespoons coconut sugar
- ¼ teaspoon vanilla
- ¼ teaspoon rock salt
- ¼ teaspoon cinnamon powder

Directions:

Add all ingredients to a Magic Bullet along with all other ingredients and pulse blend it until fully smooth. Store in a sealed container in the fridge for up to a week.

Great Crepes with Mango Cool-E

There is nothing like a great plate of crepes! These are simple to make (but leave time for mix to chill) and can also be easily frozen after making them. It is also fun to serve as a light dinner with super stuffings — let your culinary imagination run wild!

Ingredients:

Crepes:

- 1 cup water

- 3 tablespoons Delores hemp seeds

- 1 cup gluten free oat flour
  or all-purpose flour

- ¼ cup coconut oil, room temperature

- 2 tablespoons coconut sugar

- ¼ teaspoon baking powder

- ¼ teaspoon rock salt

Cool-E:

- ¾ cup fresh or frozen pineapple chunks, defrosted and drained

- ¾ cup fresh or frozen mango chunks, defrosted and drained

- 2 tablespoons Delores hemp seeds

- 2 tablespoons white ground chia

- 1 tablespoon coconut sugar

- 1 teaspoon vanilla

- Pinch of cinnamon and ginger

Directions:

For crepes

1. In a food processor, blend the water and hemp seeds until creamy.

2. Add all other ingredients and blend until creamy in texture.

3. Pour into mixing bowl and chill in fridge for 1 hour.

For filling:

In a food processor, blend all Cool-E ingredients together until creamy and chill in fridge.

To make crepes:

1. Grease a 6-inch skillet with coconut oil.

2. Heat the skillet on high heat until hot and pour a 3-4 tablespoons of batter into the skillet. Swirl batter around in order to cover the skillet's bottom (if too thick add in a little warm water). When a nice light brown, in about 1-2 minutes, carefully flip and cook on opposite side for about 1 minute. Remove to a plate.

3. Take each crepe and pour 2-3 tablespoons of Mango Cool-E into center. Fold up bottom ½ an inch and top ½ an inch. Roll in the sides and serve with a sprinkle of ground cinnamon.

Mega Bread

This bread is so delicious and full of great fiber and essential fatty acids galore. Don't worry — the fats are safe at these temperatures as research was done on this!

Ingredients:

- 2 ¾ cups gluten free oat flour or all-purpose flour

- ¼ cup plus 2 tablespoons, white ground chia

- ½ tablespoon coconut sugar

- 1 teaspoon rock salt

- 1 ¼ cups water, lukewarm

- ½ tablespoon yeast

Directions:

1. In a medium mixing bowl, mix together flour, chia, sugar, rock salt.

2. In a separate small bowl, gradually stir the yeast into the water.

3. Gradually add in the yeast mix to the dry mix, stirring together slowly and gradually.

4. On a lightly floured surface, knead the dough for about 10 minutes, until smooth and elastic.

5. In a medium sized bowl, add a tablespoon of olive oil on bottom and rub the bottom with it. Place dough in the bowl and turn it over. Cover with a towel and place on kitchen counter for 2 hours (until doubled in size).

6. Remove cover and punch down the center, place dough on floured surface and knead for 2 minutes. Return to greased bowl, recover and let sit for another hour.

7. Remove cover, punch down middle again, and place in oiled baking pan (9 inch x 5 inch).

8. Bake at 350F for about 55 minutes, or until the top of the loaf springs back when lightly pressed.

Tip: if you like a crunchy top, sprinkle 1 tablespoon of white whole seed chia on top.

Noshin' Squash Muffins

These muffins are a great way to get squash in even first thing in the morning. Easy to make and even easier to eat, this one is a simple family FLAVORite!

Ingredients:

- 1 ½ cups squash puree
- ⅓ cup maple syrup
- ⅓ cup white ground chia
- ¼ teaspoon vanilla
- 2 cups gluten free oat flour or all-purpose flour

- 2 teaspoons cinnamon powder
- 2 teaspoons baking powder
- 1 teaspoon baking soda
- ½ teaspoon rock salt

Directions:

1. Preheat oven to 300F and grease 12 muffin tins with coconut oil.

2. In a small bowl, combine squash, maple syrup, chia and vanilla.

3. In a second medium bowl, mix dry ingredients together.

4. Add dry ingredients to wet and stir well.

5. Fill muffin tins to ⅔ full and bake for 30 minutes in center rack.

Strawberry Slammer Jammer

This jam is a slam dunk. With the low glycemic load of the coconut sugar combined with the glucose stabilizing effect of the chia, this recipe allows everyone to enjoy jam with none of the guilt.

Ingredients:

- 5 cups washed and chopped strawberries (approx. 2 quarts or a 900g package)

- 2 tablespoons fresh lemon juice

- 1 cup coconut sugar

- 4 tablespoons white whole seed chia (optional — see note)

- 1 tablespoon cacao powder

- 1 teaspoon maca powder (optional)

Directions:

1. Prepare 4 small mason jars with lids washed and cleaned, place in a cook pot and cover with water. Bring to a boil and then turn to low heat.

2. Place strawberries and lemon juice in a large pot. Place on stove top and turn heat to medium/high.

3. Cook for 6-8 minutes; mashing the berries with a potato masher as you heat them.

4. Add coconut sugar and stir in and turn to high, keep stirring and bring to a hard boil (meaning that mixture will not subside when you stir it). Keep at a hard boil for one minute and continue stirring.

5. Turn heat down to low add chia and cacao powder. Simmer for 15 minutes or until desired consistency.

6. Take each mason jar and remove from water, carefully add in jam mixture to mason jar. Cover with lid and lightly tighten lid. Repeat until all of the jam is bottled.

7. Wait 10 minutes and the gently tighten each lid by hand. Ensure that the top "pops", which means it is sealed.

8. If properly sealed, can be kept for up to 2 years unless chia included, in which case keep in fridge for up to 10 days. May be frozen.

Makes 2 cups.

On the Go Hot Cocoa

Although yummy; hot chocolate conjures up images of white sugar, marshmallows, and the resulting sugar spikes in the kiddies. In the interests of "Momsanity", I developed a GOOD FOR YOU version that you can serve without any guilt at any time. Easy to make, this has a couple of "tricks" to get you from a poor choice to a great one without sacrificing any taste.

Ingredients:

- 2 cups non-dairy milk

- 3 tablespoons cacao powder

- 3 tablespoons coconut sugar

- 2 tablespoons slow roasted hemp seeds

- 1 teaspoon white ground chia

- 1 teaspoon maca powder (optional)

- ¼ teaspoon vanilla extract (or ½ teaspoon raw ground vanilla)

- Pinch of both cinnamon and nutmeg

Directions:

1. In a blender mix all ingredients until smooth.

2. In a sauce pan on medium, heat the blended mixture to desired temperature.

3. For a frothy "top" place 1 tablespoon hemp seeds and 2 tablespoons water in a blender and puree until fluffy and top off the hot cocoa with it.

4. Tip: for a "new flavor" try adding 1 tablespoon of orange juice or a little pinch of cayenne pepper or ground cardamom.

Cinna-Chick Sticks

This is a fun way for kids and adults to scoop up their favorite fruit in an interactive way.
Why not make breakfast healthy "hands on" fun?

Ingredients:

- 2 gluten free tortillas
  (or use crepes from recipe)

- 1 ½ tablespoons coconut oil, melted

- 2 tablespoons coconut sugar

- 1 tablespoon white whole seed chia

- ¼ teaspoon ground cinnamon

Directions:

1. Preheat oven to 350F.

2. On a cutting board, take a pizza cutter and cut each tortilla into 8 pieces. Place each tortilla on a cookie sheet in the original circle shape, and brush each circle of tortilla with ½ of the coconut oil, then sprinkle on coconut sugar, cinnamon and chia.

3. Bake for 10 minutes until crisp.

4. Serve with "Cutie Fruitie Salad".

Cutie Fruitie Morning Salad

This is a great way to start off the day. Fresh fruit combined with a Superfood line up of champions, this tastes great and will send you on your way with a super-boost.

Ingredients:

- 1 cup grapes, halved

- 1 golden delicious apple, peeled, cored and diced

- ½ cup raspberries

- ½ cup strawberries stem removed and diced

- 1 tablespoon coconut sugar

- 1 tablespoon goji berries

- 1 tablespoon cacao nibs

- 2 tablespoons Delores hemp seeds

- 2 tablespoons "Strawberry Slammer Jammer" (strawberry jam)

Directions:

Gently mix all ingredients together, refrigerate (preferably overnight).

Makes 2 ½ cups.

Gee-I love Strawcherry Coulis

This coulis is a lovely sweet and rich way to finish off pancakes, use it as an early morning fruit dunk or drinkable on its own! Low glycemic, with fiber, it is a great way to enjoy a sweet sauce with none of the insulin spiking guilt.

Ingredients:

- ½ cup coconut sugar
- ½ cup frozen unsweetened strawberries
- 1 tablespoon lemon juice
- 1 ½ tablespoons Delores hemp seeds
- 1 tablespoon white ground chia seeds

Directions:

1. In a medium saucepan, combine the strawberries, sugar, and lemon juice.

2. Bring to a boil over medium-high heat.

3. Transfer to a blender along with the hemp seeds and chia.

4. Purée until smooth.

Easily frozen. Makes 1 cup.

Boostberry Coulis

This coulis has the added boost of blueberries for antioxidants, and the hemp seeds for whole protein. So, go ahead and start pouring it on your morning fresh fruit, oatmeal, or muesli!

Ingredients:

- ½ cup coconut sugar

- 1 cup frozen unsweetened blueberries

- 1 tablespoon lemon juice

- 2 tablespoons Delores hemp seeds

Directions:

1. In a medium saucepan, combine the strawberries, sugar, and lemon juice.

2. Bring to a boil over medium-high heat.

3. Transfer to a blender along with the hemp seeds.

4. Purée until smooth.

Easily frozen. Makes 1 cup.

Whadda Fudge Spread

This chocolate spread is an ideal way to teach the naysayers how amazing Superfoods can taste. It is so rich and deelish you will want to eat it on every piece of gluten free toast you could ever make or on its own with a huge honkin' spoon (or shovel)!

Ingredients:

- ¼ cup coconut sugar
- ¼ cup Delores hemp seeds
- 2 tablespoons water
- 2 tablespoons cacao powder

- 1 teaspoon ground chia
- 3 teaspoon coconut oil (room temperature)
- ½ teaspoon vanilla

Directions:

1. Place all ingredients in a food processor or Magic Bullet.

2. Mix on high until creamy (add 1 more tablespoon water and remix if too thick).

3. Use on pancakes, toast, as or icing for Better Brownie or cupcakes.

Easily frozen. Makes ½ cups (thick).

Super Slurpies!

Smoothies are such an easy way to start the day or have as a meal-on-the-go healthy option. The sky is the limit in the type of options that you have, so use your creativity and shake things up when you get bored of the same old, same old! Don't forget when you are slurpin' away, let it linger in your mouth — digestion starts here so don't slurp it down too quickly enjoy it in all of its super goodness!

Lasso the Lassi Smoothie

I love mangos and they are such a refreshing way to start the day.

Ingredients:

- 1 cup frozen mango, pieces
- ¾ cup water or coconut water
- 2 tablespoons coconut sugar
- 2 tablespoons lemon juice

- 2 tablespoons Delores hemp seeds
- 1 tablespoon white whole seed chia
- ¼ teaspoon cardamom, ground

Directions:

1. In a blender, puree all ingredients on high until creamy.
2. Serve immediately.

Makes 2 servings.

Lush Flush Smoothie

This smoothie is a great way to get detoxified with the black cherries and the lemon juice. Adding in the Superfoods makes this an additional powerhouse of nutrition while flushing out the toxins.

Ingredients:

- 1 cup black cherry juice, unsweetened
- 3 tablespoons Delores hemp seeds
- 1 tablespoon fresh lemon juice
- 1 tablespoon goji berries
- ½ cup ice

Directions:

1. In a blender, puree all ingredients on high until creamy.
2. Serve immediately.

Makes 2 servings.

Mojo Mojito

Full of energy and stamina makes for some serious Mojo!
If you wanna get real frisky add a shot of mellow rum to the mix.

Ingredients:

- 1 avocado
- 1 ½-2 cups non-dairy milk or coconut water
- 3 tablespoons fresh lime juice
- 2 tablespoons Delores hemp seeds
- 2 tablespoons coconut sugar
- 1 tablespoon white whole seed chia
- 4 ice cubes
- 10 mint leaves

Directions:

1. In a blender, puree all ingredients (except the mint and ice) on high until smooth.

2. Add in mint and ice and pulse until desired consistency (I like a little bit of ice chunks in mine).

3. Serve immediately.

Makes 2 servings.

Too-Kooler Smoothie

This is such a lovely and fresh smoothie and is a great way to use up watermelon in the summer months.

- 1 ripe banana
- 1 cup diced seedless watermelon
- 1 cup pineapple juice

- 2 tablespoons slow roasted hemp seeds
- 1 tablespoon white whole seed chia
- 1 tablespoon goji berries

1. In a blender, puree all ingredients on high until creamy.

2. Serve immediately.

Makes 2 servings.

Strawsome Smoothie

Smooth and creamy with dreamy nutritional benefits — this is a super start to any day.

Ingredients:

- 1 ripe banana
- 10 frozen strawberries
- 1 ripe avocado (peeled and chopped)
- ¾ cup non-dairy milk
- ⅓ cup frozen blueberries
- 2 tablespoons slow roasted hemp seeds
- 1 tablespoon white whole seed chia

Directions:

1. In a blender, puree all ingredients on high until creamy.
2. Serve immediately.

Makes 2 servings.

Super Simple Smoothie

With very few ingredients, this smoothie is a simple way to start any day.
Can also travel well for the busy mornings when you may have to smoothie slurp en route!

Ingredients:

- 2 ½ cups orange juice (preferably freshly squeezed!)
- 1 cup frozen strawberries
- ½ cup Delores hemp seeds
- 1 tablespoon white whole seed chia
- 1 teaspoon cacao powder

Directions:

1. In a blender, puree all ingredients on high until creamy.
2. Serve immediately.

Makes 2 servings.

Smooth Operator Smoothie

Yum in a glass is the simplest way to describe it. But it also has high immune boosting properties, boosts energy, and is rich in so many vitamins and minerals.

Ingredients:

- ½ ripe banana
- 2 cups rice milk or coconut water
- ½ cup frozen peaches
- ½ cup frozen blueberries
- ½ ripe avocado

- 2 tablespoons Delores hemp seeds
- 1 tablespoon coconut oil
- 1 tablespoon goji berries
- 1 tablespoon white whole seed chia

Directions:

1. In a blender, puree all ingredients on high until creamy.
2. Serve immediately.

Makes 2 servings.

Raspberry Fields Forever Smoothie

This is a great way to get in the greens at breakie without even having to think about it.
Break on through your day with this tried and true liquid-deelish!

Ingredients:

- 1 cup frozen raspberries

- ¾ cups baby spinach, washed and dried

- ½ ripe banana

- ¾ tablespoon cacao powder

- 2 tablespoons white whole seed chia

- 2 tablespoons Delores hemp seeds

- 2 cups non-dairy milk

Directions:

1. In a blender, puree all ingredients on high until creamy.

2. Serve immediately.

Makes 2 servings.

Purple Piña Colahhhda Smoothie

If you want a delicious and easy take on the sometimes boring smoothie-standby, opt for this recipe that is easy, nutritious, and tastes so fabulous you just might want to add it to your Saturday night piña colada standby!

Ingredients:

- 2 cups frozen blueberries
- ½ cup frozen pineapple pieces
- ¾ cup canned light coconut milk
- ¾ cup non-dairy milk
- 2 tablespoons Delores hemp seeds
- 1 tablespoon whole seed chia
- 1 tablespoon coconut sugar
- ¼ teaspoon vanilla

Directions:

1. In a blender, puree all ingredients on high until creamy.
2. Serve immediately.

Makes 2 servings.

Goin' Bananas Smoothie

Kids love this smoothie for breakfast and after school good eats. One serving is all of your Omega-3 EFA's for the day and 18 grams of whole protein! It is so nutrient dense, but they won't even know it is good for them... a nice break for Mum too!

Ingredients:

- 1 frozen ripe banana, peeled

- 4 cups rice milk

- 6 tablespoons slow roasted hemp seeds

- 4 tablespoons white ground chia

- 4 scoops (32 grams) of chocolate flavored greens

- 4 tablespoons cacao powder

- 2 tablespoons coconut sugar

Directions:

1. In a blender, puree all ingredients on high until creamy.

2. Serve immediately.

Makes 4 small servings or 2 large ones.

Cacao Puff Smoothie

This smoothie is a chocolate lover's dream with the rich cacao powder combined with the silky hemp seeds.

Ingredients:

- 2 cups non-dairy milk
- ¼ cup Delores hemp seeds
- 1 tablespoon white whole seed chia
- 1 tablespoon cacao powder
- 1 teaspoon vanilla

Directions:

1. In a blender, puree all ingredients on high until creamy.

2. Serve immediately.

Makes 2 servings.

Kale-ifornia Smoothie

This smoothie has lots of natural raw uber-elements in it with great greens, anti-oxidants, high EFA's, whole protein, and lots of energy! You'll want to be surfing up a storm after this one.

Ingredients:

- 2 cups non-dairy milk

- ½ cup baby spinach, washed

- 3 kale leaves, spine removed

- 1 frozen banana (or 2 tablespoons coconut sugar with a handful of ice)

- 4 tablespoons Delores hemp seeds

- 4 tablespoons goji berries

- 1 tablespoon white whole seed chia

- 2 teaspoons ground cinnamon

- 1 teaspoon vanilla extract

Directions:

1. In a blender, puree all ingredients on high until creamy.

2. Serve immediately.

Makes 2 servings.

Mintcha Smoothie

This smoothie is a nice refreshing change with the apple, mint, and green matcha.

Ingredients:

- 1 frozen banana

- 1 cup apple juice

- 2 tablespoons Delores hemp seeds

- 2 tablespoons white whole seed chia

- 2 mint leaves

- 2 teaspoons green matcha tea powder

Directions:

1. In a blender, puree all ingredients on high until creamy.

2. Serve immediately.

Makes 2 servings.

Dream Kreemsicle Smoothie

This smoothie is a deliciously healthy take on a traditionally bad-for-you frozen sugar stick.
Slurp away my friend!

Ingredients:

- 2-3 cups non-dairy milk
  (depends how thick you like it)

- 1 ½ cups frozen mango chunks

- ½ cup freshly squeezed orange juice
  (add in pulp as well)

- 2 tablespoons Delores hemp seeds

- 2 tablespoons white whole seed chia

- 2 tablespoons goji berries

- 1 tablespoon lemon juice (optional)

Directions:

1. In a blender, puree all ingredients on high until creamy.

2. Serve immediately.

Makes 2 servings.

I just love condiments: the more the better. In fact the only reason I could choke down a hotdog as a kid was because I adored the ketchup and tangy relish that I slathered on. I honestly believe that Dim Sum would not be worth existing without the sauces. And who can really see the point in eating a quesadilla without a heaping spoonful of salsa or guac'?

Unfortunately though, many of the great tasting store bought condiments are Type 2 diabetes in a bottle. High in bad sugar and fats with little or no nutrients, most premade condiments are in the no-go nutritional zone.

But when you need a fix, you really want to have it. So welcome to my super world! I have developed these recipes to get the fix-ZING back with lots of healthy benefits and great taste. And YES it can ALL be worth it!

Super Power Sour Kreem

Growing up in a British household on a pretty small budget meant that we ate a LOT of potatoes. I still love a great baked potato (even though I know the sweet potatoes are the best choice!). And who can honestly say no to a potato covered in saturated-fat-galore sour cream? Well, it's Superfoods to the rescue as this recipe will satisfy the creamy cravings but delivers it in a very healthy vessel.

Ingredients:

- ¼ cup plus 2 tablespoons water
- 1 cup Delores hemp seeds
- 2 tablespoons lemon juice
- ½ tablespoon apple cider vinegar
- ¼ teaspoon rock salt
- ⅛ teaspoon ground pepper

Directions:

1. Blend ingredients all together until smooth.
2. Keep refrigerated. Will keep in fridge for up to 4 days.

Makes about 1 cup.

Rockin' Red Super Salsa

This salsa is my favorite to enjoy with Mexican themed foods. It has the right amount of spice with the right amount of fresh flavors. With the hemp and chia addition, it goes from fabulous to super-fabby!

Ingredients:

- 1-28-oz can diced tomatoes, no added salt

- 2 teaspoons garlic, minced

- 3 tablespoons Delores hemp seeds

- 2 tablespoons white whole seed chia

- 3 teaspoons lime juice

- ½ teaspoon rock salt

- ⅓ cup canned green chilies (1-4.5oz can), chopped (or add a few squirts of hot sauce of choice to heat you like)

- ⅓ cup fresh packed cilantro

- ⅓ cup green onions, washed and chopped

Directions:

1. Reserving the juice, strain tomatoes and place in a medium bowl

2. Place the tomato juice from can in a food processor. Add in the garlic, hemp seeds, lime juice, chia, and salt. Blend on high for about 40 seconds until blended.

3. Wash and coarsely chop cilantro and add this together with chilies and green onion to diced tomato bowl.

4. Add a ½ cup of the diced tomato mixture to the hemp/chia mix in the processor and blend on low for 5 seconds. Add in the blended hemp/chia mix to remaining diced tomato mixture.

5. Pour mixture into serving bowl and refrigerate for 20 minutes. If you want it thicker, add ½ tablespoon of whole seed chia and leave to thicken for another 20 minutes. Will keep in the fridge for 3 days. May be frozen.

Makes about 3 cups.

Note: If you are running out of time, simply buy a 16oz jar of premade salsa, and pour half into food processor and add the same amount as above of lime juice, hemp seeds, chia and the cilantro pulse 5-7 times and add back into remaining salsa. It's a fast super simple salsa version.

Super De-lite White Sauce (Béchamel)

To be super healthy you don't have to give up those rich creamy dressings and sauces that accompany gourmet foods. This sauce is a healthy take on a classy classic. It can act as the basis for moussaka, lasagna, 'Cheez' sauces, or the basis of super dips. Feel free to add a ½ tablespoon of your favorite herbs or 2 tablespoons of nutritional yeast flakes for a cheesy take on it. You can play with the flavorful possibilities — the only limit is your imagination!

Ingredients:

- ⅓ cup water
- 1 ½ cups Delores hemp seeds
- ¼ cup lemon juice
- 1 ½ tablespoons apple cider vinegar
- ½ teaspoon rock salt
- ¼ teaspoon ground pepper

Directions:

Blend all ingredients together until creamy consistency. Will keep in fridge for up to 4 days. May be frozen.

Makes about 2 cups.

Soy-not Sauce

Soya sauce is one of those things that I love to eat for the flavor but I know that the high sodium and the soy base are not great choices for any sensitive system, not to mention those with a soy allergy! But this recipe has a similar hearty flavor combined with whole food raw components to help put the shine back in any dim sum.

Ingredients:

- 1 ¼ cup water
- ¼ cup nutritional yeast flakes
- 3 tablespoons balsamic vinegar
- 2 tablespoons coconut sugar

- 4 teaspoons white ground chia
- 2 teaspoons rock salt
- 1 teaspoon minced garlic
- 1 teaspoon minced ginger

Directions:

1. Blend all ingredients together then place in a small cook pot and heat on medium, and cook at a low boil for about 5-10 minutes until it has thickened.

2. Store in a sealed container in the fridge for up to a week. It can also be frozen into ice cube trays for quick use.

Makes about ¼ cup.

Delish-No-Fish Sauce
(Khong Nuoc Mam)

Some might wonder if nuoc mam (fish sauce) runs in the veins of Vietnamese people as it is synonymous with Vietnamese cuisine and is used (as most veggies know) in pretty much every Thai or Vietnamese based dish. The basics of the sauce are simple: fish thingies, lime juice, water, crushed garlic, and chilies. Trust me when I say that if you knew how authentic fish sauce was made, you would probably never eat it again. But this plant-based sauce is a super way to enjoy the flavors with lots of whole food benefits as well. Feel free to experiment by adding in more flavors and by knocking up the heat a little or a lot.

Ingredients:

- ½ cup water

- ⅓ cup coconut sugar

- 3 tablespoons lime juice

- 2 tablespoons rice vinegar

- 3 teaspoons white ground chia

- 3 teaspoons nutritional yeast flakes

- 2 teaspoons balsamic vinegar

- 1 ½ teaspoon minced garlic

- ¾ teaspoons rock salt

- ½ teaspoon crushed dried red pepper flakes

- ¼ teaspoon minced ginger

- ¼ teaspoons rock salt

- Optional: for serving sauce on its own in a bowl add a ½ teaspoon of chili flakes and ¼ of a green onion finely chopped

Directions:

1. Blend all ingredients together then place in a small cook pot and cook on medium heat.

2. Cook at a low boil (medium/low heat) for about 5-10 minutes until it has thickened.

3. Store in a sealed container in the fridge for up to a week. It can also be frozen into ice cube trays for quick use.

Makes about ¼ cup.

May-NO-naise

Those mayo goopy sandwiches, which taste so good but are so truly NOT good-for-you, do not have to be a thing of the past. This hemp rich May-No is super delicious and so nutritious, you never have to feel sandwich-guilty again!

Ingredients:

- ½ cup Delores hemp seeds
- ¼ cup water
- 2 tablespoons olive oil

- 1 ½ tablespoons lemon juice
- ⅛ teaspoon rock salt

Directions:

1. Blend all ingredients together.

2. Will keep in the fridge up to 5 days.

Makes ¾ of a cup.

Pass The Gravy, Baby!

I love gravy. In fact one of my childhood "foodie" memory moments happened with french fries. I was a kid on a family road trip to Quebec, Canada — we stopped by the roadside at a fry stand with fries covered in a thick homemade gravy. So, as an adult veep (a veggie person), life has been a sad road of gravy-less everything... until now. This vegan healthy gravy fooled even my most extreme "carnie" friends. So go ahead — pass and pour this one on!

Ingredients:

- 2 tablespoons olive oil
- 2 cups diced Spanish purple onions
- 2 cups diced celery
- 3 tablespoon minced garlic (3-4 large cloves)
- ¾ cup warm water

- ⅓ cup slow roasted hemp seeds
- ¼ cup nutritional yeast flakes
- 1 ½ tablespoon olive oil
- ½ teaspoon black pepper
- ½ teaspoon rock salt
- ½ teaspoon poultry seasoning

Directions:

1. In a medium sized cooking pot, add olive oil and place on medium heat.
2. Once oil is heated, add onions, celery and garlic.
3. Turn heat to medium/low and cover.
4. Cook for 15-20 minutes, stirring occasionally, until vegetables are soft.
5. While the vegetables are cooking, in a blender or food processor, add in all other remaining ingredients.
6. Once vegetable mixture has cooked to desired texture, add it to blender mixture and blend on high until a creamy consistency is achieved.
7. May be kept in the fridge for up to 3 days and may be frozen for future use.

Makes about 3 cups.

Cacao Barbie-Q Sauce

This sauce is a nutritious way to enjoy your flaming foodie grill.
The raw cacao powder gives it a rich flavorful finish.

Ingredients:

- 1 cup "Catchin' Up Ketchup" recipe (or low sodium tomato paste)

- 3 tablespoons vegan gluten free Worcestershire sauce

- 2 tablespoons cacao powder

- 2 tablespoons coconut sugar

- 1 tablespoon onion powder

- 1 tablespoon garlic powder

- 1 teaspoon chili powder

- 1 teaspoon chipotle puree (or red pepper chili flakes to taste)

- ½ teaspoon rock salt

Directions:

1. Blend all ingredients together and enjoy on your favorite BBQ foods.

2. Can be refrigerated for up to 10 days.

Makes about 1 ¼ cups.

This Ain't your Mom's Cranberry Sauce

Every Christmas and Easter my Mom would proudly place her homemade cranberry sauce on the table and expect us all to dollop it on our over cooked turkey leather. It was often so tart that you had to smile… in a Joan Rivers kind of way. My recipe is a fresh take on the old version and is a great combination of: tart cranberries, healthy coconut sugar, vitamin C rich oranges, lemon, and pomegranate and super-charged goji berries. Served alongside my recipe for "Stuffin' or Nothin'", as this one is sure to please all!

Ingredients:

- ¾ cups coconut sugar

- ¾ cup pomegranate or cranberry juice, unsweetened

- ¾ cup orange juice

- 2 ½ cups fresh or frozen cranberries

- ½ cup goji berries

- 1 tablespoon lemon juice

- ⅛ teaspoon vanilla

- ⅛ teaspoon ground cinnamon

- ⅛ teaspoon rock salt

- white ground chia
  (optional and as needed)

Directions:

1. In a medium sized pot over high heat, combine coconut sugar and pomegranate/ cranberry and orange juice.

2. Stirring, bring to a boil and boil for 3-4 minutes.

3. Add cranberries, goji berries, lemon juice, cinnamon, vanilla, and salt and reduce heat to medium/low.

4. Continue to cook and stir occasionally until the cranberries pop (about 8-10 minutes).

5. Turn off the heat and cool.

6. Can be refrigerated for up to 5 days and may be frozen for future enjoyment.

7. Note: If you prefer it thicker, mix in white ground chia in 1 teaspoon amounts until desired thickness.

Makes about 2 cups.

Red Pepper Chili A-O K-li

This Aioli is a terrific spread that is super with grilled veggies, vegan "Not-So-Krabby Cakes" or simply used as a dip. Without the mayo, this is a healthy take on a usually bad choice.

Ingredients:

- ½ cup roasted red peppers, drained, patted dry, and chopped
- ¼ cup Delores hemp seeds
- 1 tablespoon water
- 2 tablespoons olive oil

- 1 ½ teaspoon garlic, minced
- 1 tablespoon hot chili sauce (Sambal Oelek)
- 1 tablespoon lime juice
- ½ tablespoon coconut sugar
- ⅛ teaspoon rock salt

Directions:

1. Add all ingredients to a food processor and blend until creamy texture.

2. May be stored in the fridge for up to 5 days. Freezes well.

Makes about ½ cup.

Spice it UP! Oil

Spiced oil is an excellent drizzle addition to soups, pastas, salads, or simply poured into a bowl and dip with bread or crudités. Avocado oil is high in vitamin E and unsaturated fats and contains more protein than any other fruit and more potassium than a banana. It can also boost absorption of carotenoids in your food, reduce blood pressure and has been shown to improve periodontal disease. Although a bit of a wait to enjoy, this oil is worth the wait!

Ingredients:

- 2 cups water

- 2 sprigs rosemary
  (each approx. 8 inches in length)

- 6 whole garlic cloves, peeled

- 4 whole dried red chili peppers

- 10 peppercorns

- 5 Cacao Beans

- 1-500ml bottle avocado or olive oil

Directions:

1. In a small pot on stove top, bring water to a boil.

2. Place rosemary, garlic cloves and cacao in boiling water for 30 seconds to blanche.

3. Remove and pat dry.

4. Pour out ¼ of the oil from the bottle into a measuring cup.

5. Pop off plastic pour spout from oil bottle and save.

6. Stuff the rosemary, garlic, red chili peppers, cacao beans and peppercorns into oil bottle.

7. Top up oil in the bottle to about 1 inch below the top of the bottle. If anything is left over in measuring cup, just store in another container for further use.

8. Put top back on the bottle and place in fridge. Shake once in a while.

9. Wait 2 weeks so the flavors combine and then shake before use and enjoy! You may also strain it if you desire but I personally love the little bits of rosemary that escape as you use it.

10. Store in fridge until ready to use but let come to room temperature.

Tar-terrific Sauce

While in Wales backpacking, before I became a vegetarian, I recall the sweet sensation of eating fish and chips — the combination of deep fried fish and the super fatty mayo-creamy tartar sauce. The tartness of the sauce combined with the sweetness of the fish was wonderful. I now know that it is not fish I miss but the sauce! So here is a healthy tartar sauce that makes a super dip for veggies, can be a nice change for a salad dressing, and better yet a super side dunk for "Not-So-Krabby Cakes!"

Ingredients:

- ⅔ cup Delores hemp seeds
- ⅓ cup pickle juice
- 2 tablespoons lemon juice
- 2 tablespoons olive oil
- 2 teaspoons Dijon mustard
- 2 teaspoons minced dill

- 2 teaspoons prepared horseradish
- 1 teaspoon whole white chia
- ¼ teaspoon rock salt
- ⅛ teaspoon ground black pepper
- 2 teaspoons finely chopped dill pickle (about ¾ of a baby dill) — set aside

Directions:

1. In a Magic Bullet or food processer, add all ingredients (except for the set aside chopped dill pickle) and blend on high.

2. Once creamy, add in the chopped dill pickle, stir and refrigerate.

3. Will keep in the fridge for up to five days. Can also be frozen.

Makes about 1 cup.

Paste Days Gone Bye!

This paste is rich in chlorophyll and is an excellent accompaniment to veggie dishes, great mixed in stir fries, easily added to quinoa dishes, or as a rich and flavorful accompaniment to rice noodles. It is so good that it won't last long and will be bye-bye in no time!

Ingredients:

- ½ cup fresh basil leaves, washed and patted dry

- ½ cup fresh cilantro, washed and patted dry

- 3 tablespoons lime juice

- 2 tablespoons Delores hemp seeds

- 1 tablespoon white whole seed chia

- 1 tablespoon "Soy-Not Sauce" (or sub in soya sauce if no SOY allergy)

- 1 tablespoon water (or more if needed)

- 2 teaspoon garlic, minced

- 1 ½ teaspoon dried red hot chili pepper flakes

Directions:

1. Place all ingredients in a food processor, except for the oil.

2. Blend in a food processor and when mixed, slowly add in oil.

3. Add additional water if too thick and blend until desired thickness.

4. Feel free to add in more chili flakes if you prefer a spicier version.

5. Place in a jar and refrigerate for up to one week or freeze in small ice cube trays.

Makes about ¾ cup.

Catchin' Up Ketchup

This homemade ketchup recipe is an easy and healthier alternative to store-bought version. Unlike the store bought, this recipe has a low glycemic load with the coconut sugar and has the benefits of the chia to reduce blood sugar levels. The apple cider vinegar is highly alkaline to counter the acid in the tomatoes. All in all, a much healthier version of the traditional American classic.

Ingredients:

- 2-6 ounce cans tomato paste (preferably low sodium)
- ¼ cup warm water
- 3 tablespoons coconut sugar
- 3 tablespoons apple cider vinegar
- 1 tablespoon garlic powder
- 1 tablespoon onion powder
- 1 tablespoon molasses
- ⅛ teaspoon allspice
- 1 teaspoon rock salt
- 2 teaspoons white ground chia

Directions:

1. Blend all ingredients in a food processor or blender.

2. Adjust seasonings and sweeteners to your taste.

Makes about 2 cups of ketchup depending on the thickness (add more chia for thicker version).

That-ziki Sauce

I lived in a big city for most of my adult life — until recently moving to a farm and saying goodbye to the chaos. But for many years of city living we were lucky enough to be very close to the Greek district. Although very meat based, the Greek culinary culture offers up delicious sides and spreads that are truly wonderful. This recipe is a vegan take on a well-deserved Greek classic.

Ingredients:

- ¼ cup water

- 1 cup Delores hemp seeds

- 2 cups English cucumbers (peeled, grated)

- ¼ cup lemon juice

- 1 tablespoon olive oil

- 2 tablespoons fresh dill, coarsely chopped

- 1 tablespoon white ground chia

- 2 large cloves garlic, peeled and coarsely chopped

- 1 tablespoon apple cider vinegar

- ¼ teaspoon rock salt

- ⅛ teaspoon ground pepper

Directions:

1. In a food processor, blend together the water and Delores hemp seeds until creamy.

2. Squeeze out the water from the cucumber with paper towel. Set aside.

3. Combine all ingredients to hemp mix and pulse until well-combined but not completely smooth and still chunky.

4. Cover and refrigerate for at least one hour for the richest flavor.

5. Serve with vegetable sticks or gluten free pita. Can be stored in the fridge for a few days.

Makes 1 cup.

Spinach Rawcotta

This is a delicious way to eat spinach and get whole protein and all of your essential fatty acids.
Use as a sandwich spread, as part of raw lasagna ingredients, or as a delicious veggie dip.

Ingredients:

- 1 cup Delores hemp seeds

- ¼ cup slow roasted hemp seeds

- ½ cup baby spinach, washed, dried and packed

- ½ tablespoon lemon juice

- ½ tablespoon nutritional yeast flakes

- 1 teaspoon, garlic minced

- ½ teaspoon rock salt

- ¼ cup to ½ cup warm veggie broth (or warm water)

Directions:

1. Blend all ingredients, (except for broth/water) in a food processor until very crumbly.

2. Gradually stream in warm broth or water until creamy, light and fluffy.

3. Add more garlic to taste!

Makes about 2 cups.

Appeteasers

One of the best parties I ever threw was a girl's-night-in where I asked a bunch of girlfriends over and I asked each one to bring an amazing homemade appetizer. With everyone excited about showing off their culinary creations, we all ended up gorging ourselves all night on incredible bite-sized delectable delights. We were so stuffed that my main dish wasn't even served.

Everyone loves appetizers: how can you not? Appetizers are meant to test and trigger your savory senses. Designed to stimulate appetite, a great appetizer should tease the taste buds and be an incredible start to a meal. Unfortunately though, many appetizers, especially the fast frozen food variety, are bad-fat fried fiends. Often sporting trans-fatty acids with simple carbs and additives and little or no nutritional benefit, appetizers can load on the pounds like no other food!

But by swapping out the bad fats for the good and essential ones, and by focusing on healthy energy boosting plant-based protein with lots of heart healthy fiber, "appeteasers" can be one of the best choices to make. So, go ahead and make these tasty delights while you nutritiously nosh the day and night away!

Ate Layer Dip

This dip is a healthy entertaining dream come true. Most layered dips are full of bad fats, huge calories, and little nutritional benefits. But say hello-to-hosting-holidays as my version is full of Omega-3's, healthy whole protein, anti-oxidants, vitamins and minerals. It's a delicious dip that will keep you coming back for more! It takes a bit of prep work but be careful, as this one will not last long on any entertaining table.

Ingredients:

- "Bean There, Yum That Dip"(see below)
- 1 cup diced tomato
- "Rockin' Guac Dip" (see below)
- 1 cup medium heat salsa (or "Rockin' Red Super Salsa")
- 1 cup shredded lettuce
- "Sour Kreem" (see recipe in fabulous fixin's)
- 1 cup Daiya vegan shredded cheddar "cheez"
- 1 cup diced green onion

Directions:

1. Wash and prepare vegetables and set aside each in a separate bowl.

2. Make "Bean There Yum That Dip" and set aside.

3. Make "Rockin' Guac" and set aside.

4. Make "Sour Kreem" and set aside.

5. In a 9x9 inch glass layer the dip as follows from bottom up: bean dip, tomato, guacamole, salsa, lettuce, sour kreem, Daiya cheez and green onion.

Bean There, Yum That Dip

This bean dip has a smoky zesty flavor with the nutritional benefits of black beans. Black beans are very high in fiber, folate, protein, and antioxidants, along with numerous other vitamins and minerals. Black beans along with chia and hemp seeds (with their high fiber) also helps to move food through the stomach to the large intestine at a healthier pace. This also helps to make you feel fuller and also reduces blood sugar spikes while digesting. So go ahead and don't stop dipping!

Ingredients:

- 1 cup sweet onion, diced

- 1 tablespoon olive oil

- 1-19oz (540ml) can black beans

- ½ cup fresh cilantro, washed, patted dry and packed

- 2 tablespoons medium heat salsa

- 2 tablespoons Delores hemp seeds

- 1 teaspoon white whole seed chia

- ¼ teaspoon rock salt

- ½ teaspoon cacao powder

- ½ teaspoon coconut sugar

- ¼ teaspoon chili powder

- ¼ cup warm water

Directions:

1. Add olive oil to a fry pan, turn heat to medium high. Add in onions and stir. Cook covered for 10 minutes stirring frequently.

2. Open beans and drain any excess liquid out. Add beans to onion mix, stir and cook uncovered for 5 minutes.

3. Measure then wash cilantro, and stir into beans and cook uncovered for 5 minutes.

4. Take bean mixture off heat and add to a food processor. Add in salsa, hemp seeds, chia, rock salt, cacao powder, coconut sugar and chili powder. Blend and mix in ¼ cup water (or more if needed) and blend until a smooth but thick paste.

Rockin' Guac'

Who can say no to guac'? With its delicious and super healthy fats that are a beauty lover's dream for healthy looking skin, this dip is a "must have" once a week. By simply adding in chia to the mix, you transform a good-for-you option to a super one!

Ingredients:

- 2 large ripe avocados

- ¼ cup diced green onion (half of a small green onion)

- ¼ cup diced tomato

- 1 tablespoon white whole seed chia

- Juice of ½ lime

- 2 tablespoons cilantro, finely chopped

- ¼ teaspoon rock salt

Directions:

1. Cut avocados in half, remove pit and spoon out flesh into bowl.

2. Mash gently with fork.

3. Wash and finely chop cilantro, add to avocado.

4. Add in all other ingredients and stir together.

Makes about 1 ½ cups.

Round-it-Up Ranch Dip

Ranch dips are a kid favorite as it is creamy and tasty without any over powering flavors. But the store-bought versions are usually full of the bad fats and usually filled with the high allergen and the not good for you soy oil. My take on this dippy favorite is a healthy one that tastes great and is full of whole protein and the essential fatty acids your body needs.

Ingredients:

- 1 cup Delores hemp seeds
- ¼ cup water
- 1 tablespoon lemon juice
- ¾ tablespoon apple cider vinegar
- 2 teaspoons dried parsley
- 2 teaspoons dried chives
- ½ teaspoon garlic powder
- ½ teaspoon rock salt
- ½ teaspoon dried dill weed
- ½ teaspoon onion powder
- ⅛ teaspoon ground black pepper

Directions:

1. In a food processor, blend ingredients all together until smooth. Keep refrigerated.

2. Will keep in fridge for up to 4 days.

3. Note: for a ranch salad dressing, simply add more water until desired consistency.

Makes about 1 ¼ cups.

Pizza Pizzazz

Pizza is a dieter's devil dream. The standard combination of the crunchy crust, acidic/sweet tomato sauce, and melt in your mouth cheese all make for an incredibly gluten-rich and fatty not-so-good-for-you dream. But you can have a healthy version of this traditionally bad choice and by making a few tweaks. And what you can get is freaky amazing! The toppings on this one are SOOOOOO yummy as a combo but feel free to make this one your own personal style.

Ingredients:

Crust:

- ¾ cup gluten free oat flour, or all-purpose flour

- 1 cup quinoa flour

- ¼ cup coconut flour

- 1 ½ teaspoon baking powder

- 1 ½ teaspoons white ground chia

- 1 ½ teaspoons rock salt

- ¼ teaspoon each of: dried basil, dried thyme, dried oregano, dried rosemary, onion powder, garlic powder.

- ½ cup water

- 2 tablespoons olive oil

Toppings:

- ½ cup tomato sauce

- ¼ cup sundried tomato, chopped

- 2 tablespoons basil leaves, thinly sliced

- 1 tablespoon capers (optional)

- Handful Daiya Mozzarella Cheez (optional)

- ½ cup baby arugula, washed

Directions:

1. Preheat oven to 400 degrees.

2. Wipe a pizza pan with olive oil, and set aside.

3. In a medium bowl, sift together the dry ingredients until well blended. Make a well in the center.

4. In a separate bowl, combine water and olive oil and pour into the dry well mixing until blended (add 1 tablespoon more water at a time, if too pasty).

5. Form dough into an even ball.

6. Sprinkle a small amount of quinoa or oat flour on kitchen counter and roll out dough through the middle of the ball and evenly roll to form a circle. Dough should be about ½inch think.

7. Turn the dough evenly onto the pizza pan. If the dough is sticky, add a little more oat flour onto your hands.

8. Bake for 15 minutes. Take crust out of the oven and top with sauce and toppings of choice (I included mine above — but for arugula add after pizza cooked) with a sprinkle of Daiya vegan Cheez, and place back in the oven and bake for another 10 minutes or until the crust is lightly browned on the bottom.

9. Add arugula to top of pizza as soon as it comes out of oven.

10. Enjoy!

Pizza Pizaz with Besto Pesto, see p. 164

Chillin' Out Kale Chips

These chips are so deelish that even kale critics will fall in love with them. With great antioxidant nutrients and anti-inflammatory nutrients, kale is also a great way to naturally detoxify. With the addition of hemp to add in tons of whole protein and nutritional yeast to boost your B12's, you can have your chips and eat them too!

Ingredients:

- Bunch of Kale (8-10 leaves with stems)
- ¼ cup olive oil
- ½ cup Delores hemp seeds
- ¼ cup nutritional yeast flakes

- 1 tablespoon chili powder
- 1 tablespoon onion powder
- ½ teaspoon rock salt

Directions:

1. Remove stems of kale, wash, dry them and tear into strips (about 2 inches to 3-4 inches) and place in a large bowl.

2. For olive oil, pour evenly over kale and hand mix together.

3. In a separate small bowl, mix all of the remaining ingredients together. Then evenly sprinkle onto kale and mix with hands until all kale coated.

4. Place in a dehydrator for about 4 hours. If you do not have access to a dehydrator, then for oven baking: preheat oven to 350 degrees F (175 degrees C); line a non-insulated cookie sheet with parchment paper and bake chips about 10-15 minutes until the edges brown but are not burnt.

5. Keep in an airtight container.

Not-a-Nut Crunch

This recipe is a great way to have the taste and texture experience of caramelized nut crunch without any of the nut allergens. Also, the hemp seeds, quinoa, chia, coconut oil and the low glycemic and healthy coconut sugar allow for an even healthier version of a snack classic. Feel free to play with the flavors by adding your own spices (like hot peppers, curry, cardamom, turmeric, etc). This is great on its own or use as a super addition to granola, trail mix, yogurt, cereal, oatmeal, salads or desserts.

Ingredients:

- ½ tablespoon coconut oil
- ¼ cup coconut sugar
- 1 teaspoon Delores hemp seeds
- 1 teaspoon slow roasted hemp seeds

- 1 teaspoon white whole seed chia
- 1 teaspoon uncooked unpolished quinoa
- ⅛ teaspoon cinnamon
- Pinch of dried ginger and nutmeg powder

Directions:

1. In a fry pan, on medium high heat melt coconut oil and then add in coconut sugar.
   Stir constantly and let it come to a gentle bubbling boil for 10 seconds
   (when sugar forms a line when you slide spoon through it — it is done).

2. Stir in all other crunch ingredients and coat evenly with oil/sugar mix.

3. Remove mix from pan onto a cool no stick cookie sheet.

4. Place in freezer, and once cooled, break into small pieces.

5. Store in a sealed container.

Makes about ¼ cup.

Healthy Hummus

Hummus is one of those personal foods. Everyone has their own idea what they like: a garlicky one, lemon based, or the uber-tahini sticky version. This recipe is safe for all, with no sesame, and "not too much of anything taste" except healthy goodness. The fresh mint finishes the whole thing off in a refreshing take-down-the-garlic-kinda way.

Ingredients:

- 1 can of chickpeas (14oz), rinsed
- ¼ cup slow roasted hemp seeds
- 3 tablespoons lemon juice
- 2 tablespoons olive oil
- ¾ teaspoon minced garlic

- ½ teaspoon rock salt
- ½ teaspoon chili powder
- 2-3 large fresh mint leaves, chopped
- 2 tablespoons warm water
- Olive oil for drizzle (optional)

Directions:

1. Drain and rinse chickpeas and add to food processor.

2. Except for water, place all other ingredients in the processor.
   Pulse a few times, then put on low speed and add water slowly.

3. Blend for 1 minute then stop and scrape sides — add more water if required.

4. Blend again for 2-4 minutes until creamy and smooth.

5. Serve cold and drizzle olive oil on top if desired.

6. Freezes well.

Makes 1 ¼ cup.

Besto Pesto

This incredible pesto recipe is super high in essential fatty acids and protein, and better yet has no nuts. It is great as a pizza dip or sauce, on crackers, or as a base for a pasta sauce. Better yet? Simply eat it by the green lovin' spoonfuls.

Ingredients:

- 3 cups loose leaf basil, washed and patted dry

- ⅓ cup olive oil

- 1 cup Delores hemp seeds

- 1 ½ tablespoons lemon juice

- ½ teaspoon of garlic, finely minced

- 3 tablespoons nutritional yeast flakes (or for a non-veg' version: ¼ cup of grated romano)

- ⅛ teaspoon rock salt

Directions:

1. Blend all ingredients until creamy in texture and store in fridge.

2. Serve with gluten free crackers or cucumber slices.

3. The chlorophyll in the basil will keep this fresh in the fridge for a number of days. You can also freeze this into ice trays for an on "a need-to-use" basis.

Makes about ¼ cup.

Great-Full Spinach Dip

Unlike the famous spinach dip that was stuffed into carved out rye bread loaves and brought to every party in the 1990's, and which is also full of super-fatty cheese and mayo, THIS recipes tastes as creamy and decadent but is awesomely good for you! Rich in whole protein, vitamin E, and Omega's, this dip is one you can enjoy guilt free. Whether you serve it with veggie sticks or plop it into a scooped out gluten free bread loaf, this one will be a favorite for the health nut and the mayo-lover alike... everyone can be great-full!

Ingredients:

- 10 oz. (300gr) frozen spinach, defrosted
- 1 can (4oz/218ml) sliced water chestnut
- ½ cup green onions, chopped
- ¼ cup red star nutritional yeast flakes

- ½ cup slow roasted hemp seeds
- ¼ cup Delores hemp seeds
- ½ cup water (or plain rice milk)
- 3 tablespoons onion powder
- 2 tablespoons olive oil

- 2 tablespoons lemon juice
- 2 teaspoons garlic powder
- ½ teaspoon rock salt
- ¼ teaspoon yellow mustard (condiment not powder)
- ¼ teaspoon chili powder
- ¼ teaspoon ground pepper

Directions:

1. Drain the spinach and squeeze out the water. Place in a large mixing bowl.

2. Drain and chop the water chestnut (should equal approx. ¾ cup) and add to spinach mix.

3. Stir in chopped green onion and nutritional yeast flakes to spinach mixture.

4. In a Magic Bullet or food processer, add all other ingredients (slow roasted and Delores hemp seeds, water/plain rice milk, onion powder, olive oil, lemon juice, garlic powder, rock salt, mustard, chili powder and ground pepper).

5. Blend on high until creamy.

6. Pour the "hemp sauce" into spinach mixture and gently stir until it is mixed throughout spinach.

7. Serve chilled with veggies or in a scooped out bread loaf (a gluten free one of course!).

Barbie Dahl Dip

I love the rich flavors of this easy recipe. The tomato and cacao addition gives it a barbecue feel but keeps the traditional flavors front and center. It is great as a dip or a make ahead paste for tortilla wraps or for yummy sandwiches: who needs bad mayo when you can use this rich and healthy spread instead?

Ingredients:

- 1 tablespoon olive oil
- 1 cup sweet onion, chopped
- 1 tablespoon garlic, finely chopped
- 3 cups vegetable broth
- 1 cup dried red lentils, rinsed
- 1 (7.5oz) can tomato paste (preferably salt free)
- 1 teaspoon cacao powder

- 1 teaspoon cumin powder
- 1 teaspoon dried coriander
- 1 teaspoon curry powder
- ½ teaspoon rock salt
- ½ teaspoon turmeric powder
- Pinch cinnamon
- ¼ cup Delores hemp seeds

Directions:

1. In a medium-sized soup pot, heat oil over medium heat and then add the onion and garlic.

2. Stir and cook until the onions are translucent (about 5 minutes).

3. Add all other ingredients (except hemp seeds) and bring to a low boil.

4. Once boiling, turn down heat to low and cover.

5. Simmer for about 15-20 minutes until lentils are tender. Add more water or broth during cooking if required.

6. Blend all in a food processor, with hemp seeds (add more water if too thick) and then place in a dip bowl. Easy to freeze.

Makes 3 cups.

Dream Bean Pâté

This pâté is made with the super creamy and nutty flavored borlotti bean. Low glycemic with great fiber, it is also a source of vitamin B1, iron, potassium, and magnesium. It is one of the simplest and fastest dips to make and a great "surprise guest" standby.

Ingredients:

- 1 (14 oz.) can borlotti* beans, drained and rinsed

- ¼ cup olive oil

- ¼ cup fresh Italian parsley leaves, (washed, patted dry and loosely packed)

- ¼ cup Delores hemp seeds

- 2 cloves garlic

- 2 tablespoons lemon juice

- ½ teaspoon rock salt

- ⅛ teaspoon ground black pepper

- 1 teaspoon dried oregano or thyme

Directions:

1. Place all ingredients in a food processor. Pulse until the mixture is coarsely chopped and mixed, but not too creamy.

2. Transfer the bean puree to a small bowl and serve with gluten free pita toasts. May be frozen.

Makes 1 cup

*Note: Borlotti beans are sometimes called "cranberry beans". If unavailable, then use cannellini beans.

Lean Bean Cakes

Black beans are packed with iron and manganese along with a large amount of protein and insoluble fiber. The fiber in the beans and the chia are key for your digestive system, and helps keep your whole digestive tract in top shape along with reduced sugar cravings. It will also help to make you feel fuller for longer. They are also a rich source of an antioxidant called anthocyanins, which help fight the free radicals to help fight against cancer and the aging process. Now you can have your cake and eat it too!

Ingredients:

- 1 cup fresh cilantro, washed, patted dry and loosely packed
- ½ cup canned black beans, drained and rinsed
- ½ cup canned diced tomato
- ½ cup green onion, chopped
- 3 tablespoons white whole seed chia
- 5 tablespoons water

- 1 ½ cup quinoa flour
- 1 tablespoon baking powder
- 1 teaspoon rock salt
- 1 teaspoon chili powder
- 1 teaspoon onion powder
- ½ teaspoon ground black pepper

Directions:

1. In a small bowl, mix the chia and water and let sit for 15 minutes, stirring occasionally.

2. Coarsely chop cilantro and place in a large bowl. Add in beans, tomato and onion.

3. In a small bowl, mix remaining dry ingredients together.

4. Slowly add in the chia mix to the bean/veggie mix. Then add dry mixture to the wet one mixing well.

5. Once mixed, heat a frying pan on medium heat along with a tablespoon of olive or coconut oil.

6. Take a ¼ cup of batter and from into a ½-inch round "cake" and fry the pancakes in batches until golden brown on both sides (or you can bake at 350F for 10 minutes each side).

7. Serve with salsa. Freeze well.

Makes about 16 cakes.

Eggplant Zippy Dip

A simple but healthy take on an old Greek classic: Melizonsalata. Great for a dip, or as an alternative to pasta sauce, or in lieu of mayo on sandwiches. This dip will keep them all coming back for more.

Ingredients:

- 2 large dark purple eggplants
- 1 garlic clove, chopped
- ¼ cup Delores hemp seeds
- 3 tablespoons lemon juice
- 2 tablespoons rice milk or water
- 1 tablespoon olive oil
- 1 tablespoon white ground chia
- 1 teaspoon rock salt
- ⅛ teaspoon ground cumin
- ⅛ teaspoon chili powder
- 1 tablespoon coarsely chopped parsley

Directions:

1. Preheat oven to 400F.

2. Cut eggplants in half and set one half aside.

3. With the eggplant half set aside, we are making an eggplant serving dish, so scoop/cut out the flesh (freeze for future use) and cut the skin bottom on a horizontal cut so that the eggplant "bowl" can sit stably on its own.

4. For each of the other three eggplant halves, wrap each in foil and place in oven fleshy side up, for 30 minutes until insides are soft and slightly mushy (or alternatively throw on high heat barbecue while in foil for 20-25 minutes).

5. Take out of oven and let cool. Once cooled, take out eggplant flesh with a spoon and discard skin.

6. Place flesh in a food processor. Add all remaining ingredients to food processor and blend until consistency is between chunky and creamy.

7. Place into eggplant bowl and serve with pita, crackers or veggie sticks. Sprinkle with parsley. Freezes well.

Oh-My-Mega Dolmas

Even though I am an uber-veggie, Greek restaurants are one of my major destinations. It all has to do with the Veggie Dolmas. I have taken this tried and true love-in-a-leaf to a new super height. It is flavorfully spicy and tart, with incredible textures. You can even skip the grape leaves it you want and serve the filling as a side salad. Grape leaves or no grapes leaves: eat, drink and yell OPA!

Ingredients:

- ¼ cup plus 2 tablespoons brown rice, uncooked
- ¼ cup unpolished quinoa, uncooked
- 1 cup vegetable broth (or water)
- ½ cup carrot, shredded
- 2 tablespoons Delores hemp seeds
- 2 tablespoons slow roasted hemp seeds
- 2 tablespoons pumpkin seeds
- 2 tablespoons nutritional yeast flakes

- 1 ½ tablespoons sesame oil
- 1 tablespoon "Soy-NOT Sauce" (or 1 ½ tablespoons soya sauce if no allergy)
- 1 tablespoon white whole seed chia
- ½ tablespoon lemon juice
- 1 teaspoon hot chili sauce (Sambal Oelek is my choice)
- ¼ teaspoon rock salt
- 1 jar grape leaves
- 4 lemon wedges (garnish)

Directions:

1. In a large pot, place the rice and quinoa in the broth.

2. Cover and bring to a boil. Once boiling, turned to low heat and leave covered for 20 minutes.

3. Remove from heat and set aside covered for another 10 minutes. Remove cover and fluff with a fork.

4. In a large bowl, mix together all ingredients including the cooked rice/Quinoa.

5. Drain and rinse the grape leaves carefully. And take them apart one by one and place each on a spread out hand towel and pat dry.

6. Place dried grape leaf on a flat surface, stem facing towards you. Put a tablespoon of filling above the stem in the middle of the leaf. Fold the bottom of the leaf up over the filling, then fold the sides inward over the stuffing, and then hold stuffing and folded in leaves and roll leaf away from you. Seal with a toothpick to secure.

7. Repeat this till you are out of stuffing. Serve with "That-ziki Sauce" and lemon wedges. Cannot be frozen.

Makes approximately 15 dolmas.

Bruchempa

This recipe is one that I initially served when visiting our awesome hemp growers. I stayed at their farm and made dinner for friends and farm hands. This recipe is so good and nutrient rich — and is worth the extra work for a super wow-factor.

Ingredients:

Bread:

- 16 pieces thinly sliced gluten free baguette bread (or sliced bread, halved)

- Daiya Vegan Cheez (optional)

Garlic Paste:

- ½ cup Delores hemp seeds

- ¼ cup plus 2 tablespoons, olive oil

- 4 medium garlic cloves, chopped

- ½ teaspoon rock salt

- ¼ teaspoon ground black pepper

Tomato Mix:

- 2 cups plum tomatoes, chopped

- 2 tablespoons olive oil

- 2 tablespoons sundried tomatoes, finely chopped

- 2 tablespoons Delores hemp seeds

- 1 tablespoon white whole seed chia

- 1 tablespoon balsamic vinegar

- ½ teaspoon garlic, minced

- 8 basil leaves, washed and finely chopped

- pinch of rock salt and pepper

- Daiya Cheez (optional)

Directions:

1. Preheat the oven on broiler setting.

2. In a Magic Bullet, blend all ingredients of garlic paste and set aside (add 1 tablespoon of water at a time if too thick).

3. In a large bowl, combine the tomatoes, sun-dried tomatoes, garlic, olive oil, vinegar, basil, hemp seeds, chia, rock salt, and pepper. Allow the mixture to sit for 10 minutes.

4. On a baking sheet, arrange bread slices in a single layer.

5. Broil for 1 to 2 minutes, until slightly brown.

6. On each slice, spread about ¾ tablespoon garlic paste thinly and evenly.

7. Place about 1 heaping tablespoon of the tomato mixture evenly over each slice.

8. Optionally, top the slices with shredded Daiya cheese (optional).

9. Broil for 2-4 minutes, or until the cheese is melted. If no cheese used, then serve immediately.

Karma-lives Popcorn

This recipe is easy to make and a real crowd pleaser — especially with the kids.
The healthy benefits make this a super karmic experience — so go ahead and get poppin'!

Ingredients:

- 6 cups air-popped organic non-GMO corn (if corn issues, use popped rice, quinoa, or sourghum)

- ½ cup, plus one tablespoon, coconut sugar

- ¼ cup water

- 1 tablespoon coconut oil

- 1 teaspoon vanilla

- ⅛ teaspoon rock salt

- 2 tablespoons Delores hemp seeds

- ⅛ teaspoon rock salt

Directions:

1. Place the popped popcorn on a non-stick cookie sheet.

2. In a saucepan add coconut sugar, water, coconut oil, vanilla, and rock salt (leave aside hemp seeds and last ⅛ teaspoon salt).

3. Turn to high heat, stir constantly, and bring to a boil. Once boiling, turn to medium and keep at a low boil for about 10 minutes until thickened (should be thick enough that when you take a small amount on a spoon and place liquid on a plate, as you lift spoon, a line of thin sugar remains about 4-6 inches high).

4. Turn off the heat and stir in the hemp seeds.

5. Pour mixture onto popcorn in a steady drizzle stream.

6. Sprinkle remaining ⅛ teaspoon of rock salt onto drizzled popcorn.

7. Store in an airtight container for up to 1 week.

Karma-lives Popcorn, see p. 180

Oh-My-Mega Dolmas with That-Ziki Sauce, see p.176

All It's Cracked Up to Be Crackers

These crackers are great to make in large batches and place them in a cool container for easy dipping access. Nothing but pure natural goodness in these crackin' babies!

I n g r e d i e n t s :

- ¼ cup white ground chia

- ¾ cup water

- ¼ cup gluten free oat flour

- ¼ cup plus 2 tablespoons gluten free quick flake oats

- ¼ cup white whole seed chia

- ¼ cup plus 2 tablespoons unpolished quinoa

- ½ cup Delores hemp seeds

- ¾ teaspoon rock salt

- ¾ teaspoon each of: garlic powder and onion powder

- ½ teaspoon chili powder

D i r e c t i o n s :

1. Preheat oven to 350F.

2. Grease a non-stick baking sheet with olive oil.

3. In a small bowl, mix the chia and water and set aside for 20 minutes, stirring occasionally.

4. In a large bowl, mix together all other ingredients, add chia mix when hydrated.

5. On baking sheet, flatten out the mixture until evenly spread out in shape of a rectangle. Using hard edge of a wooden spatula, gently cut the rectangle in half.

6. Bake for 10 minutes on top rack. Using the flat spatula cut the dough, and make 2-inch squares. Flip each square over. Bake another 10 minutes on top rack or until lightly browned.

7. Keep in an air tight container.

Makes about 20 crackers.

Quickie Bickies

These biscuits are a lovely addition to a super soup, or fast way to have some fiber, great fats, and Omegas on the go! An easy and worth it quickie!

Ingredients:

- ¼ cup white ground chia

- ¾ cup water

- 2 cups gluten free oat flour, or gluten free all-purpose flour

- 1 ½ tablespoons coconut sugar

- 1 tablespoon baking powder

- 1 ½ teaspoons rock salt

- 2 teaspoons each of: garlic powder, onion powder, dried basil and parsley flakes

- ⅔ cups plain rice milk

- ¼ cup plus one tablespoon coconut oil, room temperature

Directions:

1. Preheat oven to 425F.

2. Grease a non-stick baking sheet.

3. In a mixing bowl, mix dry ingredients together.

4. To dry ingredients, add in rice milk and stir.

5. With a pastry cutter, cut in the coconut oil.

6. Take ⅛ cup of batter and make into a circle that is ½ inch deep. Drop on baking sheet.

7. Place on top rack, and bake for 10-12 minutes until bottom is a light brown.

8. Cool on baker's rack.

Makes 14-16 biscuits.

Be Souper!

A great soup makes me think of childhood home-from-school lunches. I loved to slurp down hot spoonfuls while dunking buttery thick bread. There is something about soup that is nurturing and homey — a medley of flavor and ingredients that all come together to comfort and soothe. The way a good soup tastes better the day after is another benefit — you know like a great wine it just gets better with time and promises an even better taste experience just waiting for you.

Although my Mom's creamy and buttery concoctions were wonderful tasty delights, I now know that their deliciousness was found mostly in their high saturated, fattening fats. Instead of cream based bad fatty soups, my recipes offer all of the fabby flavor with none of the flabby costs. High in nutrients these soups are a wonderful addition to your family's favorites! So soupies unite and take over! Slurp ON my friend!

Vichy-Suave (Leek & Potato) Soup

There are a number of things that I have really missed being a veggie. One of them has been cream based soups, especially leek and potato (or as the French call it: "Vichyssoise"). This was a special treat soup in our house and was consumed really quickly due to its smooth, creamy, and subtle flavors. This recipe captures all of those notes but without the guilt — so seek no further my suave friend!

Ingredients:

- ¾ cup unpolished quinoa

- 1 ½ cups water

- 2 tablespoons olive oil

- 2 cups chopped onion (Spanish or white or a combo)

- 1 ½ cup chopped green onion

- 3 cups chopped leeks (white part only of 3 large leeks)

- 5 cups vegetable broth

- 2 ½ cups diced potatoes (½-inch thick)

- ¾ cup slow roasted hemp seeds

- ¼ cup nutritional yeast flakes

- ½ cup water

- ¼ teaspoon rock salt

- ½ teaspoon garlic powder

- ½ teaspoon ground black pepper

- ½ teaspoon ground celery seed OR celery salt

Directions:

1. Bring water to boil, add quinoa and cook on low heat covered for 15 minutes — take off burner, set aside and leave covered.

2. Place olive oil in a large pot over med-high heat. Add in the 2 cups chopped onions and cook covered for 5 minutes, stirring occasionally.

3. Add in green onions and leeks and cover for 5 minutes, stirring occasionally.

4. Add in broth and potatoes, cover and let simmer on low-medium heat for about 30 minutes, stirring occasionally until potatoes are firm but fully cooked.

5. In a food processor, add in ¾ cups of the cooked soup mixture and add the cooked quinoa, hemp seeds, nutritional yeast, water, salt, garlic powder, pepper and celery salt and blend until smooth.

6. Add blended mixture back into the soup, stir and serve. Can be frozen.

Makes 7 cups.

Vichy-Suave (Leek & Potato) Soup, see p. 186 and All It's Cracked Up to Be Crackers, see p. 183

Thai One On Soup

This soup is not as much work as it initially looks — especially if you use a food processor to slice and shred. The sauce is easy to make as you just blend everything up. It is so worth it though as this soup is high on flavor and nutritional benefits and is very filling as a dinner meal. Better yet, the flavors seep through the longer it sits, so as a left over, it is a super lunch break the following day!

Ingredients:

Base:

- 2 tablespoons coconut oil
- 1 cup sweet onion, diced
- 1 tablespoon garlic, minced
- 2 cups brown mushrooms, thinly sliced
- ½ red pepper, thinly sliced lengthwise
- 1 ½ cups broccoli florets, chopped
- 1 cup carrots, shredded

Sauce:

- ½ cup sweet onion, chopped
- 4 garlic cloves
- 2 cans lite coconut milk
- 1 cup Delores hemp seeds
- 3 tablespoons coconut sugar
- Juice of 1 lime
- 2 tablespoons nutritional yeast flakes
- 1 teaspoon rock salt
- 1 inch square ginger root, chopped
- ½ teaspoon lemongrass paste/puree (or ½ lemongrass stock chopped — 6 pieces) (optional)

Toppers (Optional):

- ⅓ cup green onion, chopped
- ½ cup cucumber, seeded and diced
- 4 tablespoons washed and chopped cilantro

1. Prepare "toppers" of chopped green onion, cucumber, and cilantro and set aside.

2. In a soup pot, heat coconut oil on medium/high heat and add sweet onion and garlic.

3. Turn down to medium heat and cook covered for 5 minutes, stirring occasionally.

4. Add mushrooms, red pepper, broccoli and carrots, stir and cook covered for 10 minutes, stirring occasionally.

5. Mix all sauce ingredients together in a food processor. Blend on high until smooth.

6. Add blended sauce to vegetable mixture. Add water if needed for a thinner consistency.

7. Heat soup through until warm (don't boil it as it will spoil the healthy fats in the hemp).

8. Serve in bowls with a sprinkling of cucumber, green onion, and cilantro.

Makes 5 cups.

Wicked Pickle (or not) Soup

I love pickles and had the happiest pregnancies munching away on them. The sodium can be high on store bought ones unless you make your own at home with good-for-you rock salt. But when you need the pickle fix, this is a great soup with rich flavors that bring out all the goodness of a great pickle: texture, dill and garlic. The addition of the hemp gives it a creamy mouth feel with a whack of super high whole proteins. If you are NOT a pickle lover than omit the pickle and brine and add in a cup of vegetable stock and salt to taste for an easy veggie soup — shredding the veggies in a food processor (shredding blades) makes this souper fast to make!

Ingredients:

- 2 small gold potatoes
- 2 celery stalks
- 1 medium sweet onion
- 2 small carrots
- 1 small zucchini (or ½ a large one)

- 2 tablespoons garlic, minced
- 1 tablespoon olive oil
- 4 cups water
- 1 ½ teaspoons rock salt
- 2 tablespoons dill, minced

- 2 tablespoons lemon juice
- ½ cup garlic dill pickles, shredded or finely chopped
- ½ cup garlic dill pickle brine (from jar)
- ¼ cup Delores hemp seeds

Directions:

1. In a food processor, turn blade to shredder and shred: potatoes, celery, onions, carrots and zucchini.

2. Add olive oil to a large cook pot and turn on medium/high heat.

3. Once heated add in all shredded vegetables, garlic and water, stir and cover pot. Turn heat to medium.

4. Let it cook at a low boil, uncovered, and stirring occasionally for 20 minutes. Turn to low heat and add in rock salt, dill weed and lemon juice and cook for another 20 minutes, keeping it covered.

5. In food processor, shred pickles or finely chop them. Add pickles and brine to soup and stir. (Note: adding them at end rather than at beginning of cooking keeps them a little crunchy).

6. In a food processor, add in Delores hemp seeds, blend on high until creamy and add back into soup.

7. Stir and serve with toasted gluten free bread. Freezes well.

Makes 7 cups.

Wicked Pickle (or not) Soup, see p. 190 and Quickie Bickies, see p. 184

Magical Mushroom Soup

As a vegetarian, mushrooms can be a great addition to soups and stews as it allows the same texture and hearty taste of meat. Mushrooms contain about 80 to 90 percent water, and are very low in calories (only 100 cal/oz.). They have very little sodium and fat, and 8 to 10 percent of the dry weight is fiber so they are an excellent addition to anyone trying to downsize. Mushrooms are also an excellent source of potassium, copper, riboflavin, niacin, and selenium. With all this nutrition they become truly magical.

Ingredients:

- 3 tablespoons olive oil
- 1 cup sweet onion, chopped
- ½ cup celery, chopped
- 6 cups brown mushrooms, sliced
- 1 ½ cup shitake mushrooms, sliced
- 5 cups vegetable stock

- 1 ½ tablespoons balsamic vinegar
- ½ teaspoon rock salt
- ⅛ teaspoon black pepper
- ¼ cup unpolished quinoa
- ⅓ cup Delores hemp seeds
- ¼ cup fresh parsley, chopped (optional garnish)

Directions:

1. Wash and finely chop parsley and set aside.

2. In a large cook pot, heat olive oil on medium/high heat. Add in onion and celery and cover and cook for 3 minutes, stirring occasionaly.

3. Stir turn heat to low and add in all mushrooms. Cover and let simmer 10 minutes stirring occasionally.

4. Add stock, vinegar, salt, pepper and quinoa. Turn heat to high, bring to a boil then turn to low and cover. Let cook for 20 minutes, do not stir.

5. Place 1 cup of soup mixture along with Delores hemp seeds in a food processor or Vitamix and blend until pureed. Pour back into soup pot and stir.

6. Pour into four soup bowls evenly and serve with a sprinkle of parsley on top of each bowl. Freezes well.

Makes 8 cups.

Eat to the Beet RAWsome Soup

If you love beets like I do, this raw soup is for you! Chockfull of immune boosting antioxidants and super proteins this is a simple and fast way to beet up any potential infections! Raw beets are a great source of carbohydrates and an excellent source of potassium with phosphorus, magnesium, calcium, vitamin A, carotene and folate.

Ingredients:

- 2 cups water

- 1 ¼ cups raw red beets, cleaned and chopped (2 medium ones)

- 1 cup carrots, chopped (1 large one)

- ½ cup Delores hemp seeds

- 2 tablespoons ground white chia

- 2 tablespoons coconut sugar

- 1 inch x ½ inch ginger root (skin removed)

- 1 teaspoon garlic, minced

- ½ teaspoon rock salt

- ⅛ teaspoon ground cinnamon

Directions:

1. Blend all ingredients in a Vitamix or a powerful food processor until creamy consistency.

2. Serve chilled. Cannot be frozen.

Makes 4 cups.

En Français Onion Soup

This veggie take on an old favorite is really tasty and not too hard to make. It becomes even easier if you slice the onions in a food processor with the slicing blades. This one is even better tasting the next day and is freezable. C'est tres BIEN!

Ingredients:

- 2 tablespoons olive oil
- 1 ½ cups sweet onions, diced
- 1 ½ cups red onions. diced
- 1 tablespoon coconut sugar
- 2 thyme sprigs
- 1 bay leaf

- ½ teaspoon rock salt
- ⅛ teaspoon ground black pepper
- 1 tablespoon balsamic vinegar
- 4 cups vegetable broth
- 4 tablespoons Delores hemp seeds
- 2 teaspoons Maca Powder

Directions:

1. In a large saucepan, heat the olive oil over medium heat.

2. Stir in onions, coconut sugar, bay leaf, thyme, salt and pepper. Reduce heat to medium-low heat, cover and cook until the onions are very soft and caramelized, about 15-20 minutes.

3. Add the balsamic vinegar and broth, bring the soup back to a boil, stir and reduce heat to medium-low.

4. Cover and simmer for 20 minutes, stirring occasionally.

5. Discard the bay leaves and thyme sprigs. Take ½ cup of soup and place in a blender with hemp seeds and Maca Powder. Blend on high until creamy consistency. Pour back into soup pot and stir.

6. Place into 4 bowls and place gluten free toast on top and sprinkle the slices with Delores hemp seeds (and Daiya Cheez optionally). Voila!

Roasty Toasty Carrot Soup

Although I know how good carrots are for me, I have to admit I don't love them on their own. But I do love this soup — it is rich and kreemy with the right amount of flavor. This is a great autumn meal or a warm-me-up winter snack.

Ingredients:

- 1 cup vegetable stock

- ½ cup unpolished quinoa

- 2 tablespoon olive oil

- 8 large carrots, peeled and chopped into 1 inch pieces

- 1 cup sweet onion, chopped into 1 inch pieces

- ¼ cup celery, cut into 1 inch pieces

- 1 teaspoon ground cinnamon

- ¼ teaspoon rock salt

- 1 cup vegetable stock

- ¼ cup Delores hemp seeds

- ⅛ teaspoon ground black pepper

Directions:

1. Preheat oven to 375F.

2. In a small pot, add vegetable stock, quinoa and rock salt. Cover and place on high heat. Once it comes to a boil, turn to low heat and let cook covered for 20 minutes.

3. Remove from heat and let sit 5-10 minutes covered.

4. While quinoa is cooking, in a small roasting pan, smear oil on bottom of pan and then toss together carrots, onion, celery and cinnamon. Roast in oven for 25-30 minutes until veggies are tender with fork.

5. Place roasted vegetables, cooked Quinoa, 1 cup stock, Hemp and pepper in a food processor and blend until smooth. Add more stock if it needs to be thinned. Reheat and serve.

Serves 4.

Ginger Top Soup

If you want a satisfying myriad of fresh zingy flavors, with great protein, fiber, and anti-oxidants this one's for you. Great chilled or wonderfully soothing hot, this soup will blow your top off all year long!

Ingredients:

- 1 tablespoon coconut oil
- ¾ cup sweet onions, diced
- ½ tablespoon garlic, minced
- 1 tablespoon ginger, minced
- 5 cups vegetable stock

- ¼ cup unpolished quinoa
- 5 cups carrots, peeled and cut into ½" pieces
- 1 teaspoon rock salt
- 1-400ml/14oz can coconut milk, not lite
- ¼ cup Delores hemp seeds

Directions:

1. In a large pot, place coconut oil and turn to medium heat.

2. Melt oil, then add onions, stir and cook until softened — about 5 minutes.

3. Add garlic and ginger, stirring for about a minute.

4. Add quinoa, carrots, stock and salt, turn to medium/high heat and bring soup mixture to a boil, then reduce to low heat. Cover and simmer for 20 minutes, stirring occasionally.

5. Stir in coconut milk and hemp seeds and take off heat, allow to cool.

6. In a Vitamix or food processor, blend all until smooth. Freezes well.

Makes about 6 cups.

Come Kale Away Soup, see p. 198 and Chilin' Out Kale Chips, see p. 167

Come Kale Away Soup

This soup has lots of protein from the quinoa, chia and the chickpeas. The kale is a nutrient-packed powerhouse of a green that offers you anti-oxidants, vitamin A, and C, and provides plenty of fiber. Not only a low-fat and low-calorie vegetable, kale is recognized as one of the best to eat to help defend against cancer. If you want to speed up the preparation, use a food processor slicing blades to slice up the carrots, celery and potato — so easy!

Ingredients:

- 2 tablespoons olive oil
- 3 tablespoons garlic, chopped
- 2-6 inch sprigs fresh rosemary (or 1 teaspoon dried)
- 2 bay leaves
- 1-6 inch sprig fresh thyme (½ teaspoon dried)
- 2 large onions, sliced (2 cups)
- 1 large carrot, sliced (1 cup)

- 1 stalk celery, sliced (⅓ cup)
- 1 large potato, sliced (1 cup)
- 8 cups vegetable broth
- 2-14oz cans chickpeas (2 ½ cups)
- 1 bunch kale (thick center ribs removed), coarsely chopped (at least 8 cups)
- ¼ cup uncooked unpolished quinoa
- 2 tablespoons white whole seed chia
- rock salt to taste

Directions:

1. In a large cook pot, add oil and put on medium heat.

2. Add garlic, bay leaves, rosemary, and thyme and stir constantly for 2 minutes.

3. Add onion and stir until softened but not brown (about 4 minutes). Then turn up heat to medium high and add carrot and celery. Cook for about 2 minutes and stir.

4. Add potato and broth, turn heat to medium/high and bring to a boil; then turn to low heat and add chickpeas, kale, quinoa and chia. Cover and cook for 20–25 minutes, until all vegetables are tender.

5. Season to taste with salt. Remove bay leaves, and thyme sprigs.

6. Serve hot or cold. Freezes easily.

Makes about 8 cups.

Zuccha' Soup

This soup is easy to make and is a super go to when time is tight. A great way to start a meal as well as it is light and fresh tasting. A perfect way to use up the summer garden bounty zucchini too.

Ingredients:

- ½ cup white whole seed chia
- ¾ cup vegetable broth
- 1 tablespoon coconut oil
- ½ cup onion, chopped
- 2 cups zucchini, sliced (2 medium ones)

- ¼ cup Delores hemp seeds
- 4 cups vegetable stock
- ¼ teaspoon rock salt
- ⅛ teaspoon ground black pepper

Directions:

1. In a small bowl, soak chia and ¾ cup broth for 10 minutes, stirring occasionally.

2. In a large pot, heat the coconut oil on medium heat. Add and sauté the onion and zucchini until they are tender and transparent.

3. Transfer the mixture to a blender or food processor, add the hydrated chia along with hemp seeds and stock, and carefully blend until smooth.

4. Return pureed mixture to cooking pot, add salt and pepper and more stock if needed, reheat and serve. Can be frozen.

Makes about 5 cups.

Tomorrow's Tomato Soup

There is something so satisfying about a great tomato soup. This recipe is super on the day you make it but even better reheated (at a low temperature) for the day after. Also transitions nicely on day three as a pasta sauce, but given the taste of this soup, it will not be likely that anything will be left over!

Ingredients:

- 750g fresh tomatoes
  (approx. 6-7 medium or 5 large), quartered

- 2 ½ cups vegetable stock

- 1 cup onion, diced

- ½ cup carrot, peeled and chopped

- ¼ cup unpolished quinoa

- 1 bay leaf

- 1 teaspoon dried oregano

- ½ teaspoon rock salt

- ¼ teaspoon black ground pepper

- ¼ cup white ground chia

- 3 tablespoons Delores hemp seeds

- 2 tablespoons: parsley, chopped (garnish)

Directions:

1. Wash tomatoes and cut in halves.

2. In a large pot, add in tomatoes, stock, onion, carrot, quinoa, bay leaf, oregano, pepper, and salt. Bring to a boil then turn down heat to low. Cover and allow to simmer for 20 minutes.

3. Remove bay leaf and carefully add soup to a Vitamix or food processer, add chia and hemp seeds and blend until creamy consistency (add more water or stock if too thick).

4. Pour into 4 soup bowls and garnish with parsley (and oregano sprigs if on hand) to serve.

Green Kreem Gazpacho Soup

This cold super-charged soup is perfectly refreshing and nutrient rich. Not only is it rawsome, it is also rich in anti-oxidants, fiber, protein, vitamins and minerals. With in-season veggies, this cool raw soup is a great way to enjoy a hot summer day.

Ingredients:

- 1 ½ cups English cucumber, diced
- 2 cups fresh baby spinach, washed, patted dry and packed
- ½ cup Delores hemp seeds
- 2 tablespoons lemon juice

- 1 teaspoon rock salt
- 2 tablespoons white whole seed chia
- ½ cup water
- ¼ teaspoon nutmeg
- 1 teaspoon lemon zest (garnish)

Directions:

1. In a food processor or Vitamix, add all the ingredients except the lemon zest.

2. Blend until smooth and creamy. If the consistency is too thick, use some extra water.

3. In four soup dishes, spoon equal amounts of soup.

4. Sprinkle with lemon zest. Serve immediately. Cannot be frozen.

Makes 3 cups.

Sentilentil Soup

This recipe is one of my favorite go-tos. It is easy to make, rich in flavor, and even better the next day. Lentils are a good source of cholesterol-lowering fiber which can help to lower blood-sugar levels from rising. They are also a good source of minerals, vitamin B, and protein with virtually no fat. So good for you and tasty, it'll put a tear in your eye!

Ingredients:

- 2 tablespoons olive oil
- 2 teaspoons garlic, minced
- 1 cup onion, chopped
- 1 cup dried red lentils
- 3 tablespoons ground cumin
- 3 tablespoon ground coriander
- 2 tablespoons turmeric powder
- 2 tablespoons lemon juice
- 2 cups canned crushed tomato
- 5 cups vegetable stock
- ½ cup white whole seed chia
- Ground pepper to taste

Directions:

1. Heat olive oil on medium heat.

2. Add garlic and onions and sauté until golden.

3. Stir in pre-rinsed lentils, then add in cumin, coriander, turmeric, lemon juice, crushed tomatoes, and the stock. Stir well and let simmer on low heat for 20 minutes.

4. Add chia, and stir until thickened.

5. Serve with ground fresh pepper to taste. Freezes well.

Makes 7 cups.

Shrek Would Shriek Spinach Soup

When my kids were younger and I wanted them to eat green things I would tell them it was from Shrek. They now love the color green! This soup is a green dream as the spinach is rich in calcium, vitamins A and C, fiber, folic acid, and with flavonoids to help protect against age related memory loss. Spinach's secret weapon, lutein, makes it a super choice to help prevent cataracts and possibly reduce risks of cancer. So go ahead and join the supreme green team!

Ingredients:

- 1-10oz package chopped frozen spinach
- 2 tablespoons olive oil
- 1 cup onion, chopped
- 2 teaspoons garlic, minced
- 3 cups vegetable stock
- 2 tablespoons white whole seed chia
- 2 tablespoons Delores hemp seeds
- ¼ teaspoon rock salt
- Pepper to taste
- Lemon wedge (garnish)

Directions:

1. Defrost spinach, squeeze out excess water and set aside.

2. In skillet, heat oil on medium heat and sauté onion and garlic until soft.

3. Add vegetable stock and simmer for 10 minutes.

4. Mix spinach, chia and hemp seeds into soup. Heat it through, but don't bring to boil.

5. Carefully pour soup into a Vitamix or blender and puree. Serve immediately.

Makes 4 cups.

Awesome Avocado Soup

This soup is a nice balance of raw ingredients and canned ones if you opt for a fast prep.
The high amounts of chia and hemp seeds pump this up to a super soup in no time.

Ingredients:

- ¼ cup white whole seed chia
- ¾ cup water
- 1 large ripe avocado
- 2 tablespoons lemon juice
- 1 tablespoon olive oil
- 1 cup leek, washed and chopped (1 leek — bulb and lower leaf only)
- ¾ cup canned (or cooked) corn kernels, drained
- ¾ cup tomato, diced (either canned or fresh — peeled and seeded)
- ¾ teaspoon garlic, minced
- 2 cups vegetable broth
- ¼ cup Delores hemp seeds
- Rock salt and pepper to taste

Directions:

1. In a small bowl, place chia and water, and soak for 20 minutes, stirring occasionally.

2. Peel and pit the avocado. Place in small bowl, lightly mash and drizzle with lemon juice, set aside.

3. In a large pot, heat olive oil on medium heat and add leeks, corn, tomato, and garlic. Sauté for 5 minutes until leeks are soft.

4. Take half the sautéed vegetables and place in food processor along with chia gel, avocado, broth, and hemp seeds. Blend until creamy.

5. Add creamed vegetables back to soup pot, heat and stir. Garnish with chili flakes, parsley or corn kernels. Cannot be frozen.

Makes 4 cups.

Tomato Kreem Dream Soup

We grew up on the much loved canned tomato cream soup. On special days our Mom would add in more cream to make it even unhealthier. So, how to get that creamy mouth feel without the real cream (or additives from canned soups)? Well this soup will solve your cream-dream problems! With a lovely flavor combination of the thyme and basil and the nutty creaminess of the slow roasted hemp seeds, this will be eaten up so quickly it may barely get its 15 minutes of fame.

Ingredients:

- 1 tablespoon garlic, minced

- 1 cup sweet onion, chopped

- 3-6inch springs thyme
  (or 1 ½ teaspoons dried)

- ½ cup water

- 2 cans of diced tomato
  (2x796ml size or 2x28oz)

- 1 tablespoon coconut sugar

- ½ cup slow roasted hemp seeds

- ½ teaspoon rock salt

- 3 teaspoons fresh basil, minced
  (3 large leaves or 1 teaspoon dried)

Directions:

1. Place garlic, onion, thyme and water in a large pot. Turn to medium high, cover with lid and cook for 5 minutes stirring once.

2. Stir in all of canned tomatoes (do NOT drain) and add in coconut sugar.

3. Reduce to medium heat keeping lid slightly ajar.

4. Cook at a low boil for 15-20 minutes (until fresh thyme has turned a dark green) stirring a few times.

5. Remove from heat, stir and remove thyme sprigs (if used fresh).

6. In a food processor or Vitamix, carefully add in soup, slow roasted hemp seeds and basil. Blend until smooth and creamy.

7. Serve immediately and garnish with a sprig of thyme on side and a sprinkle of hemp seeds.

Makes 4 cups.

Middle Eat-stern Salad, see p. 208

Sumptuous Salads

As a child, my Brit born and influenced parents always insisted on having a salad at each meal. Great choice right? Yet, our salad consisted of a head of iceberg lettuce chopped into 5 pieces (there were five of us) and then drowned in Cross & Blackwell's dressing (which is just a British, Royalty-approved, form of mayonnaise). If my parents really felt like living on the edge, our salad may have also been accompanied by picked onions and a few slices of cucumber that were soaked in white vinegar.

Mostly made up of water, head lettuce is probably the only vegetable that has no nutrients to speak of. Likewise the "C&B" provided a huge array of unusable sat-fat ridden calories while the onion and cucumber's poor vinegar choice probably killed off all of our childhood good intestinal gut flora. So salad and I began green life with an odd relationship.

When I announced that I was a vegetarian at the ripe old age of eighteen I endured the many snarky comments from so many about how I "only ate salads". Ironically, whenever I went to a restaurant or (gulp) a wedding, and I explained that I was a veg', I always begrudgingly received a plate of inedible greens that was thrust in my face with some disgusting dressing slathered on top. I would then have to ward off the prying oddly defensive questions by people about why I was a vegetarian. I awaited the invariable comment by the dude who thought he was smarter than all others who accusatorily denounced that I now slaughtered plants instead of animals. If there was another veg' at the table we clung together in veg' unity like two Sesame Street characters who were identified as being "not like the others". Needless to say, I don't miss those days.

Thankfully, as a food community, we seem to have evolved a little bit more over time. In a short period of time has become far more common and accepted to be vegetarian, vegan, raw, or have other food issues and allergies that people have become more sensitive to and accepting of. What has also evolved is our perception of salads generally. Even franchise chain restaurants now occasionally offer up tasty vegetarian options.

Not only a green slathered side, salads can be complete and delicious meals in and of themselves. Rich in nutrients and enzymes with delectable possibilities for combinations, salads are only limited by our own imaginations and creative juices. In effect, salads have grown up. So enjoy these salads daily — as we've all come a long way baby!

Middle Eat-stern Salad

This salad is fresh and crunchy with a nice nutty finish due to the slow roasted hemp seeds. The smaller the dicing the better as this one is even better the next day when the dressing has had time to soak in.

Ingredients:

Salad:

- 3 cups English cucumber, diced (5-6 miniature ones work best for this recipe)

- 3 cups plum tomatoes, diced

- 1 cup red onion, finely chopped

- ⅓ cup slow roasted hemp seeds

Dressing:

- ⅓ cup olive oil

- 3 tablespoons balsamic vinegar

- 1 tablespoon coconut sugar

- ¾ teaspoon rock salt

Directions:

1. Mix together the salad ingredients in a large bowl.

2. In a separate bowl mix together the Dressing ingredients.

3. Drizzle dressing over vegetable mixture and serve. Will keep in fridge up to 3 days.

Makes about 7 cups.

What-the-Waldorf Salad

My Mom brought out the Waldorf Salad for every "event" dinner. It was our reminder that even swanky dishes served in the dining rooms of expensive hotels like the Waldorf-Astoria could make it to our table. The Cross & Blackwell English mayonnaise was in full use for her dish and, whenever she felt especially funky, she added colored marshmallows for more sticky-sweet "oomph". My version takes all of those wonderful flavors with none of the bad saturated mayo fats… or marshmallows. Sweet, sour, crunchy and refreshing, this salad is not only a special events dish but a daily dish mainstay.

Ingredients:

Dressing:

- ¼ cup Delores hemp seeds
- 3 tablespoon water
- 1 tablespoon coconut sugar
- 1 tablespoon apple cider vinegar
- ½ teaspoon rock salt
- ½ teaspoon celery seed
- ¼ teaspoon pepper
- ½ lemon, peel zested

Salad:

- 2 large Gala apples
- 1 cup seedless red grapes, halved (or whole if feeling lazy)
- 1 cup celery, sliced into ½-inch-thick pieces
- ¼ cup one green onion, finely chopped
- ¼ cup goji berries
- Juice from ½ a lemon
- 1 head Boston lettuce, trimmed, washed, and dried (optional for serving)

Directions:

1. Blend all dressing ingredients in Magic Bullet or food processor and set aside.

2. Halve, core, and cut the apples into ¾-inch pieces, leaving the skin intact.

3. In a medium bowl, add the apples, grapes, celery, onion and goji berries and sprinkle with the lemon juice; then toss with the dressing.

4. When ready to serve, arrange the lettuce leaves on 4 salad plates. Place the salad on top and sprinkle with the "Not-So-Nut Crunch" toppers (see Fabulous Fixin's) and serve.

What-the-Waldorf Salad with Not-A-Nut Crunch, see p. 209

Pass-Da Arugula Salad

Arugula is a cruciferous cancer fighting vegetable (along with broccoli, cauliflower and cabbage) that is rich in compounds called glucosinolates that are converted and help to regulate immune function reduce risks of some cancers. Arugula also contains super anti-oxidants like: beta carotene, lutein and zeaxanthin!
So go ahead and pass-da greens!

Ingredients:

- 4 cups baby arugula, washed and dried

- ⅔ cup vegetable stock

- ⅓ cup sun dried tomatoes, patted dry and coarsely chopped

- 3 tablespoons olive oil

- 2 tablespoon nutritional yeast flakes

- 2 tablespoons slow roasted hemp hearts

- 1 tablespoon "Catchin' Up Ketchup" (recipe) or tomato paste

- 1 teaspoon garlic, minced

Directions:

1. Wash arugula and place in a serving bowl.

2. Blend all remaining ingredients together (except for sundried tomatoes) and put on high in a Magic Bullet or blender until creamy. Add in sundried tomatoes and pulse until coarsely blended but not smooth.

3. Mix dressing with arugula and serve with a drizzle of "Spice It UP! Oil" (recipe in Fabulous Fixin's).

Sleek Greek Quinoa Salad

This is an amazing update to an old favorite. With a hemp based dressing and quinoa as the main ingredient, this salad quickly goes from great to super.

Ingredients:

Salad:

- 1 cup unpolished quinoa
- 2 cups veggie stock
- ¼ teaspoon rock salt
- 2 ½ cups cherry tomatoes, halved (1 pint)
- 1 cup diced cucumbers
- 1 cup diced red pepper
- ½ cup diced red onion
- 2 tablespoons flat leaf parsley, minced

Dressing:

- ¼ cup olive oil
- 2 tablespoons balsamic vinegar
- 2 tablespoons Delores hemp seeds
- 2 teaspoons dried oregano flakes
- 1 ½ teaspoons coconut sugar
- ⅛ teaspoon rock salt

Directions:

1. In a medium pot, add quinoa, salt and water.

2. Stir and place on stove top covered on high heat. Once it comes to a boil, reduce to low and let cook for 20 minutes. After 20 minutes, turn off heat and set quinoa aside still covered or 10 minutes. Then gently flake with a fork, until lightly fluffy.

3. In a mixing bowl, add tomatoes, cucumber, red pepper, red onion and parsley. Add quinoa and gently mix.

4. Blend dressing ingredients together and drizzle on top of salad. Mix well and serve. Can be refrigerated for up to 3 days.

Makes about 6 cups.

Gotta Matcha Raspberry Salad

I love raspberries, especially in season, and I am addicted to the interesting flavor of matcha tea. This recipe is a great refreshing summer salad with incredible anti-oxidants and is easy to make.

Ingredients:

Salad:

- Pint of raspberries
  (don't use overly ripe ones)

- Large mint leaves, finely minced

- tablespoon Delores hemp seeds

- ½ tablespoon cacao nibs

Dressing:

- 3 tablespoons coconut sugar

- 3 tablespoons lemon juice

- 1 tablespoon Delores hemp seeds

- 3 teaspoons matcha green tea powder

- ⅛ teaspoon vanilla

- ⅛ teaspoon rock salt

Directions:

1. Place berries, mint, Delores hemp seeds and cacao nibs in a small bowl.

2. In a separate bowl whisk together all other ingredients.
   Once fully mixed, drizzle over raspberries. Serve chilled.

Silly Lemon Dilly Salad

This salad is simple to make with really fresh flavors of lemon and dill. It is delicious as a satisfying lunch break or a simply super side dish. It's so simple, it's plain silly!

- 1 cup unpolished quinoa
- 1 ½ cups water
- ¼ teaspoon rock salt
- ¼ cup green onion, finely chopped
- 2 tablespoons nutritional yeast flakes (more to taste)

- ¼ cup slow roasted hemp seeds
- 1 ½ tablespoon fresh dill, finely chopped
- 1 tablespoon lemon juice
- 1 tablespoon olive oil

Directions:

1. In a medium cook pot, add quinoa, salt and water. Stir and place on stove top covered on high heat. Once it comes to a boil, reduce to low and let cook for 20 minutes. After 20 minutes, turn off heat and set quinoa aside still covered or 10 minutes.

2. Cool, then gently flake with a fork, until lightly fluffy.

3. In a mixing bowl, add remaining ingredients and gently mix.

4. Pour onto cooked and cooled quinoa, mix and serve.

Serves 4.

Note: if you are not vegan, you can take out the yeast flakes and add in a ¼ cup crumbled feta.

Tu-No Salad

Growing up, every Mom on our street made tuna salad with 3 ingredients: tuna, relish and tons of mayonnaise. To get a healthy mayo-type consistency requires a bit of blending but the ingredients are simple to use and it is well worth the work. This recipe is a great addition to any hearty table whether you eat real tuna or Tu-NOT!

Ingredients:

Sauce:

- 3 tablespoons water
- ½ cup Delores hemp seeds
- 2 tablespoons lemon juice
- 1 ½ tablespoons coconut sugar
- 1 tablespoon Dijon mustard

- 1 tablespoon apple cider vinegar
- 1 teaspoon white ground chia
- ¼ teaspoon rock salt
- ¼ teaspoon ground black pepper
- ¼ teaspoon ground cumin

Salad:

- 1-15oz can chick peas, drained and rinsed
- ⅓ cup celery, finely chopped

- ⅓ cup green onion, finely chopped
- 2 tablespoons dill pickle, finely chopped

Directions:

1. In a food processor, blend together all of the sauce ingredients until creamy. Set aside.

2. Add chick peas to food processor and pulse until coarsely chopped but not smooth.

3. Add chick peas to serving bowl and stir in celery, green onion and dill pickle then mix in sauce.

4. Serve as a side or enjoy on a wrap or as a gluten free sandwich. This recipe tastes even better the next day — so try to make ahead!

Makes about 1 ¼ cups.

Orange ya Onion Way? Salad

This salad is a throwback to the early 80's and is a super-take on a salad that my Mom served on special events: when she had a sit down dinner party. At the time, us kids thought it was so funny to have oranges in a SALAD — shouldn't they be green? How salad times have luckily changed, although this recipe (like neon legwarmers) is now super timeless.

Ingredients:

Salad:

- 4 cups baby spinach, washed, dried and packed

- 1 large orange, peeled, deseeded, and diced

- ½ medium red onion, thinly sliced

- 2 tablespoons coconut cacao nibs

Dressing:

- 1 tablespoon apple cider vinegar

- 1 tablespoon orange juice

- ½ tablespoon lemon juice

- 1 teaspoon grated orange rind

- ⅛ teaspoon rock salt

- ⅛ teaspoon ground pepper

- ½ teaspoon Dijon mustard

- 3 tablespoons olive oil

- 3 tablespoons water

- 3 tablespoons Delores hemp seeds

Directions:

1. In a large salad bowl, mix all salad ingredients together (except coconut cacao garnish).

2. In a blender or Magic Bullet, blend all dressing ingredients together and pour over salad.

3. Mix, sprinkle on coconut cacao nibs and serve.

Makes 5 cups.

Tu-NO Salad, see p. 215

Let-Us Eat Salad

This salad is a zing of flavors that is alkaline, rich in anti-oxidants, protein, great fiber, and immune blasting anti-carcinogens! This one is easy to assemble and the dressing is so good it is drinkable.

Ingredients:

Dressing:

- 3 tablespoons Delores hemp seeds
- 1 tablespoon nutritional yeast flakes
- ¼ cup orange juice
- 2 tablespoons lemon juice
- 1 tablespoon minced fresh ginger
- 1 tablespoon apple cider vinegar
- ½ tablespoon orange zest
- 2 tablespoons coconut sugar

Salad:

- 6 cups packed red leaf lettuce, washed, dried and torn
- ½ cup green apple, chopped
- ¼ cup red grapes, halved
- ¼ cup goji berries
- ¼ cup green onion, chopped

Directions:

1. In a Magic Bullet or a food processor, mix dressing together in a blender until creamy and set aside. Add water if needed.

2. In a salad serving bowl put in lettuce, sprinkle all other salad ingredients on top and drizzle with dressing. Serve immediately.

Makes 6 cups.

Berry Good Salad

Strawberries are low in calories and rich in dietary fiber to help keep digestion and elimination regular, as well as lower blood pressure and curb overeating. In addition, the phenols in strawberries fight against many inflammatory disorders, such as osteoarthritis, asthma, and atherosclerosis. All in all, a berry good choice!

Ingredients:

Salad:

- 940 gram box of strawberries, washed and stems removed

- 3 tablespoons basil, finely chopped (washed and dried)

Dressing:

- 1 ½ tablespoon balsamic vinegar

- 1 tablespoon coconut sugar

- 2 tablespoons slow roasted hemp seeds

- 3 tablespoons olive oil

- ⅛ teaspoon rock salt

- ⅛ teaspoon ground black pepper

- 1 tablespoon cacao nibs (garnish)

Directions:

1. Cut off the tops of the strawberries and cut them into quarters, placing in salad serving bowl.

2. Add chopped basil to strawberry mixture.

3. In a Magic Bullet or food processor, blend all dressing ingredients together.
   Drizzle the dressing over the strawberry mixture.

4. Garnish with cacao nibs. Serve immediately.

Makes 4 cups.

Whadda Salad

Simple salads can be the savior of any meal. This recipe is a great starter or can be a meal in and of itself. This salad is a great way to start off and you can mix and match as you please. Feel free to add in various seeds, dried fruit, or any veggie leftovers.

Ingredients:

Salad:

- 6 cups torn salad greens
- ¼ cup red onion, thinly sliced
- ¼ cup cucumber, thinly sliced
- 10 grape tomatoes, cut in half
- ¼ cup goji berries
- 4 tablespoons slow roasted hemp seeds(topping)

Dressing:

- ¼ cup Delores hemp seeds
- ¼ cup vegetable stock
- 1 tablespoon coconut sugar
- ½ tablespoon Dijon mustard
- ½ tablespoon white ground chia
- 1 teaspoon prepared ground horseradish
- ½ teaspoon apple cider vinegar
- ¼ teaspoon rock salt

Directions:

1. In a large mixing bowl, mix salad ingredients together.

2. In a Magic Bullet or food processor, blend all dressing ingredients and pour over salad.

3. Mix and serve immediately with a tablespoon of the slow roasted hemp seeds over each serving.

Makes 6 cups.

Tabboul-Hey! Salad

I love Middle Eastern foods as they have the best salads and dips. This tabbouleh salad is based upon a friend's Mom's recipe, and she prided herself on it being pretty authentic. I have spiced it up a bit and superfoodied it, so it is Hey-venly!

Ingredients:

Salad:

- ⅔ cup unpolished quinoa
- 1 ⅓ cup water (or vegetable stock)
- ½ cup mint leaves, washed/dried and finely chopped
- 2 ½ cups flat leaf parsley, washed/dried and finely chopped
- ¾ cup green onion, finely chopped (about 6)
- 1 cup plum tomatoes, seeded and diced (about 5-6)
- 2 tablespoons slow roasted hemp hearts

Dressing:

- ¼ cup olive oil
- ½ cup lemon juice
- 1 teaspoon garlic, finely minced
- ½ teaspoon allspice
- ¼ teaspoon rock salt

Directions:

1. In a small cook pot, add quinoa and water or stock, cover and bring to a boil. Keep covered, turn to low and leave for 20 minutes.

2. Remove from heat, remaining covered, and leave for 10 minutes.

3. Cool, fluff with a fork.

4. While quinoa is cooking, wash, chop and measure the mint, parsley, onions and tomato.

5. In a separate bowl, mix the dressing together and set aside.

6. Mix quinoa, parsley, mint, onions and tomato together.

7. Add dressing to quinoa and mix thoroughly, adding more lemon juice if necessary to give a tart flavor. Adjust salt to taste.

8. Serve with tender lettuce heart leaves as scoops for the tabbouleh.

Perkin' Gurken Salad

After taking every odd job I could during my teens, I had the amazing experience of backpacking around Europe with my sis' for a few months when I was 18. One of my most memorable meals was sitting in a biergarten (no one asked for ID, hee hee) and slurping an Über sized beer while eating an incredible cucumber salad — there called a "gurken salat". It was heaven on earth. So as my homage to my wonderful Schwarzwald memories, or lack thereof, please enjoy this recipe and don't forget to yell "Mahlzeit" while you enjoy!

Ingredients:

- 4 cups English cucumber, thinly sliced (peeled and deseed if not an English cucumber)

- ½ cup sweet onion, thinly sliced

- ¼ cup packed fresh dill, washed, sprigs removed, patted dry and chopped

Dressing:

- 3 tablespoons olive oil

- 3 tablespoons Delores hemp seeds

- 3 tablespoons rice wine vinegar

- 2 tablespoons coconut sugar

- ½ teaspoon Dijon mustard

- ¼ teaspoon rock salt

- Pinch ground pepper

Directions:

1. Slice cucumber and onion (fastest in a food processor) and then place in a medium sized non-metal serving dish.

2. After measuring, finely chop the dill and add to cucumber/onion dish.

3. In a Magic Bullet or food processor, blend all dressing ingredients and pour over cucumber and onions mixing gently.

4. Refrigerate for 2 hours before serving.

5. Drain any excess water off before serving and gently remix.

Pro Anti-Pasta Salad

Anti-pasta are terrific condiments that often get lost and stuck in lonely jars in the back of fridges. But my love of these rich tasting accents all come together in this anti-pasta super explosion. Your jars never have to feel lonely again.

Ingredients:

Salad:

- 1 cup uncooked unpolished quinoa
- 2 cups veggie stock or water
- ¼ teaspoon rock salt
- ¾ cup artichoke hearts, chopped
- ½ cup roasted red pepper, chopped
- ¼ cup slow roasted hemp seeds
- ¼ cup sun dried tomato
  (rinsed, patted dry and chopped)
- 2 tablespoons white whole seed chia
- 2 tablespoons diced manzanilla green olives
  (rinsed, patted dry and chopped)

Dressing:

- 2 tablespoons olive oil
- 2 tablespoons lemon juice
- 3 teaspoons coconut sugar
- ⅛ teaspoon rock salt

Directions:

1. In a medium cook pot, add quinoa, salt and stock/water. Stir and place on stove top covered on high heat. Once it comes to a boil, reduce to low and let cook for 20 minutes.

2. After 20 minutes, turn off heat and set quinoa aside still covered for 10 minutes.

3. Cool, then gently flake with a fork, until lightly fluffy.

4. In a medium mixing bowl, gently mix together quinoa and all other salad ingredients.

5. Mix dressing ingredients together and drizzle over salad. Mix gently.

Makes about 3 cups.

Queen of Green Salad

Once you start eating greens regularly, you start to crave them. Kale is one of the best greens that you can have as it is full of minerals, vitamins, fiber and is highly alkaline — so will help to reduce the acid in your system. This recipe is simple and brings out the best flavors of the broccoli and kale which make a great green combo. This is a salad fit for any green queen (or any other regal being).

Ingredients:

- 3 tablespoons coconut oil

- ¼ teaspoon rock salt

- 4 teaspoons garlic, minced (about 6 cloves)

- 1 teaspoon red chili pepper flakes

- 1 head of broccoli, stem removed and florets sliced

- 1 bunch kale, stems removed

- ¼ cup sundried tomato, rinsed then thinly sliced

- 3 tablespoons slow roasted hemp seeds

- One lime, halved

Directions:

1. Wash and thinly slice kale. Set aside.

2. In a large skillet, heat coconut oil over medium/high heat. Once melted, add in garlic, salt and chili peppers and stir until garlic is lightly brown (about 2 minutes).

3. Stir in broccoli, cover and cook on medium heat for 2 minutes. Add in kale and stir then cover and cook for 3 minutes.

4. Remove from heat, and place in a serving bowl. Add in sundried tomatoes and slow roasted hemp seeds.

5. Squeeze both limes halves over the mixture and stir. Refrigerate until ready to use.

Makes about 5 cups.

Caesar's Palace Salad

This dressing is so creamy tasting that no one will believe that there is no dairy in it.
A new healthy take on an old classic makes this salad guilt and dairy free.

Ingredients:

Salad:

- 4 cups romaine lettuce, spines removed washed, dried and torn

Caesar Dressing:

- ¼ cup water

- 3 tablespoons Delores hemp seeds

- 3 tablespoons olive oil

- 2 tablespoons nutritional yeast flakes

- 2 tablespoons lemon juice

- 1 tablespoon garlic, minced

- 1 teaspoon Dijon mustard

- 1 tablespoon coconut sugar

- ¼ teaspoon white pepper

Directions:

1. In a food processor blend all dressing ingredients until smooth. Add water if need to thin.

2. In a salad bowl, add washed and dried lettuce and mix in dressing.

3. Serve with gluten free croutons.

Makes 4 cups.

Sidelines

A great side dish to me is like an awesome appetizer and super condiments. On a great food day, these are meant to provide support and compliment the main dish. But in my world, they are usually so good that you want to order them on their own. I have had many restaurant experiences just ordering a slew of sides and enjoying every one of them.

My side dish recipes are designed to satisfy even the pickiest partner or the choosiest child. Many are a healthy version of the not-so-good original. But taste-wise and nutritionally these recipes are superiorly super on all levels. These sidelines are so tasty they will quickly become the front lines!

Super Slaw, see p. 238

Co-blime Smashed Tats

Tired of boring baked potatoes? This recipe is a great way to enjoy potatoes or sweet potatoes with better and healthier options than the bad-choices of butter and sour cream. These are simple to make, tasty and nutritious.

Ingredients:

- 2 pounds Yukon gold potatoes or sweet potatoes

- 2 tablespoons coconut oil

- 2 tablespoons slow roasted hemp seeds

- ½ teaspoons rock salt

- 1 ½ tablespoon lime juice

- ½ teaspoon chipotle puree (or finely ground chili pepper flakes as a substitute)

Directions:

1. Peel and clean each potato and cut each into 6 pieces (try to make the same size).

2. In a large pot, cover potatoes with water and add a generous pinch of rock salt. Bring to a boil, then reduce the heat, placing a lid on the pot. Allow them to simmer for 15-20 minutes.

3. Once potatoes are cooked (use a fork to make sure center is soft), drain and put back into pot.

4. Add coconut oil to potatoes and smash them with a potato masher. Don't over mash as the idea is to keep them chunky.

5. Add in all other ingredients and continue to smash until mixed. Serve and enjoy!

Makes about 4 cups.

Co-blime "Pot-Cakes" (variation)

These are excellent, even healthier, leftover delights!

Directions:

1. With a full recipe of Co-Blime Smashed Tats, make these coconut lime "pot cakes", by adding in a ½ cup of coconut flour and 2 more tablespoons of lime juice. Stir thoroughly.

2. Roll mixture into golf ball sized balls and then squish and pat into patties. Fry patties on a heated skillet with ½ tablespoon of coconut oil or olive oil per skillet. Mixture should make about 18 pot-cakes.

3. Serve with a side of "Sizzlin' Salsa" and "Rockin' Guac'".

Stuffin' or Nothin'

My mother made the best stuffing ever and it was the only food reason that I looked forward to Thanksgiving and Christmas turkey dinners. Her version was full of butter, nuts, white bread and sometimes sausage... and boy did it taste good. In memory to her, my plant-based version is a Stuffin' Lover's dream come true. It is honestly delicious, healthy, gluten free and won't pack on any holiday pounds. It is easy to make ahead as the batter and cooked version freeze beautifully.

Ingredients:

- ¼ cup white whole seed chia

- 1 cup vegetable stock

- 3 tablespoons olive oil

- ¼ cup olive oil

- 1 ½ cups green onions, finely chopped (about 6 onions)

- 1 ½ tablespoons garlic, minced

- 2 ½ cups sweet onions, chopped (about 2 medium ones)

- 2 cups celery, diced (about 3 stalks)

- ¼ cup chopped flat leaf parsley, washed/dried and chopped (a large handful)

- ½ tablespoon fresh rosemary, sprigs removed and finely minced

- ¼ cup gluten free quick flake oats

- ½ cup gluten free oat flour, or gluten free all-purpose flour

- 5 cups gluten free bread (don't use raisin!), diced — about 9 slices

- 1 teaspoon rock salt

- 1 ½ tablespoons coconut sugar

- 1 ½ teaspoon poultry seasoning (or more to taste)

- ¼ teaspoon black pepper

- 1 ¼ cups apple, chopped (about one medium)

1. In a small bowl, soak chia, stock and 3 tablespoons olive oil for 20 minutes, stirring occasionally. Set aside.

2. Add ¼ cup olive oil to a large cook pot and place on stove at medium/high heat. Once heated, add all onions and garlic and cover for 4 minutes and stir occasionally

3. Add celery, parsley and rosemary, stir and cover for 4 minutes, stirring occasionally.

4. Remove from stove top and turn off heat.

5. In a large mixing bowl, mix together oat flakes and flour, bread pieces, coconut sugar, poultry seasoning and pepper. Slowly add in apples, chia mixture and cooked onion mixture to dry mix until all evenly mixed together.

6. Place in a 9x12 oiled baking pan and bake in a preheated oven at 375F for 45 minutes. Can be baked ahead and frozen.

Sizzilin' Super Salsa

I love salsa as a side dish and eat a LOT of it. I have included my favorites both with different flavors and wow-wonderful tastes. Put the super-zing back in your salsa with this wonderful recipe that is raw power! This one is great as a side salad or a great addition to any Mexican themed meal. And what the Mex'? Why not just have it as THE meal!

Ingredients:

- ¾ cup tomato, diced
- ½ cup mango, diced
- ½ cup peach, diced
- ¼ cup red onion, diced
- ¼ cup canned black beans, drained and washed
- 2 tablespoons jalapeno pepper, seeded and finely chopped

- 2 tablespoons Delores hemp seeds
- 1 ½ tablespoons coconut sugar
- 1 ½ tablespoons cilantro, finely chopped
- 1 ½ tablespoons lime juice
- ¾ teaspoon cacao powder
- ¼ teaspoon rock salt

Directions:

Mix all ingredients together and serve as a side salad or with gluten free tortilla chip.

Simplicious Salsa

This salsa is really easy to make with a fresh flavor as the sweetness of the mangoes combined with the tang of the lime and the crunch of the cucumbers is a satisfying culinary break. The enzymes in mangos helps to relieve indigestion and the high level of soluble dietary fiber, pectin and vitamin C present in mangoes helps to lower bad cholesterol Mangos are also rich in iron and contain Glutamine acid which is good to boost memory and keep cells active. A simply super choice to make: Eat Mangos!

Ingredients:

- 3 ripe mangos, skinned and diced

- 3 green onions, finely chopped

- 1 cup cucumber, diced

- 3 teaspoons lime juice

- 1 tablespoon white whole seed chia

- 2 teaspoons cilantro, washed/dried and finely chopped

- ¼ teaspoon rock salt

Directions:

1. Add all ingredients together and refrigerate before serving.

2. Can be served with tortilla chips, crackers or pita.

3. Can be refrigerated for a few days.

Bok a 'Room Tonight Salad

Bok Choy is a veggie from the cabbage family that is a low-calorie food high in antioxidants, folic acid, vitamin C and potassium. Combined with the high antioxidants in the red pepper, this is an easy way to get in super nutrients with little work... but with big flavors. So relax and enjoy!

Ingredients:

- ½ cup unpolished quinoa
- 1 cup vegetable stock
- ⅛ teaspoon rock salt
- 1 tablespoon coconut oil
- 6 baby bok choy, halved
- ½ red pepper, thinly sliced
- 12 shitake mushrooms, stems removed
- 3 tablespoons vegetable stock
- 2 tablespoons fresh basil, chopped (garnish)

Dressing:

- 2 tablespoons rice wine vinegar
- 2 tablespoons slow roasted hemp seeds
- 1 ½ teaspoon lime zest
- 1 ½ tablespoon "No-Fish Sauce" (or soy sauce if no allergy)
- 1 tablespoon lime juice
- 1 tablespoon coconut sugar

Directions:

1. In a small pot, place quinoa, ¾ cup stock and salt and cover. On high heat bring to a boil, then turn to low and let cook covered for 20 minutes.

2. Remove from heat, turn heat off, and let sit for 5 minutes then fluff it up and place on bottom of a serving bowl.

3. To make dressing, place all ingredients in a small food processor and blend until creamy consistency. Set aside.

4. In a skillet, add coconut oil and turn to high heat. Once heated, add mushrooms, bok choy and peppers.

5. Add 3 tablespoons of stock, cover and cook for about 4 minutes, stirring occasionally until all veggies are tender and the bok choy is "sweating".

6. Remove from heat, and place on top of quinoa (including juices) in the serving bowl. Pour dressing over it and garnish with basil.

7. Serve immediately.

Even Greater Tater Salad

The basis for this salad was included in my first book "Better Being". I have revamped it slightly but have also included it here because it is just such a perfect illustration of how rockin' hemp seeds are. I have served this salad so many times and people cannot believe that it has NO mayo and is a healthy version of what is usually the worst choice at the family picnic table.

Ingredients:

Salad:

- 3 ½ cups yellow potatoes, cubed ½"pieces, (5 medium sized ones)

- ½ cup green onions, chopped

- ¼ cup dill pickles, thinly sliced and finely chopped

- ½ tablespoon white whole seed chia

- ½ tablespoon fresh dill, washed/dried and finely chopped

Sauce:

- ⅔ cup Delores hemp seeds

- ½ cup dill pickle juice from the jar

- 3 tablespoons olive oil

- 1 ½ teaspoons Dijon mustard

- 2 tablespoon water

- ¼ teaspoon ground black pepper

- ¼ teaspoon garlic powder

- ¼ teaspoon celery salt or ground celery seed

- 1 pinch of ground cumin

Directions:

1. In a large pot, boil 1 liter of water. Once boiled, add potato turn heat to medium/high and cook until fork tender (about 10 minutes).

2. Blend sauce ingredients in a food processor on high and set aside.

3. Once potatoes are cooked and tender/firm, drain and add to a serving bowl and let cool.

4. Add in all other salad ingredients.

5. Drizzle sauce over salad, mix gently and serve.

Makes 4 cups.

Note: If you do eat eggs you can add in 2-4 boiled and chopped organic free range eggs.

Oddles of Noodles with Gimme Ginger Dressing

This colorful salad has it all: crunchy textures with rich flavors of nut-free nutty, hot, sweet, savory and salty. The hemp in the dressing gives it a boost of protein, while the raw veggies create a crispy vitamin rich experience. The soba noodles are gluten free, buckwheat based, and are rich in anti-oxidants, essential amino acids, and essential nutrients. This recipe is a wonderful side salad but also a terrific main event. Can also be saved for a next day high protein lunch! Your guests will be screaming: 'gimme another servin'!

Ingredients:

Salad:

- 1 (9.5oz) package gluten free soba noodles
- 1 cup cucumbers, peeled, and sliced
- ½ cup radishes, thinly sliced
- ½ cup green onions, chopped
- ½ cup red peppers, thinly sliced
- ½ cup shredded carrots
- ½ cup bean sprouts

Dressing:

- ¼ cup rice wine vinegar
- ¼ cup slow roasted hemp seeds
- 2 tablespoons "No-Soy Sauce" (or 1 tablespoon soy sauce if no allergy)
- 3 tablespoons coconut sugar
- 2 tablespoons lime juice
- 1 tablespoon roasted sesame oil
- 1 tablespoon freshly grated ginger
- 1 teaspoon hot sauce (Sambal Oelek) or ½ teaspoon dried chili pepper flakes
- ¼ teaspoon rock salt

Directions:

1. In a large cook pot, make gluten free soba noodles according to package. Drain and rinse in cold water and set aside in a large serving bowl.

2. For the dressing, in a Magic Bullet blend all ingredients together and pour over noodles, tossing gently.

3. Add in the radishes, green onions, peppers, cucumbers, and carrots. Gently mix.

4. Serve chilled with optional garnish of slow roasted hemp seeds on top and green onions.

Makes 7 cups.

Spiced "Chic" Peas

This recipe is great for keeping off the pounds: the coconut oil helps to speed up the metabolism, the chickpeas are full of protein and fiber, turmeric is a known weight loss tool, the ginger boosts digestive enzymes, and the chia allows you to feel fuller for longer. During the winter months serve it hot over cooked Quinoa or in the summer as a spicy summer side. Stay "Chic" looking all year long... the super smart way!

Ingredients:

- 2 cups sweet onions, chopped

- 1 ½ square inch piece of ginger root, finely minced (1 ½ tablespoons minced)

- 3 teaspoons garlic, minced

- 1 teaspoon ground cumin

- 1 teaspoon turmeric powder

- 1 teaspoon cacao powder

- ¼ teaspoon ground cinnamon

- Juice of one lime

- 2 tablespoons coconut oil

- 1-15oz can diced tomato (or 1 ½ cups fresh)

- 2 tablespoons white whole seed chia

- 1-15oz can chickpeas

- ½ cup cilantro, washed/dried and coarsely chopped

- 2 tablespoons Delores hemp seeds

- Rock salt to taste

Directions:

1. In a food processor, place onion, ginger, garlic, cumin, turmeric, cacao powder, cinnamon and lime juice. Blend into a paste (add more water if needed) and reserve.

2. In a large saucepan, add coconut oil and heat on medium. When hot, add paste and sauté for 2 minutes.

3. Add tomato and white chia and sauté for 5 minutes stirring occasionally.

4. Add cooked chickpeas, turn heat to low-medium and cook for 10 minutes, stirring occasionally.

5. Remove from heat, add in cilantro, Delores hemp seeds and salt to taste. Serve hot or cold. Freezes well.

Makes 3 cups.

Super Slaw

This is both a Mom-on-the-run or single person's delight. Easy to throw together with excellent nutritional benefits, this slaw is a super way to have a delicious and nutritious dinner. Also great for an after gym-I-gotta-eat-NOW meal!

Ingredients:

- 1 tablespoon coconut oil

- ½ tablespoon roasted sesame oil

- 1-340g bag of raw broccoli cole slaw

- 2 tablespoons "Soy-Not Sauce"
  (or 1 ½ tablespoons soy sauce if no allergy)

- ¼ cup slow roasted hemp seeds

- 2 tablespoons goji berries

- 1 tablespoon white whole seed chia

- 1 tablespoon cilantro, finely chopped

- 1 teaspoon nutritional yeast flakes

Directions:

1. In a fry pan, heat coconut oil and sesame oil on medium to high heat. Once heated, add in broccoli slaw along with "Soy-Not Sauce" (recipe) and stir on medium heat until slaw is firm but cooked (about 5 minutes).

2. Add in remaining ingredients stirring quickly. Serve immediately.

Makes 5 cups.

Sub-Lime Stuffed Tat

Baked potatoes can be so delicious and creamy with the loaded up butter and sour cream. It is basically a way to dynamite any weight loss diet. But these potatoes are a healthy version of an old classic. So start the BBQ, and go get stuffed!

Ingredients:

Tats:

- 4-6 medium sized Russet potatoes

- 1 teaspoon rock salt (¼ teaspoon for each potato)

- 4-6 12 x 12-inch sheets heavy duty foil

- Olive oil or olive oil spray

Stuffing:

- 1 teaspoon garlic, minced

- 6 tablespoons salsa

- ¼ cup Delores hemp seeds

- 2 tablespoons lime juice

- 1 ½ teaspoon cacao powder

- ¼ teaspoon rock salt

- 2 handfuls cilantro springs, washed

Topping for each Potato:

- 1 teaspoon slow roasted hemp hearts

Directions:

1. Wash and scrub potato, remove any eyes. (Do not use potatoes with green tinged skins). Poke with a fork three times.

2. Place potato in center of a sheet of foil (shiny side in).

3. Spray well or drizzle each with a little olive oil and sprinkle each with ¼ teaspoon salt. Wrap up ends of foil around potato.

4. Place over indirect heat of gas grill or put into preheated oven 425F. Turn frequently and bake for about an hour or until potato is fork-tender.

5. In meantime, place stuffing ingredients into a small blender and blend until a smooth paste.

6. Once potato is cooked, cut off the top third of each potato and scoop out insides into a separate bowl leaving a ¼ inch shell.

7. Add the stuffing paste to the potato flesh and mash together until creamy. Spoon stuffing back into potato skins and top each potato with a teaspoon of roasted hemp seeds. Serve and enjoy!

Let's face it: main dishes are the focus of most meals. They are what we think of as being rich and satiating. Their satisfying and fulfilling nature is what we love about them. Unfortunately, so many common main dishes are high in butter, cream and animal based protein. The high saturated content, low nutritional content and limited fiber makes them difficult to digest and even harder to burn off. Although these poor nutritional choices may taste so great, they are not often worth the proverbial girth. So what gives?

My "main" focus is on foods that deliver the "awww" factor while ensuring that the belt buckle doesn't go out another notch. Additionally, the following recipes will help to speed up your metabolism, increase energy levels and deliver powerful nutritional benefits. Their incredible taste will ensure that everyone will love these dishes as their new favorite Main Event.

Over the 'Shroom Lasagna, see p. 242

Over the 'Shroom Lasagna

This kreemy dream is a vegan and dairy lover's delight. It is so rich tasting that you won't believe it is dairy free. It is a perfect meal for a large group and will satisfy all — whether vegan or not! Great as a day-after-meal as well, the flavors get more complex as it sits and sets.

Ingredients:

Lasagna:

- 2 tablespoons olive oil

- 2 cups sweet onion, diced

- 5 cups brown mushrooms, diced (or 1-454g pre-sliced package)

- 2 tablespoons balsamic vinegar

- 6 cups baby spinach (one 200gr package)

- 3 tablespoons white whole seed chia

- "Béchamel tarragon sauce recipe" (below)

- 1 package gluten free lasagna noodles (need 12 noodles total)

- 1 tablespoon olive oil

- 1 cup Daiya vegan mozzarella (optional)

Directions:

1. In a large fry pan, sauté onions and olive oil on a medium/high heat for 6-8 minutes or until onions are translucent.

2. Make "Béchamel Sauce" (below) while waiting for onions to cook and set aside.

3. In onion mix, stir in balsamic vinegar and mushrooms and cover and cook 10 minutes, stirring occasionally.

4. After 10 minutes, add spinach to onion/mushroom mix, cover and turn heat to medium/low. Cook for 15-20 minutes stirring occasionally until mushrooms are tender and fully cooked.

5. While mushrooms are cooking, in a separate large pot, add in 8 cups water and bring to a boil then turn to low heat.

6. Once mushrooms have cooked, stir in chia, turn off heat and remove from stove. Let sit for 10 minutes and then stir.

7. Cook pasta noodles according to package directions and drain once al dente.

8. In a 9x11 pan, grease bottom and sides with 1 tablespoon olive oil.

9. Add a thin layer of the béchamel sauce on bottom of pan. Place one layer of noodles on bottom so that noodles touch at edges but do not overlap. (For the lasagna, there should be four layers total, so when spooning visually separate the sauce and mushroom mix into 4 equal amounts.) Spoon a thin layer of the béchamel sauce and then top with a layer of mushroom spinach mix. Repeat until done.

10. Sprinkle Daiya cheez on top (optional) and carefully cover with foil so it is not touching the lasagna.

11. Cook in a preheated oven at 350F on the middle rack for 30 minutes. Remove from oven and let sit for 5 minutes, then cut. Garnish with parsley flakes.

Ingredients:

Béchamel Sauce

- ½ cup water
- 1 ½ cups Delores hemp seeds
- ¼ cup lemon juice
- 1 ½ tablespoons apple cider vinegar
- ½ tablespoon dried tarragon
- ½ teaspoon rock salt
- ½ teaspoon ground pepper

Directions:

In a food processor, blend all ingredients together until creamy consistency.
Add a tablespoon more water, one by one, if too thick.

Fry-Goodbye! Eggplant Parm'

This baked version of an Italian fried classic is a delicious and healthy alternative. It takes a bit of preparation, but is well worth it! It can be easily reheated the next day and is wonderful hot or cold. Once cooked it can also be frozen into individual servings for a thawed out super lunch!

Ingredients:

- 2 large Italian eggplants
- 1 ½ tablespoons rock salt
- Coating mix (below)
- 1 cup olive oil
- Sauce (below)
- ¾ cup Daiya mozzarella shredded cheez (optional)

Directions:

1. Slice eggplant into ¼ inch pieces. Lay pieces on 2 large cookie sheets.

2. Sprinkle ¾ tablespoon of salt evenly on first side of eggplant slices. Let sit and "sweat" for an at least ½ an hour. Blot the water off of the first side with a kitchen towel. Flip eggplant pieces over and sprinkle the remaining salt on the other side of the eggplant slices. Let sit for ½ hour.

3. While waiting for eggplant, make Tomato Basil Sauce (below) and set aside.

4. Mix the coating mix together and set aside.

5. Rinse eggplants under warm water, shake and place in bowl.

6. Rinse off the two cookie sheets and dry. Spread ¼ cup olive oil on each sheet.

7. Place each eggplant piece in coating and flip over so each side gets coated then place on cookie sheets — don't overlap them.

8. Bake in preheated 450F oven for 8-10 minutes (until eggplant browns).

9. Take out of oven and drizzle ¼ cup of olive oil over eggplant pieces on each cookie sheet and then flip each one over. Bake another 8-10 minutes and remove from oven.

10. Turn oven to 350F.

11. In a 9x9 inch baking dish, add a small amount of sauce to cover bottom. Add a layer of eggplant pieces, spoon a layer of sauce on top and then sprinkle ¼ cup Daiya vegan cheez (or for non-vegan version, shredded mozzarella). Repeat layers — you should get 3-4 layers.

12. Cover dish with foil, making sure not to have foil touch top. Bake for 30 minutes, remove from oven, keeping covered and let sit 5-10 minutes before cutting.

Coating Mix

- 1 cup gluten free oat flour

- ½ cup gluten free quick flake oats

- ½ cup coconut flour

- 1 tablespoon onion powder

- ½ tablespoon garlic powder

- ¼ teaspoon rock salt

- ¼ teaspoon ground black pepper

Directions:

In a large bowl, mix all ingredients together, and use accordingly.

Roma Chia Sauce

Ingredients:

- 1 tablespoon olive oil

- ½ cup onion, diced

- 1 garlic clove, mined

- 4 cups unsweetened, unsalted and unseasoned tomato sauce

- 2 tablespoons of white whole seed chia

- 1 tablespoon coconut sugar

- 1 teaspoon rock salt

- 5 large leaves of basil — finely chopped

Directions:

1. In a medium pot, add olive oil and place on medium/high heat.

2. Add onion and garlic, cover and cook for 5 minutes.

3. Add in sauce, sugar, chia, and salt. Mix well.

4. Turn heat to low and simmer 5-10 minutes.

5. Just before about use, add in basil, stir and turn off heat.

Wanna Cry Sheppard's Pie

There are a few things that I really miss being a veggie and one of them was my Mom's Sheppard's Pie. There is something so satisfying about the layered yums and the different flavors and textures of soft and creamy juxtaposed against the chewy and savory. It is a wonderful reminder of childhood comfort food memories — it's so good it'll bring tears to your eyes!

Ingredients:

Base Layer:

- 2 tablespoon olive oil
- 2 cups yellow onions, diced
- ½ cups celery, diced
- 3 tablespoons garlic, minced (3-4 large cloves)

- 4 ½ cups Portobello Mushrooms, chopped (4-5 large ones)
- 3 cups Crimini mushrooms, chopped
- 1 cup vegetable broth

- 1 ½ tablespoons balsamic vinegar
- ½ cup uncooked unpolished quinoa
- 1 cup water
- 2 tablespoons whole chia seeds

Directions:

1. In a large cook pot, heat olive oil on medium/high heat. Once heated, add in onion and cook covered for about 5 minutes, stirring occasionally.

2. Add in garlic and celery, cover and cook for 5 minutes, stirring occasionally.

3. Reduce heat to low and add in mushrooms, veggie broth and vinegar and cook uncovered at a low boil 20-30 minutes stirring occasionally.

4. Cook until mushrooms are tender and most of water is gone.

5. While cooking down mushrooms, put quinoa and water in a pot, cover and turn on high. Once it comes to a boil, reduce heat to low and cook for 20 minutes.

6. Set aside and keep cover on.

7. Make Veggie Layer (below).

8. Make Potato Layer (below)

9. Once quinoa and mushroom mixture are cooked, add quinoa and chia to mushroom mix. Stir and let sit 5 minutes.

10. In an olive oil greased 9x11 pan, pack in base layer and then top with veggie and then potato layer. Make sure each layer is relatively evenly spread out.

11. Cook in a preheated oven at 375 F for 30 minutes until heated through and bubbling. You can also broil once baked for 5 minutes to brown potatoes if desired.

Veggie Layer

Ingredients:

- 1 ½ cups frozen corn and/or peas

Directions:

1. Boil ½ cup of water in a pot.

2. Place veggies in, cover and turn down to medium heat.

3. Cook for 5-10 minutes until cooked but firm. Drain and set aside.

Potato Layer

Ingredients:

- 5 cups peeled Yukon gold potatoes, cut into ½ inch cubes (3-4 large potatoes)

- ¼ cup olive oil

- ½ cup slow roasted hemp seeds

- 3 tablespoons nutritional yeast flakes

- 2 teaspoons garlic powder

- 1 teaspoon rock salt

- ½ teaspoon ground black pepper

- ½ cup non-dairy milk (unsweetened and not flavored) — or more if required

Directions:

1. Boil potatoes in a pot of water until fork can easily go through pieces. Drain and set aside.

2. Add in olive oil and gently smash potatoes.

3. Place all other ingredients in a food processer and blend until creamy.

4. Add to potatoes and mash gently until creamy with no lumps. If more non-dairy milk is required add and mash until creamy. Make sure not to over mash as the potato starch gets too sticky if overworked.

Power Veggie Burgers

I love veggie burgers and crave them especially during the summer months. These are full of whole, protein, essential fatty acids and lots of nutrients. Baked or barbecued these are a year round mainstay.

Ingredients:

- 1 ½ tablespoon white whole seed chia
- ¼ cup water
- ½ cup dried red lentils
- ½ cup unpolished quinoa
- 2 cups water
- 19 oz can black beans (drained and rinsed)

- ½ cup flat leaf parsley, washed, stems removed and coarsely chopped
- ¼ cup dill, washed, stems removed and coarsely chopped
- ½ cup chopped sweet white onion
- 2 teaspoons chili powder

- 1 ½ teaspoon dried oregano
- 1 teaspoon dried rosemary
- 1 teaspoon garlic powder
- ¾ teaspoons rock salt
- 4 liberal splashes of Tabasco (optional).
- ¼ cup Wheat Free oat flour

Directions:

1. Soak the chia and water in a bowl for 20 minutes. Stir occasionally.

2. While chia is soaking, place water, lentils and quinoa in a pot with a secure lid on. Bring to a boil, stir once, place lid on and turn to low and cook for 20 minutes.

3. Remove from heat, turn heat off and set aside keeping lid on.

4. In a food processor, add beans, parsley, dill, onion oregano, salt, rosemary, garlic, chili and Tabasco and pulse on high 4 times, stir and repeat 5 times (for a total pulse of 20 times). Mixture should NOT be smooth but be mixed and remain a little chunky.

5. Place bean mix in a medium sized mixing bowl.

6. Add chia mixture and quinoa mixture to bean bowl and hand mix. Form into patties about ½ inch in thick and dunk each side in a bowl filled with the oat flour.

7. Patties may be cooked one of three ways: (i) fried in a fry pan on medium high heat with 1 tablespoon of oil of choice for 10 minutes each side; or (ii) baked in a preheated oven at 375F for 40 minutes, flip them over at the 20 minute mark; (iii) Barbecued at a very low heat on a non-stick BBQ pan, flipping carefully, until browned.

8. Serve with "Cacao Barbie-Q's Sauce".

Zucchini Raw-sagna

This lasagna is so great tasting and rich in live enzymes. A great way to get a noodle kind of experience with green veggies as the base! Feel free to experiment with flavors and sauces.

Ingredients:

- 3 medium zucchinis

- Few pinches rock salt

- 4 medium tomatoes

- 1 tablespoon lemon juice

- 2 tablespoons coconut sugar

- 2 tablespoons white chia seed

- "Spinach Rawcotta" recipe (Fabulous Fixin's)

- "Besto Pesto" recipe (Fabulous Fixin's), or store bought if short on time!

Directions:

1. Wash zucchini and tomatoes. Cut off ends of zucchini and remove tomato core.

2. With a mandolin, or a sharp knife, slice the zucchini lengthwise into ¼ inch strips and lay on a cookie sheet. Sprinkle with a few pinched of salt and leave for ½ an hour. Then pat dry.

3. Quarter tomatoes and place in a Vitamix or food processor, along with lemon juice, coconut sugar and chia Seed. Blend on high until smooth. Set aside in a separate bowl.

4. Make "Rawcotta" and "Besto Pesto" recipes, and set each aside in separate bowls.

5. When zucchini is ready, place lengthwise in one layer in a 9x13 pan.

6. Layer on top with pesto, tomato sauce and "Rawcotta" (Note: should make 3 layers so keep in mind when allocating amounts).

7. Continue layering until all zucchini and sauce used.

8. Let set for an hour then serve. Cannot be frozen.

9. Will keep in fridge for 2 days.

Power Packin' Mac n' Cheez

This mac n' cheez not only tastes great but is a fabulous way to enjoy Superfoods in a retro way. The new nutritious take on an old classic is a super way to get great essential fatty acids, whole protein, anti-oxidants and minerals galore. Make the bright orange boxed "Krap Macaroni" a thing of an unhealthy past, and get super powered up!

Ingredients:

- 1-375g or 13oz bag gluten free elbow pasta
- 2 ½ cups non-dairy unflavored milk
- ½ cup plus 2 tablespoons nutritional yeast
- 2 tablespoons white ground chia
- 1 tablespoon lemon juice
- 1 ½ teaspoons rock salt

- 2 teaspoons garlic, chopped
- 1 teaspoon Dijon mustard
- 1 teaspoon paprika
- ¾ teaspoon turmeric
- ½ cup Delores hemp seeds
- ½ teaspoon ground black pepper

Directions:

1. Cook the gluten free pasta according to the directions on the bag or box until al dente (don't overcook).

2. While pasta is cooking, place all other ingredients into a food processor and blend until creamy. Don't worry it looks runny but will thicken when added to pasta and simmered.

3. Drain cooked pasta and add sauce and pasta back into pasta pot.

4. Simmer over medium/low heat for 5-10 minutes, to allow it to thicken.

Makes 4 cups.

Power Packin' Mac n' Cheez, see p. 250

Quin-Wow! Coconut Curry

A well-made curry is like a great pair of well-worn shoes: comfortable, familiar and satisfying, and will keep you going for a long time. Well, this one will not disappoint. With lots of nutrients and protein, this curry will fill you up and satisfy your taste buds, belly, and body.

Ingredients:

- 1 ½ cups sweet onions, diced
- 1 ½ tablespoons garlic, minced
- 2 tablespoons coconut oil
- 4 cups yams, diced (3 small ones)
- 2 cups vegetable broth
- 2 cups cauliflower florets, chopped (about ½ head)
- 2 cups broccoli florets, chopped (about ½ a head)
- ⅓ cup dried red lentils

- ⅓ cup uncooked unpolished quinoa
- 2-14oz cans lite coconut milk
- 3 tablespoons lime juice
- 1 tablespoon garam masala powder
- 1 tablespoon cacao powder
- 1 teaspoon minced ginger (or ginger puree)
- 1 teaspoon finely chopped basil
- 1 ½ teaspoons lemon grass puree (optional — at most grocery stores in produce)

Directions:

1. In a large pot on medium heat, heat coconut oil until melted then add onions and garlic.

2. Cover and cook for 5-10 minutes until onions are slightly translucent, stir occasionally.

3. Add in yams and vegetable broth, cover and cook for another 15 minutes, stirring occasionally.

4. Turn down heat to medium/low and add in remaining ingredients. Cover and cook for another 25 minutes, stirring occasionally until all vegetables are cooked through.

5. Serve on its own or over brown rice or rice noodles.

Makes 8 cups.

Quin-Wow! Coconut Curry, see p. 252

Great Goulash

Goulash is such a satisfying meal and is great reheated the next day. This recipe is herb and spice rich with just the right amount of balance to bring out all of the goulash goodness for a hearty and fulfilling dish.

Ingredients:

- 2 tablespoons olive oil
- 1 cup sweet onion, diced
- 1 tablespoon coconut sugar
- 4 garlic cloves, crushed
- 1 teaspoon dried caraway seeds
- 2 tablespoons sweet Hungarian paprika
- ⅓ tablespoon dried marjoram
- 1 teaspoon fresh thyme leaves (or 1 teaspoon dried)
- 2 bay leaves

- 2 tablespoon balsamic vinegar
- 1 ½ pounds Portobello mushrooms cut into one-inch pieces
- 1 medium carrot, peeled and diced
- 1 medium celery stalk, diced
- 1 can (28 oz./796 ml) diced tomatoes
- 2 cups vegetable stock/broth
- 1 medium yellow potato, diced
- 1 teaspoon rock salt
- ½ tablespoon cacao powder

Directions:

1. In a large covered sauté pan, heat the olive oil and sauté the onions and sugar for about 4 minutes until caramelized.

2. Add the garlic and caraway seed and cook another minute. Add the paprika, marjoram, thyme, bay leaf, and vinegar. Sauté another minute, until fragrant. Add the remaining ingredients: mushroom, carrot, celery, tomato, stock, potato, quinoa, salt and pepper.

3. Bring to a boil, then lower to a simmer. Cover and cook until very tender, about 1 hour, stirring occasionally.

4. Taste and adjust seasoning with salt and pepper.

Makes 8 cups.

Fettuccine Ate-It-All-Fredo

This dish used to be my go-to dish when out at restaurants as it was usually worth the "cheat". What used to happen was that I would eat it and love it and then feel sick for days from the gluten, butter, and cream. With this recipe, there is no morning-after pill required (aka. digestive enzyme poppers) required for this nighttime love affair with All-fredo!

Ingredients:

- 1-375gr or 13oz gluten free fettuccine noodles
- 1 ½ cups Delores hemp seeds
- ½ cup water
- ½ cup nutritional yeast flakes
- 3 tablespoons olive oil
- 2 tablespoons lemon juice
- ½ teaspoon lemon zest, grated
- 1 teaspoon garlic, minced
- ½ teaspoon rock salt
- ¼ teaspoon ground white pepper
- Pinch nutmeg
- 1 tablespoon flat leaf parsley, finely minced (garnish)

Directions:

1. In a large pot of boiling salted water cook pasta until tender but still firm to the bite (about 4-5 minutes) while stirring occasionally. Drain, drizzle with a little olive oil, stir and set aside in pot.

2. For remaining sauce ingredients, blend together in a food processor or Magic Bullet until it is a creamy consistency. Add more water if too thick. Add more garlic or lemon to taste.

3. Add sauce back to pasta pot and toss over a medium low heat until pasta and sauce are heated through, stirring gently.

4. Serve with a sprinkle on top of parsley to garnish.

5. Serves four.

Arrabbi-Ate-a Pasta

This recipe is a Superfood take on an Italian based recipe. I ate a lot of Pasta Arrabbiatta while at law school as it was tasty, cheap and easy. This dish has a subtle spiciness with flavorful depth — especially if you use fresh rosemary. Nutritionally, the hemp just pumps this pasta up with terrific protein and a creamy consistency. This is one of my all time, feel good, favorite dishes.

Ingredients:

- 2 tablespoons olive oil

- 2 ½ cups sweet white onions (about 2 medium ones)

- 2 tablespoons minced garlic (garlic cloves)

- 1 fresh rosemary sprig, 6 inches long

- 1 can diced tomato (28fl oz.)

- 1 tablespoon finely chopped pickled banana peppers

- ½ cup roasted red pepper, diced

- 1 cup vegetable stock/broth

- ¼ cup Delores hemp seeds

- 3 teaspoons white ground chia

- 4 cups gluten free pasta noodles, uncooked

Directions:

1. In a large pot, turn heat to medium/high and add olive oil. Once heated, stir in onions, cover and cook for 3-4 minutes until they sweat, stirring occasionally.

2. Stir in garlic, cover and cook 3-4 minutes, stirring occasionally.

3. Add in rosemary sprig, cover and stir for 8 minutes. This will release the oils and aroma.

4. Add in canned tomatoes, red pepper, banana peppers and stock.

5. Simmer on a low heat for 25 minutes.

6. In a medium pot, make the pasta based upon directions on box/bag. Drain and set aside.

7. Remove rosemary sprig and then place 3 cups of cooked sauce into a blender, along with the Delores hemp seeds and ground chia.

8. Blend on high until creamy.

9. Add hemp/chia sauce back in to sauce pot and mix well.

10. Once pasta is cooked and drained, return to pot.

11. Add in all or desired amount of sauce to pasta and stir gently and serve. If you prefer less sauce (I like all of it) then use as bread dunk — super yummy.

Makes 6 cups.

Arrabbi-Ate-a Pasta, see p. 256

Not-So-Krabby Cakes, see p.260; Tar-Terrific Sauce, see p. 154; Red Pepper Chili A-OK-li, see p. 152

Not-So-Krabby Cakes

The only bad thing about actual crab cakes is that they are made from crab. These cakes are a plant-based dream and are really easy on the pocketbook! You won't believe that they are vegan and are a healthy alternative. Try tricking shellfish lovin' friends and family with this one! Save your money and a crab — eat these!

Ingredients:

- 2 cups grated zucchini
- Generous pinch of rock salt
- 1 tablespoon white whole seed chia
- 3 tablespoons water
- 3 tablespoons Delores hemp seeds
- 1 ½ tablespoons lemon juice
- 1 tablespoon olive oil
- 1 teaspoon vegan Worcestershire sauce*
- 1 teaspoon Dijon mustard

- ½ teaspoon rock salt
- 1 tablespoon water
- ¼ teaspoon garlic powder
- ¼ teaspoon ground celery seed
- ½ cup gluten free quick flake oats
- ½ cup green onions, finely chopped
- ¼ cup red bell pepper, finely chopped
- ½ cup gluten free oat flour, for dusting
- Oil for frying

Directions:

1. In a small bowl, mix together chia and water. Set aside for 20 minutes stirring occasionally.

2. Grate zucchini and place around sides of a colander. Place colander in sink. Sprinkle zucchini with generous pinch of rock salt. Leave for 25 minutes and then squeeze against sides of colander to help remove excess water. Set colander aside.

3. In a Magic Bullet or food processor blend together until creamy: hemp seeds, lemon juice, olive oil, Worcestershire sauce, Dijon, salt, garlic powder, celery seed, salt and water.

4. In a large bowl, mix together zucchini, hydrated chia mix, hemp blend, red pepper and onion.

5. Shape into patties about ¾ inch thick and dust with oat flour.

6. Heat oil in a large skillet over medium/high heat. When oil is hot, fry cakes until browned, about 4 to 5 minutes on each side. Serve warm with "Red Pepper A-OK-ioli Sauce" or "Tar-terrific Sauce".

Makes about 12 cakes.

*- Note that vegan Worchester sauce may contain soy products — so be careful if there are any allergen issues.

Bestest Biriyani!

A good friend of mine at law school was of Pakistani descent and she and her Mom taught me some wonderful recipes. One of my favorites was their Biriyani recipe, which usually is meat based. This recipe takes the best of both worlds: spices from Pakistan but with some super additions to make this the most beautiful, nutrient boosting Bestest Biriyani ever!

Ingredients:

Rice Mix:

- ½ cup brown basmati rice
- ½ cup unpolished quinoa
- 2 cups water
- 1 tablespoon olive oil
- 1 tablespoon lemon juice
- ½ tablespoon mild curry paste (store bought)
- ¼ teaspoon ground cinnamon
- 3 green cardamom pods

Topping:

- 2 tablespoons olive oil
- 3 cardamom pods
- ¼ teaspoon fennel seeds
- ¼ teaspoon coriander seeds
- ½ tablespoon ginger paste
- ½ tablespoon garlic paste
- ½ tablespoon mild curry paste
- ⅓ cup tomato paste
- ¼ cup water
- ¼ cup goji berries
- 1 ½ cups vegetables, diced (½ cup each: frozen green peas, diced carrots, chopped green beans)
- 1 cup onions, diced
- ¼ teaspoon rock salt
- 1 teaspoon coconut sugar
- ½ cup cilantro, washed dried and packed

1. For Rice Mix, combine rice and quinoa, and stir in all other ingredients in a cook pot with a secure lid on.

2. Bring to a boil, stir once, place lid on and turn to low and cook for 20 minutes.

3. Remove from heat, turn heat off and set aside keeping lid on.

4. In a medium-large frying pan, turn heat to medium-high and add 3 tablespoons olive oil. Once heated add in cardamom, coriander, and fennel seeds and cook for 1 minute, stirring.

5. Add garlic and ginger paste and cook for 2 minutes, stirring.

6. Add in water, curry paste, and tomato paste and stir.

7. Bring to a low boil then add in vegetables, onions, and goji berries, salt, and coconut sugar. Cover and turn heat to low. Let vegetables cook until tender but firm (about 8-10 minutes)

8. Gently add in rice/quinoa to topping mix, gently folding in.

9. Coarsely chop cilantro and add in to Biriyani at very end.

10. Serve immediately. Great as a leftover.

Makes 6 cups.

Fala-full with "Rawgurt" Dressing

Falafel is one of those "personal" tastes. Some love a fried one, some love a baked one, and others opt for a spicy taste while children often enjoy a milder palate. Well, this falafel has it all. It is adult and kid-friendly and it is a mild version that can be pumped up for spiciness if need be. You can also make large batches to freeze and just simply reheat on a greased pan at 350F for 10-15 minutes. The sauce is a great dairy-free experience of cool freshness; which is a lovely addition to the more complex tastes of the falafel. Enjoy!

Ingredients:

Cucumber Mint "Rawgurt" Dressing:

- 6 inches of an English Cucumber (peeled) approx. 6"
- ⅓ cup slow roasted hemp seeds
- 1 tablespoon olive oil
- 1 tablespoon lime juice
- 3 large fresh mint leaves
- ¼ teaspoon rock salt
- ⅛ teaspoon cumin

Directions:

Blend all ingredients together in a food processor and serve as a drizzle or on the side of the falafel.

Falafel Ingredients:

- 2 cups presoaked chickpeas (equals 1 ½ cups dried chickpeas soaked in 3-4 cups water for 12 hours)*
- 1 tablespoon white whole seed chia
- 3 tablespoons lemon juice
- 1 ½ cups diced white onion (approx. 2 medium ones)
- ½ cups cooked (or canned) Fava Beans
- ½ cups slow roasted hemp seeds
- ⅓ cup washed, dried and chopped cilantro
- ⅓ cup washed, dried and chopped Italian parsley
- 5 large peeled cloves garlic
- 1 ½ teaspoon dried cumin
- 1 ½ teaspoon baking powder
- 1 ½ teaspoon rock salt
- ¼ cup plus 2 tablespoons coconut flour
- ¾ cup coconut oil (optional)

Directions:

1. Wash 1 ½ cups of dried chickpeas in 3-4 cups of water and soak in the fridge for 12 or more hours (change water every 12 hours if you soak for a day or two).

2. Rinse and drain when ready for use. (Note: the dried chickpeas will now be larger as they retain water after soaking).

3. Add the 2 cups of soaked chickpeas to a food processor along with all other ingredients, excluding the coconut flour and coconut oil (leave these 2 aside).

4. Pulse mixture until it starts to break apart. Then blend until mixture is well mixed and still textured but is not smooth.

5. Place chickpea mix in a bowl and mix in coconut flour.

6. If frying, place ½ cup of the coconut oil in a large fry pan and place on medium/high heat. Once pan and oil are hot, take ½ of chickpea mixture and form into 2 inch balls. Gently press down and shape each falafel so thickness is about ¾ inch thick.

7. Carefully drop the falafel into the oil. Turn frequently until a light crispy brown exterior forms. Remove and drain on paper towel.

8. Use remaining oil and make falafel out of the remaining chickpea mixture.

9. If baking, preheat oven to 350F.

10. Oil a baking sheet with coconut oil or other cooking oil.

11. Make 2 inch balls out of entire chickpea mixture and gently press down on each until flat and approx. ¾" thickness. Place on sheets and cook for 15 minutes. Turn falafel over and cook a remaining 15 minutes or until falafel is a light brown on both sides.

12. Serve with "Cucumber Mint Rawgurt Dressing".

Note: If you use canned and drained chickpeas, your mix will become much runnier. To counter this, add 4-5 more tablespoons of coconut flour or more, until mix is no longer runny/sticky and can be easily formed into balls for frying. For a spicier version, add 1-2 more garlic cloves and double the cumin. Feel free to add chili flakes if you like heat.

Bean Dream Gnocchi

Gnocchi is a personal favorite so here's a healthful gnocchi (dumpling) recipe to play with.
Some people dream of genies but I have gnocchi ones! Dream on!

Ingredients:

Gnocchi:

- 2-19 oz. canned white beans, drained and rinsed

- 2 teaspoons white ground pepper

- ¼ cup white ground chia

- ½ cup gluten free oat flour

Sauce:

- 4 tablespoons olive oil

- 1 ½ teaspoons garlic, minced

- 1 cup red onion, thinly sliced

- ¼ cup water

- 6 cups chard leaves, veins removed and chopped

- 1-15-oz can diced tomatoes

- ¼ teaspoon of each of these dried herbs: basil, thyme, oregano, rosemary

- ¼ teaspoon freshly ground pepper

- ¼ cup Delores hemp seeds

Directions:

1. In a medium sized mixing bowl, use a hand wand and puree beans the beans until smooth (can use a potato ricer as well).

2. Stir in white pepper and white ground chia.

3. Sprinkle oat flour onto clean counter and knead flour into bean dough, keeping counter dusted throughout process.

4. Divide dough into 18 pieces and roll into a 6 inch snake and slice into 1 inch sections.

5. Lay on an oiled baking sheet and bake in 350F oven for 10 minutes. Turn over and bake 5 more minutes.

6. Place on serving plates.

7. In a frying pan, add olive oil and onion and cook, stirring, over medium heat, for 2 minutes.

8. Stir in garlic and water and cover and cook until the onion is soft, 4 to 6 minutes.

9. Add chard and cook for 1-2 minutes, stirring, until it begins to wilt.

10. Stir in tomatoes, seasonings and hemp seeds and bring to a simmer.

11. Pour sauce over gnocchi and serve.

Makes 6 cups.

On the Go Hot Cocoa, see p. 121, Gotta Goji Oatmeal Cookie see p.287, and Better Than a Butter Cookie see p. 287

Sweet-Um's

I remember that during every Sunday dinner, we would be reminded that only if we ate everything on our plate, we would we be able to have our dessert. Store bought butter tarts or the homemade cheese cake with canned goopy cherry sauce on top, were like the Holy Grail that was offered up as retribution (for me at least) to finishing my Brussels sprouts (I still cannot eat them-not even on a dare), and a gristly slab of roast beef that I had to choke down every Sunday night. Our dog Brandy patiently waited for me to pass him chunks of spat out meat (via my napkin) under the table while my parents were distracted.

A good dessert is like a vacation: the less you have the more you appreciate it when you finally get to enjoy it. The fact that not many people vacation 24/7, nor do most people eat desserts at every meal, is what makes each experience so special. But unlike the unfulfilling goop-stuffed doughnut or deep fried fast food apple "pie" (more like "why?"), a good sweet treat should be worth it.

Not only should a well-deserved dessert taste incredible, but it should be good for you as well. Yes, desserts CAN and SHOULD be good for you! Once again, the key to healthy eating, including desserts, is the choice of excellent ingredients that are enjoyed in the right combinations and amounts.

Our old school attitude that desserts are the bad treat earned for eating the good food first is O-V-E-R. Like our food motto "make all of your food count", desserts are no different. The following sweet dreamy delights will provide your body with rich amounts of whole protein, fiber, great-for-you fats, anti-oxidants, vitamins and minerals. When you make the right choices, life can and should be truly super sweet.

Better Brownie

This brownie does not get much better.
Rich in anti-oxidants, protein, vitamins and minerals, this is a heart healthy treat with no regrets!

Ingredients:

Wet Ingredients:

- 1 cup unsweetened apple sauce
- 2 tablespoons coconut oil (melted)
- ½ teaspoon vanilla

Dry Ingredients:

- ¾ cup coconut sugar
- ¼ cup Delores hemp seeds
- 3 tablespoon cacao nibs
- ½ cup oat flour
- ⅓ cup cacao powder
- ¼ cup coconut flour
- 1 teaspoon baking soda
- ½ teaspoon rock salt

Directions:

1. Preheat oven to 350F.

2. Lightly grease a 7x11 (or 9x9) glass pan with coconut oil.

3. In a small bowl, mix together all WET ingredients.

4. In a separate bowl, mix DRY ingredients: coconut sugar, hemp hearts, and cacao nibs; then sift in: oat flour, coconut flour, cacao powder, baking soda and salt.

5. In dry mix bowl, make a center and slowly mix in the wet ingredients.

6. Evenly spoon batter in to greased pan.

7. Bake at 350F for 30 minutes.

8. Remove from oven and let cool in pan before frosting or cutting.

Whadda Fudge Icing

- ¼ cup coconut sugar
- ¼ cup Delores hemp seeds
- 2 tablespoons water
- 2 tablespoons cacao powder

- 1 teaspoon ground chia
- 3 teaspoon coconut oil (room temperature)
- ½ teaspoon vanilla

Directions:

1. Place all ingredients in a food processor or Magic Bullet.

2. Mix on high until creamy (add 1 more tablespoon water and remix if too thick).

3. Once Brownie base is fully cooled, spread icing evenly on top.

4. Cut into squares and keep refrigerated.

Better Brownie , see p. 270

Magnifimint Mouse with Ca-Wow Kale Chips and Terrific Truffle, see p. 281

Choco-Knockout Cookie

This cookie puts the POW! back in power. Heart healthy cacao combined with anti-inflammatory oats and blood sugar reducing chia combine to make a healthy cookie that tastes terrific.

Ingredients:

Wet Ingredients:

- 2 tablespoons white whole seed chia
- 6 tablespoons water
- 2 teaspoons vanilla
- ½ cup coconut oil (melted)

Dry Ingredients:

- 1 cup coconut sugar
- 1 teaspoon baking soda
- ¼ teaspoon Himalayan rock salt
- ¼ cup cacao powder
- 1 cup gluten free oat flour
- 2 cups gluten free quick flake oats
- ½ cup cacao nibs

Directions:

1. Stir chia and water in a bowl and let sit for 20-30 minutes. Stir in vanilla and coconut oil.

2. In a large bowl, mix together all dry ingredients and then add wet ingredients to it.

3. Hand mix until all is combined.

4. Take a tablespoon of dough and form into a cookie shape and place on a pre-oiled cookie sheet (I use coconut oil) one inch apart.

5. Bake in a preheated oven of 350F for 10-12 minutes.

6. Once out of oven, cool on a cookie rack.

7. Once cooled, ice them.

Great Balls of Energy!

These balls are a Superfood dream come true. Loaded with massive nutrients, including major fiber, EA, and whole protein it is great to pop one in for a fast breakie or an after workout treat. These are easy to make and even easier to eat!

Ingredients:

- 1 cup Delores hemp seeds

- ¼ cup white ground chia

- 3 tablespoons coconut oil, melted

- 2 tablespoons coconut sugar

- 2 tablespoons cacao powder

- 3 tablespoons sprouted buckwheat (or 1 ½ tablespoons coconut flour)

- 1 tablespoon white whole seed chia

- ¼ teaspoon rock salt

- 12 goji berries (optional)

Directions:

1. In a large bowl, mix all ingredients together.

2. Roll into 1 inch balls (add water if mix is too thick).

3. Insert one goji on top of each ball.

4. Refrigerate for at least an hour.

Goin' Bananas Ice Kreem

This dish is simple to make and is a frozen dessert lover's delight.
The high levels of good-for-you essential fatty acids make this recipe an ice kreem dream.

Ingredients:

- ½ cup Delores hemp seeds

- ¼ cup maple syrup

- ⅛ teaspoon rock salt

- ⅛ teaspoon vanilla

- Pinch of each ground: ginger, cinnamon and cardamom

- 3 cups frozen sliced bananas (4-5 medium ones)

Directions:

1. In a food processor, add all ingredients but for the bananas and blend on high until creamy consistency.

2. Then add in bananas and blend again until creamy but not runny.

3. Serve immediately. Great as a popsicle as well!

Makes 2 servings or 4 sides.

Sportbread Cookies

Shortbread cookies have a bad rap for a good reason, but not these ones! With immune boosting coconut oil, excellent fiber, and low glycemic — these cookies are terrific for pre or post workout. Who knew that short bread could be so sweet?

Ingredients:

- 1 tablespoon white whole seed chia
- 3 tablespoons water
- ½ cup coconut oil (melted)
- ½ teaspoon vanilla
- ½ cup coconut sugar

- ½ cup coconut flour
- 1 cup gluten free oat flour
- ½ teaspoon baking powder
- ⅛ teaspoon rock salt

Directions:

1. Pre heat oven to 350F.

2. Soak chia, water, coconut oil and vanilla in a small bowl for 20 minutes stirring occasionally.

3. In a separate mixing bowl mix together all dry ingredients.

4. Slowly stir in the wet mix to the dry mix.

5. Mix with hands until pliable (put in fridge for 10 minutes if dough is too sticky).

6. Take a tablespoon of mix and roll out into 1-inch balls and place on oiled cookie tray.

7. Gently push the center of the balls down (note: you can also firmly pack into a 9x9 glass pan to have shortbread squares).

8. Bake at 350F for 10-15 minutes, until lightly brown on bottom. Remove from oven and leave on pan to cool.

9. For added decadence, once cooled, dip into melted dark chocolate and sprinkle on coconut cacao nibs.

Makes about 16-20 cookies or one 9x9 pan.

Hemp-ease Poppies

These pop in your mouth lovelies are so easy to make you won't believe that you lived without them. Rich in anti-oxidants, energy boosting, and full of whole protein, these are an awesome before workout snack or a wake-me-up-it's-time-to go power popper.

Ingredients:

- ½ cup cacao nibs

- ¼ cup coconut oil

- 1 cup Delores hemp seeds

- 3 tablespoons coconut sugar

- 1 teaspoon grated orange zest

Directions:

1. In a food processor, pulse the cacao nibs about 5 times. Add in all other ingredients and pulse 4 times.

2. Mix well and form into balls or use a fun chocolate mold and press mixture firmly into them.

3. Place in freezer for 2 hours and store in fridge or freezer.

Makes about 16.

Terrific Truffles

I love the fact that you can have a truffle that is healthy and delicious.
"Wow" friends and family with this simply and healthy truffle treat!

Ingredients:

- ¼ cup coconut oil, melted
- ¼ cup agave or maple syrup
- ½ cup cacao powder
- 1 tablespoon coconut sugar
- ¾ cup Delores hemp seeds
- ¼ teaspoon vanilla
- Pinch of rock salt
- 2 tablespoons each of coconut cacao nibs and slow roasted hemp seeds (garnish)

Directions:

1. Melt coconut oil and mix in agave or maple syrup, cacao powder, coconut sugar, hemp seeds, vanilla and salt.

2. Refrigerate for one hour, then take a tablespoon of batter and roll into balls.

3. In 2 small bowls place coconut cacao nibs and hemp seeds in each, and roll the truffles in each (works even better if you put a dollop of agave/syrup on top of each truffle).

4. Can be frozen. Keep in refrigerator up to 2 weeks.

Makes about 20 truffles.

Ca-Wow Kale Chips

Kale is one of the best greens you can eat. It is a great source of fiber, highly alkaline and rich in vitamins and minerals such as vitamin A, calcium, beta-carotene, vitamin C, folic acid, vitamin B6, manganese, and potassium. These chips are not only tasty but are full of health benefits with high anti-oxidants, pure protein and immune boosting. WOW is right.

Ingredients:

- 2 bunches of kale (14-16 leaves)

- ⅓ cup coconut oil

- ¼ cup cacao powder

- ¼ cup Delores hemp seed

- ¼ teaspoon rock salt

- ⅓ cup coconut sugar

- 2 tablespoons coconut cacao nibs (or cacao nibs)

Directions:

1. Remove stems of kale, wash, pat dry and tear into strips (3-4 inches) and place in a large bowl.

2. Melt coconut oil over low heat, cool and pour evenly over kale and hand mix together.

3. In a separate small bowl, mix all of the remaining ingredients together. Then evenly sprinkle onto kale and mix with hands until all kale coated.

4. Place in a dehydrator for about 4 hours. If you do not have access to a dehydrator, then for oven baking: preheat oven to 350 degrees F (175 degrees C); line a non-insulated cookie sheet with parchment paper and bake chips about 10-15 minutes until the edges brown but are not burnt.

5. Keep in an airtight container.

Magnifimint Mousse

This recipe is easy to make, tastes great, and has a number of Superfoods included in it.
This is a good recipe to have as a super simple stand by!

Ingredients:

- 20 dates, pitted 1 cup water
- 2 avocados, pitted and peeled
- 4 tablespoons cacao powder
- 4 tablespoons white ground chia
- 2 tablespoons Delores hemp seeds
- 3 large mint leaves
- ¼ teaspoon rock salt

Directions:

1. Place dates in a large bowl and add 2 cups warm water. Soak for 3 hours or until soft.

2. In a food processor, blend all of the ingredients together until the mousse is smooth and creamy. Add more mint if desired.

3. Pour into four dessert bowls and serve chilled. Note: due to avocados this should be eaten same day made.

Berry Easy Pudding

This pudding is easy to make and is a crowd pleaser with the li'l peeps.
Their frozen alternatives are fun to eat as well.

Ingredients:

- ¾ cups water

- ¼ cup plus 1 tablespoon white whole seed chia

- 2 cups blueberries

- 1 cup raspberries

- ⅓ cup Delores hemp hearts

- 1 tablespoons coconut oil

- 5 tablespoons coconut sugar

- 1 teaspoon cacao powder

- ¼ teaspoon vanilla

Directions:

1. Add chia and water, stir and soak for 20 minutes.

2. Once soaked, blend chia mix along with all ingredients in a high speed food processor for about 3 minutes until mixed well (blend longer if you prefer a completely smooth pudding).

Makes about 2 cups.

Cherry Good Pops!

1. Make pudding as "Easy Berry Pudding" above.

2. Take 12 cherries and gently split down middle and remove pit.

3. In an ice cube tray, place a teaspoon of pudding at bottom of each ice cube spot.

4. Add in cherry and place pudding on top until reach top of ice cube tray.

5. Place a small miniature wooden popsicle stick into center of each (can find these at craft stores).

6. Place in freezer for a few hours. Remove and run back under hot water and pop each one out.

Pin-Yah Colada Pudding

One of the best parts of heading south to vacation is the lovely mix of fresh fruits and coconut. This pudding is a healthy way to boost your Omegas and bring back the wonderful holiday memories of Pina Colada drinkie-poos, but in a super healthy delivery system!

Ingredients:

- ¼ cup white whole seed chia
- 2 cups lite canned coconut milk
- 1 cup diced frozen pineapple
- 1 cup diced frozen mango
- 1 frozen ripe banana

- 2 tablespoons Delores hemp seeds
- 1 tablespoon coconut sugar
- 1 teaspoon pure vanilla extract
- 1 pinch of cinnamon

Directions:

1. Mix the white whole seed chia and the coconut milk together and let sit for at least 20 minutes (stir occasionally).

2. Add the chia mix along with all ingredients to a food processor and mix everything together until smooth and creamy. If too thick, add a little more coconut milk.

3. Serve immediately in four bowls. Note: these can also be frozen into popsicle molds for a super Omega-3 healthy frozen snack!

Peach POWer Pudding

Nothing says summer like a super ripe peach. If you can, make this pudding using in season peaches. If not, opt for using frozen ones or canned ones. But either way this is a super nutrient rich pudding that everyone will enjoy.

Ingredients:

- 3 cups ripe peaches, peeled and sliced (can use canned as well)

- ⅔ cups lite canned coconut milk

- ¼ cup Delores hemp hearts

- 5 tablespoons coconut sugar

- 3 tablespoons ground chia

- 1 tablespoon coconut oil

- ¼ teaspoon ground cinnamon

- ¾ teaspoon vanilla

- ½ cubic inch ginger root, peeled and chopped

Directions:

1. Place all ingredients in a high speed food processor and blend on high for a few minutes until creamy consistency.

2. Place in serving cups and chill in fridge for at least 2 hours. You can also place into popsicle molds and freeze for at least 5 hours.

So-Free Apple Goji Crisp

This apple crisp is protein-rich with the benefit of oats and is free of butter and refined sugar, but you would never know it! The coconut oil is a far better choice than butter, and the goji berries are the best answer to high glycemic raisins.

Ingredients:

Base:

- 4 cups thinly sliced apples, skin removed (approximately 5 apples)
- ½ cup coconut sugar
- ⅛ teaspoon cinnamon
- ⅛ teaspoon vanilla
- 3 tablespoons goji berries

Topping:

- 1 tablespoon whole seed chia
- 3 tablespoons water
- ⅓ cup coconut oil, melted
- ¼ teaspoon vanilla
- 1 cup quick flake oats
- ¼ cup unsweetened shredded coconut flakes
- ¼ cup oat flour
- ¼ cup coconut flour
- ½ cup coconut sugar
- ¼ teaspoon ground cinnamon

Directions:

1. Preheat oven to 350F.

2. For base, in a 6x10 inch baking dish, mix apples, coconut sugar, cinnamon and vanilla. Then place goji berries on top.

3. In small bowl, mix chia, water, melted coconut oil and vanilla together and let sit 10 minutes.

4. In a medium bowl, mix all chia and other topping ingredients together and sprinkle on top of base.

5. Bake in oven for 45 minutes.

Gotta Goji Oatmeal Cookies

These cookies are always a super pleaser. They are easy to make, taste terrific, and freeze well (baked cookies and dough). So go ahead and make a huge batch and draw down on them when you need them — if they last that long!

Ingredients:

Wet Ingredients:

- 2 tablespoons whole seed chia
- 6 tablespoons water
- 2 teaspoons vanilla
- ½ cup coconut oil (melted)

Dry Ingredients:

- 1 cup coconut sugar
- 1 teaspoon baking soda
- ½ teaspoon cinnamon
- ¼ teaspoon rock salt
- 1 cup oat flour
- 2 cups quick flake oats
- ¼ cup goji berries

Directions:

1. Stir chia and water in a bowl and let sit for 20 minutes, stirring occasionally. Stir in vanilla and coconut oil.

2. In a large bowl, mix together all ingredients in dry mix and then add wet chia mix, hand mixing until all is combined.

3. Take a tablespoon of dough and form into a cookie shape and place an inch apart on a pre-oiled cookie sheet (I use coconut oil).

4. Bake in a preheated oven of 350F for 8-10 minutes.

5. Remove from oven when bottom of cookie is a light brown. Once out of oven, let sit on cookie sheet for 10 minutes, and then remove with a spatula (this allows them to "set").

Makes 20-24 small cookies or 12 larger ones.

Lemon Cook-Ease

These easy to make cookies are refreshing snacks that have great nutritionals like whole protein, essential fatty acids, low glycemic, and immune boosting properties.

Ingredients:

- ¾ cup gluten free oat flour

- ¼ cup quinoa flour

- ¼ teaspoon baking powder

- ⅛ teaspoon rock salt

- ¼ cup softened coconut oil

- ½ cup coconut sugar

- 2 teaspoons lemon rind, grated

- 1 tablespoon lemon juice

Directions:

1. Preheat oven to 350F.

2. In a medium sized mixing bowl, mix together dry ingredients: oat and quinoa flour, baking powder and rock salt.

3. In a separate mixing bowl, use an electric mixer to beat together the coconut oil and the coconut sugar.

4. Beat in rind and juice then beat in slowly the dry flour mixture.

5. Roll dough into a one inch balls then squish down in center, making a cookie shape.

6. Place on a greased cookie sheet and bake oven for 10 minutes. Once done, place on a baker's rack to cool.

Makes about 2 dozen.

Better Than a Butter Cookie

These cookies not only taste like butter cookies but are even better! With no butter, egg or bad-for-you white sugar, these cookies are yummy nutritional goodness!

Ingredients:

Wet Ingredients:

- ⅔ cup coconut oil (melted)
- 1 teaspoon vanilla
- 2 tablespoons white whole seed chia
- 6 tablespoons water

Dry Ingredients:

- 2 cups gluten free oat flour or an all-purpose flour
- 1 cup unsweetened coconut flakes
- ⅔ cup coconut sugar
- 3 tablespoons Delores hemp seeds
- 1 ½ teaspoon baking powder
- ½ teaspoons rock salt

Directions:

1. Preheat oven to 350F.

2. In a small bowl, mix wet ingredients together (coconut oil, vanilla, whole chia and water). Let it sit and soak for 15 minutes, stirring occasionally.

3. In a large mixing bowl, mix all dry ingredients together. Once chia mix has soaked, add wet mix to dry mix and hand stir until all combined.

4. Take a tablespoon of cookie dough and press and shape into 1/4 inch round cookie. Place on slightly greased (with coconut oil) cookie sheet.

5. Bake for 8-10 minutes, until bottom of cookies are a light brown. Cool on a cookie rack.

6. Dough and cookies freeze well.

Makes 24 cookies.

RAPPIN' IT UP!

So my friend, we have finally reached the end of our travels together — at least this rockin' recipe round.

I am so grateful for the opportunity to share these recipes with you and some of the personal stories that formed them. I hope that you have enjoyed the materials in this book and the recipes within to be shared with friends and family. If this book inspires you to make (and tweak) these recipes, and to use Superfoods daily, then my job is done. It is truly one of the greatest honors to feed loved ones with delicious and nutrient rich foods — so keep on makin' 'em and stuffin' 'em!

This book is in no way perfect, nor am I. I have done my best to provide relevant and current information and research. Yet information is never static so things do change, and I look forward to learning as more research is done as time goes on. I hope that this book provides you with a useable resource and inspires and encourages you to pursue your own personal journey of better choices and Superfood eating.

The beauty of embarking upon any journey is that it never truly ends, as your direction and knowledge is changed forever and new facts, information, and ingredients are around every corner.

The road to healthy living is one that takes time and is part of a daily commitment. By learning and educating yourself about how your body works and how food affects your body's ability to function, you will make more informed and healthier choices. By choosing to eat Superfoods on a daily basis that feeds your body, mind and planet, you will become an even better version of YOU!

So what are you waiting for? Get going and BE SUPER!

Best wishes to you and yours,
Ann

NOTES

(Endnotes)

[1] See: http://www.who.int/mediacentre/factsheets/fs311/en/index.html

[2] See full report at: https://www.idf.org/sites/default/files/Global_Diabetes_Plan_Final.pdf

[3] WAO White Book on Allergy 2011-2012: Executive Summary

[4] Ibid.

[5] Biomed Pharmacother. 2002 Oct;56(8):365-79. The importance of the ratio of Omega-6/Omega-3 essential fatty acids. Simopoulos AP.

[6] Danaei G, et al. The Preventable Causes of Death in the United States: Comparative Risk Assessment of Dietary, Lifestyle, and Metabolic Risk Factors. PLoS Med 2009;6(4), and Raffaele De Caterina, n-3 Fatty Acids in Cardiovascular Disease, New England Journal of Medicine 2011; 364: 2439–50

[7] Postgrad Med J 2009;85:84-90 doi:10.1136/pgmj.2008.073338, Omega-3 fatty acids: a comprehensive review of their role in health and disease, B M Yashodhara1, S Umakanth1, J M Pappachan1, S K Bhat2, R Kamath3, B H Choo1

[8] For an excellent resource and overview of research see link at http://www.umm.edu/altmed/articles/Omega-3-000316.htm.

[9] Yurko-Mauro, K., et al., Beneficial effects of docosahexaenoic acid on cognition in age-related cognitive decline. Alzheimers Dement, 2010. DHA Improves Memory and Cognitive Function in Older Adults, Study Suggests. ScienceDaily, 2010.

[10] PLoS One. 2010; 5(3): e9434. Published online 2010 March 2. doi: 10.1371/journal.pone.0009434 PMCID: PMC2830458. Effect of Animal and Industrial Trans Fatty Acids on HDL and LDL Cholesterol Levels in Humans — A Quantitative Review. Ingeborg A. Brouwer,1,* Anne J. Wanders,1,2 and Martijn B. Katan1

[11] Ibid.

[12] Excellent summary of research on trans fatty acids is set out here: http://en.wikipedia.org/wiki/Trans_fat

[13] Position of the American Dietetic Association and Dietitians of Canada: Vegetarian diets. JADA, 2003; 103(6) 748-765.

[14] "Effects of Fructose vs Glucose on Regional Cerebral Blood Flow in Brain Regions Involved With Appetite and Reward Pathways", Kathleen A. Page, MD; Owen Chan, PhD; Jagriti Arora, MS; Renata Belfort-DeAguiar, MD, PhD; James Dzuira, PhD; Brian Roehmholdt, MD, PhD; Gary W. Cline, PhD; Sarita Naik, MD; Rajita Sinha, PhD; R. Todd Constable, PhD; Robert S. Sherwin, MD. JAMA. 2013;309(1):63-70. doi:10.1001/jama.2012.116975.

[15] J Clin Endocrinol Metab. 2011 Oct;96(10):E1596-605. doi: 10.1210/jc.2011-1251. Epub 2011 Aug 17. Consumption of fructose and high fructose corn syrup increase postprandial triglycerides, LDL-cholesterol, and apolipoprotein-B in young men and women. Stanhope KL, Bremer AA, Medici V, Nakajima K, Ito Y, Nakano T, Chen G, Fong TH, Lee V, Menorca RI, Keim NL, Havel PJ.

[16] J Am Soc Nephrol. 2010 September; 21(9): 1543–1549. doi: Increased Fructose Associates with Elevated Blood Pressure Diana I. Jalal, Gerard Smits, Richard J. Johnson, and Michel Chonchol

[17] (Cui, X.; Zuo, P.; Zhang, Q.; Li, X.; Hu, Y.; Long, J.; Packer, L.; Liu, J. (2006). "Chronic systemic D-galactose exposure induces memory loss, neurodegeneration, and oxidative damage in mice: protective effects of R-alpha-lipoic acid". Journal of neuroscience research 84 (3): 647–654.

[18] Cramer D, Harlow B, Willett W, Welch W, Bell D, Scully R, Ng W, Knapp R (1989). "Galactose consumption and metabolism in relation to the risk of ovarian cancer". Lancet2 (8654): 66–71.

6) 748-765.

[19] See: Pereira MA, Pins JJ. Dietary fiber and cardiovascular disease: Experimental and epidemiologic advances. Curr Athero Rep. 2000;2(6):494-502. Glore SR, Van Treeck DV, Knehans AW, Guild M. Soluble fiber and serum lipids: A literature review. J Am Diet

Assoc. 1994;94(6):425-436. Davidson MH, Maki KC. Effects of dietary inulin on serum lipids. J Nutr. 1999;129(7 Suppl):1474S-1477S. Reaven GM. Compensatory hyperinsulinemia and the development of an atherogenic lipoprotein profile: The price paid to maintain glucose homeostasis in insulin-resistant individuals. Endocrinol Metab Clin North Am. 2005;34(1):49-62. Blake GJ, Ridker PM. Inflammatory bio-markers and cardiovascular risk prediction. J Int Med. 2002;252(4):283-294. King DE. Dietary fiber, inflammation and cardiovascular disease. Mol Nutr Food Res. 2005(6);49:594-600.

[20] Nutr Rev. 2001 May;59(5):129-39. Dietary fiber and weight regulation. Howarth NC, Saltzman E, Roberts SB.

[21] Note: I have only included food source references that are vegan and not a high allergen.

[22] Although this relationship is hard to prove scientifically as Monsanto (the privately held seed mega-giant who is responsible for GMO crops) requires any user/grower to sign an intellectual property based agreement that prevents any study of the Monsanto seed without their prior permission. They have basically used the legal argument of IP rights to prevent any scientific review of GMO seeds for their long term safety. This issue is continuing in the US court system and patent office.

[23] http://www.cdc.gov/nchs/data/databriefs/db10.htm

[24] Bhattacharyya S, Dudeja PK and Tobacman JK (2010) Tumor necrosis factor alpha-induced inflammation is increased but apoptosis is inhibited by common food additive carrageenan. Journal of Biological Chemistry 285(50): 39511-22, and see: Borthakur A, Bhattacharyya S, Anbazhagan AN, Kumar A, Dudeja PK and Tobacman JK (2012). Prolongation of carrageenan-induced inflammation in human colonic epithelial cells by activation of an NFκB-BCL10 loop. Biochimica and Biophysica Acta 1822(8): 1300-7

[25] Bhattacharyya S, O-Sullivan I, Katyal S, Unterman T and Tobacman JK (2012) Exposure to the common food additive carrageenan leads to glucose intolerance, insulin resistance and inhibition of insulin signalling in HepG2 cells and C57BL/6J mice. Diabetologia 55(1): 194-203

[26] Malatesta M, Biggiogera M, Manuali E, Rocchi MBL, Baldelli B, Gazzanelli G. Fine structural analyses of pancreatic acinar cell nuclei from mice fed on genetically modified soybean. European Journal of Histochemistry. Oct-Dec 2003; 47: 385–388; Malatesta M, Caporaloni C, Gavaudan S, et al. Ultrastructural morphometrical and immunocytochemical analyses of hepatocyte nuclei from mice fed on genetically modified soybean. Cell Struct Funct. Aug 2002; 27(4): 173–180; Vecchio L, Cisterna B, Malatesta M, Martin TE, Biggiogera M. Ultrastructural analysis of testes from mice fed on genetically modified soybean. Eur J Histochem. Oct-Dec 2004; 48(4): 448-454.

[27] Malatesta M, et al. A long-term study on female mice fed on a genetically modified soybean: effects on liver ageing. Histochem Cell Biol. 2008; 130: 967–977.

[28] Tudisco R, Lombardi P, Bovera F, et al. Genetically modified soya bean in rabbit feeding: Detection of DNA fragments and evaluation of metabolic effects by enzymatic analysis. Animal Science. 2006; 82: 193–199.

[29] Brasil FB, Soares LL, Faria TS, Boaventura GT, Sampaio FJ, Ramos CF. The impact of dietary organic and transgenic soy on the reproductive system of female adult rat. Anat Rec (Hoboken). Apr 2009; 292(4): 587–594.

[30] Séralini GE, Mesnage R, Clair E, Gress S, de Vendômois JS, Cellier D. Genetically modified crops safety assessments: Present limits and possible improvements. Environmental Sciences Europe. 2011; 23(10)

[31] http://alzheimers.org.uk/site/scripts/documents_info.php?documentID=99

[32] Cornucopia Institute (2009-05-18) Behind the Bean — The Heroes and Charlatans of the Natural and Organic Soy Foods Industry and Toxic Chemicals: Banned In Organics But Common in "Natural" Food Production soy Protein and chemical solvents in Nutrition Bars and Meat alternatives (November 2010).

[33] For the Us and Canadian Government's n position on "gluten Free" labelng see the following: Canada CFIA: http://www.inspection.gc.ca/food/labelling/other-requirements/gluten-free-claims/eng/1340194596012/1340194681961; and the US FDA: http://www.fda.gov/ForConsumers/ConsumerUpdates/ucm265212.htm#How_Is_FDA

[34] Catassi, C. Response to P.Collin et al, AmJ Clin Nutr, 2007 ; 86:260-9; and Catassi, C., Fabiani, E., Iacono, G., D'Agate, C., Francavilla, R., Biagi, F., Volta, U., Accomando, S., Picarelli, A., Vitis, I. de, Pianelli, G., Gesuita, R., Carle, F., Mandolesi, A., Bearzi, I.,Fasano, A. A prospective, double-blind, placebo-controlled trial to establish a safe gluten threshold for patients with celiac disease. Am J Clin Nutr. 2007;85(1):160-166

[35] I personally don't agree with the Canadian governments characterization of oats as being a gluten rich food and I believe that their inclusion is misleading and misinformed. Much better would be for them to explain the risks of cross contamination of all foods, and set standards higher for manufacturers to provide test results annually for ALL foods that contain a gluten free label. Only then will celiac be able to make the most informed and risk free choice.

[36] See research at: www.ncbi.nlm.nih.gov/pubmed/16960024

[37] See section on What was Not Included for flax research. How Flax Compares to chia:

- Flaxseeds and flaxseed oil can spoil if they are not kept refrigerated. It should be protected from light, heat, air, and moisture. Chia does not spoil due to the high anti-oxidants.

- Flaxseed has less dietary fiber (27% vs. 33%), and can hold less water (approx. 6 times its weight) than chia although it has more soluble fiber (ratio insoluble: soluble = 2:1, vs. 8:1).

- Flaxseed contains 60% less calcium, but has more magnesium and potassium.

- The ratio of Omega-3 and Omega-6 content is almost equal.

- Flaxseed has to be milled to be able to absorb its nutrients.

- Chia has very similar benefits of flax, without the additional risks.

[38] Alvarez-Jubete L, Wijngaard H, Arendt EK et al. Polyphenol composition and in vitro antioxidant activity of amaranth, quinoa buckwheat and wheat as affected by sprouting and baking. Food Chemistry, Volume 119, Issue 2, 15 March 2010, Pages 770-778. 2010.

[39] Pasko P, Zagrodzki P, Barton H et al. Effect of quinoa seeds (Chenopodium quinoa) in diet on some biochemical parameters and essential elements in blood of high fructose-fed rats. Plant Foods for Human Nutrition65. 4 (2010): 333-338. 2010.

[40] Quignard-Boulange A, Foucault AS, Mathe V et al. Quinoa extract enriched in 20-hydroxyecdysone protects mice from diet-induced obesity and modulates adipokines expression. Obesity (silver spring) 20. 2 (2012): 270-277. 2012

[41] The four ancient crops were: maize (corn), beans, chia, and amaranth. The history of chia and ancient crops is supported by Codices written about the time the Spanish conquest especially the Florentine Codex which was written between 1548 and 1585 by Fray Bernardino de Sahagun, and is titled the General History of the Things of New Spain which describes various aspects of Aztec chia production.

[42] Vulkan, V., D.Whitham, J. Sievenpiper A. L. Jenkins, A, L. Rogovik, R. P. Bazinet, Edward Vidgen, and A. Hanna. 2007. Supplementation of Conventional Therapy With the Novel Grain Salba (Salvia hispanica L.) Improves Major and Emerging Cardiovascular Risk Factors in Type 2 Diabetes: Results of a randomized controlled trial. Diabetes Care 30: 11 2804-2810.

[43] Vulkan, V., D.Whitham, J. Sievenpiper A. L. Jenkins, A, L. Rogovik, R. P. Bazinet, Edward Vidgen, and A. Hanna. 2007. Supplementation of Conventional Therapy With the Novel Grain Salba (Salvia hispanica L.) Improves Major and Emerging Cardiovascular Risk Factors in Type 2 Diabetes: Results of a randomized controlled trial. Diabetes Care 30: 11 2804-2810.

[44] Vuksan V., A L Jenkins, A G Dias, A S Lee, E Jovanovski, A L Rogovik and A Hanna. 2010. Reduction in postprandial glucose excursion and prolongation of satiety: possible explanation of the long-term effects of whole grain Salba (Salvia Hispanica L.)European Journal of Clinical Nutrition 64, 436-438.

[45] Prostaglandins Leukot Essent Fatty Acids. 1994 Nov;51(5):311-6. Clinical and experimental study on the long-term effect of dietary gamma-linolenic acid on plasma lipids, platelet aggregation, thromboxane formation, and prostacyclin production. Guivernau M, Meza N, Barja P, Roman O. Source — Department of Medicine, School of Medicine, University of Chile, Santiago.

[46] Little C, Parsons T. Herbal therapy for treating rheumatoid arthritis. Cochrane Database Syst Rev. 2001;(1):CD002948; Remans PH, Sont JK, Wagenaar LW, Wouters-Wesseling W, Zuijderduin WM, et al. Nutrient supplementation with polyunsaturated fatty acids and micronutrients in rheumatoid arthritis: clinical and biochemical effects. Eur J Clin Nutr. 2004 Jun;58(6):839-45.

[47] Kankaanpaa P, Nurmela K, Erkkila A, et al. Polyunsaturated fatty acids in maternal diet, breast milk, and serum lipid fattty acids of infants in relation to atopy. Allergy. 2001;56(7):633-638.

[48] Kenny FS, Pinder SE, Ellis IO et al. Gamma linolenic acid with tamoxifen as primary therapy tn breast cancer. Int J Cancer.

2000;85:643-648.

[49] The Mayan's sacred book, Popul Vuh, contains their story of the creation, and instead of an apple tree, there's a cacao tree.

[50] Hunter, J. Edward; Zhang, Jun; Kris-Etherton, Penny M. (January 2010). "Cardiovascular disease risk of dietary stearic acid compared with trans, other saturated, and unsaturated fatty acids: a systematic review". Am. J. Clinical Nutrition(American Society for Nutrition) 91 (1): 46–63. doi:10.3945/ajcn.2009.27661.ISSN 0002-9165. PMID 19939984.

[51] Bayard V, Chamorro F, Motta J, Hollenberg NK (2007). "Does flavonol intake influence mortality from nitric oxide-dependent processes? Ischemic heart disease, stroke, diabetes mellitus, and cancer in Panama". Int J Med Sci 4 (1): 53–8. PMC 1796954.

[52] Contemporary Reviews in Cardiovascular Medicine. Cocoa and Cardiovascular HealthRoberto Corti, MD*; Andreas J. Flammer, MD*; Norman K. Hollenberg, MD, PhD; Thomas F. Lüscher, MD

[53] Waterhouse AL, Shirley JR, Donovan JL. Antioxidants in chocolate. Lancet.1996; 348: 834.

[54] Weiss C, Dejam A, Kleinbongard P, Schewe T, Sies H, Kelm M. Vascular effects of cocoa rich in flavan-3-ols. JAMA. 2003; 290: 1030–1031; Heiss C, Kleinbongard P, Dejam A, Perre S, Schroeter H, Sies H, Kelm M. Acute consumption of flavonol-rich cocoa and the reversal of endothelial dysfunction in smokers. J Am Coll Cardiol. 2005; 46: 1276–1283.

[55] Ottaviani JI, Carrasquedo F, Keen CL, Lazarus SA, Schmitz HH, Fraga CG. Influence of flavan-3-ols and procyanidins on UVC-mediated formation of 8-oxo-7,8-dihydro-2'-deoxyguanosine in isolated DNA. Arch Biochem Biophys. 2002; 406: 203–208.

[56] Adamson GE, Lazarus SA, Mitchell AE, Prior RL, Cao G, Jacobs PH, Kremers BG, Hammerstone JF, Rucker RB, Ritter KA, Schmitz HH. HPLC method for the quantification of procyanidins in cocoa and chocolate samples and correlation to total antioxidant capacity. J Agric Food Chem. 1999; 47: 4184–4188.; and Rein D, Lotito S, Holt RR, Keen CL, Schmitz HH, Fraga CG. Epicatechin in human plasma: in vivo determination and effect of chocolate consumption on plasma oxidation status. J Nutr. 2000; 130: 2109S–2114S.

[57] Flammer AJ, Hermann F, Sudano I, Spieker L, Hermann M, Cooper KA, Serafini M, Luscher TF, Ruschitzka F, Noll G, Corti R. Dark chocolate improves coronary vasomotion and reduces platelet reactivity. Circulation. 2007; 116:2376–2382.

[58] http://www.medscape.com/viewarticle/770473

[59] Andres-Lacueva C, Monagas M, Khan N, Izquierdo-Pulido M, Urpi-Sarda M, Permanyer J, Lamuela-Raventos RM. Flavanol and flavonol contents of cocoa powder products: influence of the manufacturing process. J Agric Food Chem. 2008; 56: 3111–3117.

[60] A 2012 report by an independent auditor, the Fair Labor Association (FLA), says it found "multiple serious violations" of Nestle's own supplier code. SHAME ON YOU! See what organizations are trying to do to stop this: http://www.laborrights.org/stop-child-labor/cocoa-campaign and http://www.fairlabor.org/search/node/cocoa

[61] http://circ.ahajournals.org/content/116/21/2360.full

[62] Huang Di Nei Jing (Yellow Emperor's Classic of Internal Medicine) Chinese medical textbook dating to the Qin and Han periods (221 B.C.-220 A.D.). Tianjin Scientific Technology Publishing Press, 1986. Chinese version translated by research scientist Sue Chao. Shen Nung Ben Tsao (25-220 A.D.)

[63] Huang Guifang, Luo Jieying. Immune Boosting Effects from Fu Fang Wu Zi Yang Zong Wan (a Chinese patent herb containing Lycium barbarium fruit). Zhong Cao Yao (Chinese Herbs). 1990, 12(6): 27.

[64] State Scientific and Technological Commission of China, Clinical Experiment on Lycium, Register No. 870306; Lycium barbarum Medical Effects, improves eyesight, Ningxia Scientific and Technological Commission, July 1982-Jan. 1984.

[65] Optometry & Vision Science: "Goji Berry Effects on Macular Characteristics and Plasma Antioxidant Levels;" Peter Bucheli, Karine Vidal, Lisong Shen et al.; February 2011

[66] A study published in The International Journal of Biological Macromolecules in 2010.

[67] Park HJ, Shim HS, Choi WK, Kim KS, Shim I Basic Oriental Medical Science and Acupuncture and Meridian Science Research Center, Kyung Hee University, Seoul 130-701, Korea. Experimental Neurobiology [2011, 20(3):137-143]

[68] Kim HP, Kim SY, Lee EJ, Kim YC. Zeaxanthin Dipalmitate from Lycium Barbarum Has Hepatoprotective Activity. Res. Commun Mol Pathol Pharmacol. 1997, Sep.; (3): 301-314; He Jie, Pan Li, Guo Fuxiang, et al. Hepatoprotective Effects from Lycium Barbarum Fruit

in a Mouse Experiment. China Pharmacology and Toxicology. 1993, 7(4): 293; Li yuhao, Deng Xiangchao, Wu Heqing, et al. The Effect on Lipid Metabolism of Injured Liver Cells in Rat. Zhong Guo Zhong. Yao Za Zhi (Journal of Chinese Herbal Medicine). 1994, 19(5):300.

[69] Cao GW, Yang WG, Du P. Observation of the Effects of LAK/IL-2 Therapy Combined with Lycium Barbarum Polysaccharides in the Treatment of 75 Cancer Patients. Chunghua Chung Liu Tsa Chih. 1994, Nov.; 16(6): 428-431, Lu CX, Cheng BQ. Radiosensitizing Effects of Lycium Barbarum Polysaccharide of Lewis Lung Cancer. Chung His I chieh Ho Tsa Chih. 1991, Oct.: 11(10): 611-612. A study published in the Chinese Journal of Oncology , 1994 found that 79 people with cancer responded better to treatment when goji juice was added to their regimen. 79 patients in advanced stages of cancer were treated with the cancer drug LAK/IL-2 combined with Lycium Barbarum polysaccharides . Regression of the several cancers was observed. The response rate of patients treated with LAK/IL-2 and LBP was 40 percent while that of patients treated only with LAK/IL-2 was 16 percent study. A study published in the March 2011 edition of the journal Medical Oncology reveals that the polysaccharide components of goji inhibit the growth of colon cancer cells.

[70] The State Scientific and Technology Commission of China, 1988 Report.

[71] Jackson, Eric. (August 20 — September 2, 2006). From whence come coconuts?.The Panama News (Volume 12, Number 16). Retrieved April 10, 2011.

[72] A study of the clinical activity of a gel combining monocaprin and doxycycline: a novel treatment for herpes labialis. J Oral Pathol Med. 2011 Apr 30; Short- and medium-chain fatty acids exhibit antimicrobial activity for oral microorganisms. Arch Oral Biol. 2011 Jul;56(7):650-4. Epub 2011 Feb 17; Antibacterial study of the medium chain fatty acids and their 1-monoglycerides: individual effects and synergistic relationships. Pol J Microbiol. 2009;58(1):43-7; The Effect Of Virgin Coconut Oil Supplementation For Community-Acquired Pneumonia In Children Aged 3 To 60 Months Admitted At The Philippine Children's Medical Center: A Single Blinded Randomized Controlled Trial, CHEST, October 29, 2008; Novel antibacterial activity of monolaurin compared with conventional antibiotics against organisms from skin infections: an in vitro study. J Drugs Dermatol. 2007 Oct;6(10):991-8. Virucidal activities of medium- and long-chain fatty alcohols and lipids against respiratory syncytial virus and parainfluenza virus type 2: comparison at different pH levels. Arch Virol. 2007;152(12):2225-36. Epub 2007 Sep 22; In vitro antimicrobial properties of coconut oil on Candida species in Ibadan, Nigeria.

J Med Food. 2007 Jun;10(2):384-7; Effect of fatty acids on arenavirus replication: inhibition of virus production by lauric acid. Arch Virol. 2001;146(4):777-90; In vitro killing of Candida albicans by fatty acids and monoglycerides. Antimicrob Agents Chemother. 2001 Nov;45(11):3209-12; Inactivation of visna virus and other enveloped viruses by free fatty acids and monoglycerides. Ann N Y Acad Sci. 1994 Jun 6;724:465-71. Lauric acid inhibits the maturation of vesicular stomatitis virus. J Gen Virol. 1994 Feb;75 (Pt 2):353-61.

[73] The ketogenic diet reverses gene expression patterns and reduces reactive oxygen species levels when used as an adjuvant therapy for glioma. Nutr Metab (Lond). 2010 Sep 10;7:74; Growth of human gastric cancer cells in nude mice is delayed by a ketogenic diet supplemented with omega-3 fatty acids and medium-chain triglycerides. BMC Cancer. 2008 Apr 30;8:122; Efficacy of medium-chain triglycerides compared with long-chain triglycerides in total parenteral nutrition in patients with digestive tract cancer undergoing surgery. Kaohsiung M Med Sci 2005;21:487-494; Antitumor effect of medium-chain triglyceride and its influence on the self-defense system of the body. Cancer Detect Prev. 1998;22(3):219-24. Implementing a ketogenic diet based on medium-chain triglyceride oil in pediatric patients with cancer. J Am Diet Assoc. 1995 Jun;95(6):693-7; Effects of a ketogenic diet on tumor metabolism and nutritional status in pediatric oncology patients: two case reports. J Am Coll Nutr. 1995 Apr;14(2):202-8; Influence of various fatty acids on tumour growth in total parenteral nutrition. Eur Surg Res 1994;26:288-297; Menhaden, coconut, and corn oils and mammary tumor incidence in BALB/c virgin female mice treated with DMBA. Nutr Cancer. 1993;20(2):99-106.

[74] Influence of coconut oil administration on some hematologic and metabolic parameters in pregnant rats. J Matern Fetal Neonatal Med. 2011 Oct;24(10):1254-8. Epub 2011 Jul 7. In vivo antinociceptive and anti-inflammatory activities of dried and fermented processed virgin coconut oil. Med Princ Pract. 2011;20(3):231-6. Epub 2011 Mar 29; Coconut oil is associated with a beneficial lipid profile in pre-menopausal women in the Philippines. Asia Pac J Clin Nutr. 2011;20(2):190-5; Dietary fatty acids and oxidative stress in the heart mitochondria. Mitochondrion. 2011 Jan;11(1):97-103. Epub 2010 Aug 5; Successful treatment of severe hypertriglyceridemia with a formula diet rich in omega-3 fatty acids and medium-chain triglycerides. Ann Nutr Metab. 2010;56(3):170-5. Consumption of coconut milk did not increase cardiovascular disease risk in mice, International Journal of Current Research Vol. 6, pp.063-064, July, 2010; Saturated fat and cardiometabolic risk factors, coronary heart disease, stroke, and diabetes: a fresh look at the evidence. Lipids. 2010 Oct;45(10):893-905. Epub 2010 Mar 31. Anti-inflammatory, analgesic, and antipyretic activities of virgin coconut oil. Pharm Biol. 2010 Feb;48(2):151-7. A good response to oil with medium- and long-chain fatty acids

in body fat and blood lipid profiles of male hypertriglyceridemic subjects. Asia Pac J Clin Nutr. 2009;18(3):351-8; Medium-chain fatty acids: functional lipids for the prevention and treatment of the metabolic syndrome. Pharmacol Res. 2010 Mar;61(3):208-12. Epub 2009 Nov 30; Medium-and long-chain fatty acid triacylglycerol reduce body fat and serum triglyceride in overweight and hypertriglyceridemic subjects. Zhonghua Yu Fang Yi Xue Za Zhi. 2009 Sep;43(9):765-71; A ketogenic diet increases succinic dehydrogenase activity in aging cardiomyocytes. Ann NY Acad Sci. 2009 Aug;1171:377-84; The benefit of medium-chain triglyceride therapy on the cardiac function of SHRs is associated with a reversal of metabolic and signaling alterations. Am J Physiol Heart Circ Physiol. 2008 Jul;295(1):H136-44. Epub 2008 May 2. Medium-chain fatty acids as metabolic therapy in cardiac disease. Cardiovasc Drugs Ther. 2008 Apr;22(2):97-106; The effect of virgin coconut oil on the cholesterol level of patients with hypercholesterolemia. Fil Fam Phy. 2008 Jan-Mar 46(1):9-17.

[75] Anti-inflammatory activity of virgin coconut oil. Philipp J Intern Med. 2007;Mar-Apr 45(2):85-88.

[76] Medium-chain fatty acid nanoliposomes suppress body fat accumulation in mice. Br J Nutr. 2011 Nov;106(9):1330-6. Epub 2011 Jun 28. Medium-and long-chain triacylglycerols reduce body fat and blood triacylglycerols in hypertriacylglycerolemic, overweight but not obese, Chinese individuals. Lipids. 2010 Jun;45(6):501-10. Epub 2010 May 15; Effects of dietary medium-chain triglyceride on weight loss and insulin sensitivity in a group of moderately overweight free-living type 2 diabetic Chinese subjects. Metabolism. 2007 Jul;56(7):985-91; Medium chain triglyceride oil consumption as part of a weight loss diet does not lead to an adverse metabolic profile when compared to olive oil. J Am Coll Nutr. 2008 Oct;27(5):547- 52; Effects of dietary coconut oil on the biochemical and anthropometric profiles of women presenting abdominal obesity. Lipids. 2009 Jul;44(7):593-601. Epub 2009 May 13.

[77] Caprylic triglyceride as a novel therapeutic approach to effectively improve the performance and attenuate the symptoms due to the motor neuron loss in ALS disease PLoS One. 2012;7(11):e49191. doi: 10.1371/journal.pone.0049191. Epub 2012 Nov 7; 2-Deoxy-D-Glucose Treatment Induces Ketogenesis, Sustains Mitochondrial Function, and Reduces Pathology in Female Mouse Model of Alzheimer's Disease. PLoS One. 2011; 6(7): e21788. Published online 2011 July 1. doi: 10.1371/journal.pone.0021788; Caregiver Reports Following Dietary Intervention with Medium Chain Fatty Acids in 60 Persons with Dementia. International Symposium of Dietary Interventions for Epilepsy and Other Neurologic Diseases, Edinburgh, Scotland, October 2010; Efficacy of dietary treatments for epilepsy. J Hum Nutr Diet. 2010 Apr;23(2):113-9. Case Study: Dietary intervention using coconut oil to produce mild ketosis in a 58 year old APOE4+ male with early onset Alzheimer's disease. 25th International Conference of Alzheimer's Disease International (ADI), March 10-13, 2010, Greece. Ketone bodies as a therapeutic for Alzheimer's disease. Future treatments in Alzheimer's disease. 25th International Conference of Alzheimer's Disease International (ADI), March 10-13, 2010. Ketogenic diets: an historical antiepileptic therapy with promising potentialities for the aging brain. Ageing Res Rev. 2010 Jul;9(3):273-9. Epub 2010 Feb 24.

[78] Kidney: In vivo antinociceptive and anti-inflammatory activities of dried and fermented processed virgin coconut oil. Med Princ Pract. 2011;20(3):231-6. Epub 2011 Mar 29; Anti-inflammatory, analgesic, and antipyretic activities of virgin coconut oil. Pharm Biol. 2010 Feb;48(2):151-7; Anti-inflammatory activity of virgin coconut oil. Philipp J Intern Med. 2007;Mar-Apr 45(2):85-88; Comparison of the fat elimination between long-chain triglycerides and medium-chain triglycerides in rats with ischemic acute renal failure. Ren. Fail. 2002 Jan;24(1):1-9; Protective effect of coconut oil on renal necrosis occurring in rats fed a methyl-deficient diet. Ren. Fail. 1995 Sep; 17 (5):525-37. Liver: Opposite effects of dietary saturated and unsaturated fatty acids on ethanol-pharmacokinetics, triglycerides and carnitines. J Am Coll Nutr. 1994 Aug;13(4):338-43; Hepatoprotective Activity of Dried-and Fermented-Processed Virgin Coconut Oil, Hindawi Publishing Corporation, Evidence-Based Complementary and Alternative Medicine Volume 2011, Article ID 142739, 8 pages; In vivo antinociceptive and anti-inflammatory activities of dried and fermented processed virgin coconut oil. Med Princ Pract. 2011;20(3):231-6. Epub 2011 Mar 29; Toll-like receptor-2 deficiency enhances non-alcoholic steatohepatitis. BMC Gastroenterol. 2010 May 28;10:52; Anti-inflammatory, analgesic, and antipyretic activities of virgin coconut oil. Pharm Biol. 2010 Feb;48(2):151-7; Role of medium-chain triglycerides in the alcohol-mediated cytochrome P450 2E1 induction of mitochondria. Alcohol Clin Exp Res. 2007 Oct;31(10):1660-8. Epub 2007 Aug 6; Review: nutritional support for patients with cirrhosis. J Gastroenterol Hepatol. 1997 Apr;12(4):282-6; Beneficial effects of enteral fat administration on liver dysfunction, liver lipid accumulation, and protein metabolism in septic rats. J Nutr Sci Vitaminol (Tokyo) 1995;41:657-669.

[79] Effect of topical application of virgin coconut oil on skin components and antioxidant status during dermal wound healing in young rats. Skin Pharmacol Physiol. 2010;23(6):290-7. Epub 2010 Jun 3; Novel antibacterial and emollient effects of coconut and virgin olive oils in adult atopic dermatitis. Dermatitis. 2008 Nov-Dec;19(6):308-15; A randomized double-blind controlled trial comparing extra virgin coconut oil with mineral oil as a moisturizer for mild to moderate xerosis. Dermatitis. 2004 Sep;15(3):109-16

[80] Effect of topical application of virgin coconut oil on skin components and antioxidant status during dermal wound healing in young

rats. Skin Pharmacol Physiol. 2010;23(6):290-7. Epub 2010 Jun 3; Novel antibacterial and emollient effects of coconut and virgin olive oils in adult atopic dermatitis. Dermatitis. 2008 Nov-Dec;19(6):308-15; A randomized double-blind controlled trial comparing extra virgin coconut oil with mineral oil as a moisturizer for mild to moderate xerosis. Dermatitis. 2004 Sep;15(3):109-16

[81] European Journal of Clinical Nutrition, January 2010; 64:62-67, doi:10.1038/ejcn.2009.113 and

The European e-Journal of Clinical Nutrition and Metabolism, December 2009; e315-e320

[82] Cunnane, SC, Ganguli, S, Menard, C, et al. High alpha-linolenic acid flaxseed (Linum usitatissimum): some nutritional properties in humans.Br J Nutr. 1993 Mar: 69(2): 443-53; Dorea, JG. Maternal Thiocyanate and Thyroid Status during Breast-Feeding. J Am Coll Nutr. 2004. Vol. 23, No. 2, 97–101.

[83] Klosterman et al., Biochemistry 6, 170 (1967); Lamoureux, Diss. Abstr. B 28, 4908 (1968). Bacterial inhibition: Parsons et al., Antimicrob. Agents Chemother. 1967, 415

[84] Milder, IE, Arts, IC, van de Putte, B, et al. Lignan contents of Dutch plant foods: a database including lariciresinol, pinoresinol, secolariciresinol, and matairesinol. Br J Nutr. 2005 Mar; 93(3): 393-402.

[85] Tou, JCL, Chen, J, Thompson, LU. Flaxseed and its lignin precursor, secoisolariciresinol diglycoside, affect pregnancy outcome and reproductive development in rats. J. Nutr. 1998; 128: 1861-1868;Adlercreutz, H. Lignans and human health. Critical reviews in Clinical Laboratory Sciences. 2007; 44: 483-50; Velentzis, LS. Do phytoestrogens reduce the risk of breast cancer and breast cancer recurrence? What clinicians need to know. Eur J Cancer. 2008 Jul 7; Thompson, LU, Chen, JM, Li, T, et al. Dietary flaxseed alters tumor biological markers in postmenopausal breast cancer. Clin Cancer Res 2005; 11(10): 3828-35.

[86] Khan, G, Penttinen, P, Cabanes, A, et al. Maternal flaxseed diet during pregnancy or lactation increases female rat offsrping's susceptibility to carcinogen-induced mammary tumorigenesis. Reproductive Toxicology. 2007; 23: 397-406.

[87] Johnson, MD, Kenney, N, Stoica, A, et al. Cadmium mimics the in vivo effects of estrogen in the uterus and mammary gland. Nat med. 2003;9: 1081-4; Stoica, A, Katzenellenbogen, BS, Martin, MB. Activation of estrogen receptor-alpha by the heavy metal cadmium. Mol Endocrinol. 2000; 14: 545-53.

[88] Pan, A, Sun, J, Chen, Y, et al. Effects of flaxseed derived lignan supplement in type 2 diabetic patients: a randomized, double-blind, cross-over trial. Plos One 2007 nov; 2(11): e1148; Barre, DE, Mizier- Barre, KA, Griscti, O, et al. High dose flaxseed oil supplementation may affect fasting blood serum glucose management in human type 2 diabetics. J Oleo Sci. 2008;57(5):269-7; Mc Manus, Clandinin, Jumpson, J, et al. A comparison of the effects of n-3 fatty acids from linseed oil and fish oil in well-controlled type 2 diabetes. Diabetes Care 1996; 19, 463-467; Goh, Y, Jumpson, J, Ryan, R. Effect of n-3 fatty acids on plasma lipids, cholesterol, and fatty acid content in NIDDM patients. Diabetologica 1997; 40: 45-52.

[89] Bloedon LT, Balikai S, Chittams J, et al. Flaxseed and cardiovascular risk factors: results from a double blind, randomized, controlled clinical trial. J Am Coll Nutr. 2008 Feb;27(1):65-74.

[90] Bloedon LT, Balikai S, Chittams J, et al. Flaxseed and cardiovascular risk factors: results from a double blind, randomized, controlled clinical trial. J Am Coll Nutr. 2008 Feb;27(1):65-74; Hallund J, Tetens I, Bügel S. The effect of a lignan complex isolated from flaxseed on inflammation markers in healthy postmenopausal women. Nutr Metab Cardiovasc Dis. 2008 Sep;18(7):497-502; Jenkins, DA, Kendall, WC, Vidgen E, et al. Health aspects of partially defatted flaxseed, including effects on serum lipids, oxidative measures, and ex vivo androgen and progestin activity: a controlled crossover trial. Am J Clin Nutr 1999;69: 395-402; Zhang, W, Wang, X, Liu, Y, et al. Dietary flaxseed lignin extract lowers plasma cholesterol and glucose concentrations in hypercholesterolemic subjects. Br J Clin Nutr.2008; 99: 1301-1309; Dodin, S, lemay, A, Jacques, H, et al. The effects of flaxseed dietary supplement on lipid profile, bone mineral density, and symptoms in menopausal women: a randomized, double-blind, wheat germ placebo-controlled clinical trial. J Clin Endocrinol Metab 2005; 90: 1390-1397; Stuglin C, Prasad K. Effect of flaxseed consumption on blood pressure, serum lipids, hemopoietic system and liver and kidney enzymes in healthy humans. J Cardiovasc Pharmacol Ther. 2005 Mar;10(1):23-7; Paschos, GK, Magkos, F, Panagiotakos, DB, et al. Dietary supplementation with flaxseed oil lowers blood pressure in dyslipidemic patients. Eur J Clin Nutr. 2007; 61: 1201-1206.

[91] See comprehensive analysis of breakfast research results for 47 studies at Journal of the American Dietetic Association, Volume 105, Issue 5, May 2005, Pages 743–760, Breakfast Habits, Nutritional Status, Body Weight, and Academic Performance in Children and Adolescents, Gail C. Rampersaud, MS, RD, Mark A. Pereira, PhD, Beverly L. Girard, MBA, MS, RD, Judi Adams, MS, RD, Jordan D. Metzl, MD.

Notes

Notes

Notes